T0305892

Understanding the Law for Physicians, Healthcare Professionals, and Scientists

A Primer on the Operations of the Law and the Legal System

Understanding the Law for Physicians, Healthcare Professionals, and Scientists

A Primer on the Operations of the Law and the Legal System

Marshall S. Shapo

CRC Press
Taylor & Francis Group
Boca Raton London New York

CRC Press is an imprint of the
Taylor & Francis Group, an **informa** business

A PRODUCTIVITY PRESS BOOK

CRC Press
Taylor & Francis Group
6000 Broken Sound Parkway NW, Suite 300
Boca Raton, FL 3487-2742

First issued in paperback 2021

ISBN-13: 978-1-03-209560-8 (pbk)
ISBN-13: 978-1-138-48345-3 (hbk)

Library of Congress Cataloging-in-Publication Data

Names: Shapo, Marshall S., 1936- author.
Title: Understanding the law for physicians, healthcare professionals, and scientists : a primer on the operations of the law and the legal system / Marshall S. Shapo.
Description: Boca Raton : Taylor & Francis, 2018. | Includes bibliographical references and index.
Identifiers: LCCN 2017055526 (print) | LCCN 2017056802 (ebook) | ISBN 9781351054829 (eBook) | ISBN 9781138483453 (hardback : alk. paper)
Subjects: | MESH: Physicians--legislation & jurisprudence | Legislation, Medical | Research Personnel--legislation & jurisprudence | Health Personnel--legislation & jurisprudence | United States
Classification: LCC K3601 (ebook) | LCC K3601 (print) | NLM W 33 AA1 | DDC 344.03/21--dc23
LC record available at https://lccn.loc.gov/2017055526

Visit the Taylor & Francis Web site at
http://www.taylorandfrancis.com

and the CRC Press Web site at
http://www.crcpress.com

For Helene, the nonpareil

To the memory of my parents

Mitchell Shapo and Norma S. Shapo

And for

Aaron, Gabrielle, Joshua, Jonathan, Michaela, Noah (the closer)

Contents

Author

Marshall S. Shapo, the Frederic P. Vose Professor at Northwestern University Pritzker School of Law, is a nationally recognized authority on injury law. He received an AB, summa cum laude, from the University of Miami, where he was first in his class. He was magna cum laude at the University of Miami School of Law, where he was first in his class and editor-in-chief of the *Law Review*. Professor Shapo's graduate degrees are an AM in history and an SJD, both from Harvard. Before his appointment to the Northwestern faculty, he was the Joseph M. Hartfield Professor of Law at the University of Virginia and a member of the faculty at the University of Texas School of Law. Professor Shapo was a visiting fellow at Wolfson College, Oxford University, and twice at Wolfson College, Cambridge University. He also served as a visiting professor at the Juristisches Seminar, University of Gottingen. In 2005 he was the principal speaker, delivering five lectures on various aspects of tort and injury law, at a seminar attended by leading European tort scholars at the University of Girona. He has also lectured in Portugal, Germany, Italy, Japan, and Brazil.

A reviewer of one of Professor Shapo's books called him "[a] towering presence in American tort law." Among his approximately thirty books and book-length works is the magisterial four-volume treatise *The Law of Products Liability*, which in its recently published seventh edition has grown to

3,640 pages. A reviewer of an earlier edition wrote that "[m]ore than any other scholar on the planet, Marshall Shapo views and portrays the world of products liability as a living portrait." Professor Shapo was the principal author of *Towards a Jurisprudence of Injury: The Continuing Creation of a System of Substantive Justice in American Tort Law*, a thousand-page commentary written in his capacity as Reporter for the Special Committee on the Tort Liability System of the American Bar Association.

A published trilogy has carried forward Professor Shapo's ideas about experimentation on mass publics in products and the environment: *A Nation of Guinea Pigs* (1979), *Experimenting with the Consumer* (2009), and *The Experimental Society* (2016). He has written various other works and engaged in numerous activities focused on the relation between law and science. Among other writings, he contributed an essay to the volume *Compensation for Research Injuries*, published by the President's Commission for the Study of Ethical Problems in Medicine, Biomedical, and Behaviorial Research. He also acted as coreporter for the Symposium on Legal and Scientific Perspectives on Causation, sponsored in 1990 by the Tort and Insurance Practice Section (TIPS) of the American Bar Association and the Center for Epidemiology and Public Policy at the Johns Hopkins School of Hygiene and Public Health.

Professor Shapo has testified several times before congressional committees on various aspects of injury law. A recent honor is the coveted William L. Prosser award for "outstanding contributions in scholarship, teaching, and service" from the Torts and Compensation Law section of the Association of American Law Schools. He has also received the Robert B. McKay Law Professor Award of the TIPS section of the American Bar Association.

Introduction

Many workers in science, technology, and medicine, no matter how strong their academic degrees or how distinguished their careers, find themselves baffled, frustrated, and even angered by their encounters with the law. Some of those occasions may lead to the need for a lawyer. But many of the bafflements and frustrations arise from ignorance about what the law is, including how it operates.

Over more than half a century of inquiry into the relation between law and science, I have had many conversations with physicians, scientists, and business professionals whose work rests on technological development. I have come to realize that these people often desire more knowledge about the operations of law and the legal system. This book seeks to provide basic knowledge about the law in realms where those persons—for whom I sometimes use the shorthand term *scientists*—often encounter it, primarily in areas where activities pose risks of personal injury.

Here I discuss two basic types of law: Civil litigation and other remedies afforded to persons who ascribe injuries to the conduct or products of others and direct regulation by the government of the levels of safety in those areas. Principal practical applications of this knowledge lie in ways to minimize risk, both in the primary sense and in efforts to avoid litigation over injuries, and in how to present arguments about policy to government officials who write laws and regulations. The book is descriptive and generally does not make judgments about the fairness or efficacy of the law or the legal system. Those judgments I leave to my readers.

Chapter 1

Different Cultures, Different Lenses

It is useful as a preliminary matter to describe the approaches that scientists and lawyers take to situations involving various kinds of risk—approaches that often are in conflict but that are sometimes in harmony.

1.1 A Line of Clash: Falsifiability and Propositions That Cannot Be Falsified

A frequent line of clash between lawyers and scientists has to do with a method of problem solving that is common to scientists. This method embraces a winnowing process in which investigators define a hypothesis and collect data in an effort to test whether that hypothesis can be "falsified." This process is continuous. Testing proceeds in a way that narrows the inquiry in the direction of what might provisionally be called truth.

An important distinction concerns the criterion of falsifiability, the possibility of empirically testing a hypothesis. One might investigate, for example, the question of whether contact of a particular chemical with the skin of human beings causes a specific kind of irritation or illness. This might be termed a "scientific" question. We can contrast the question of whether a supermarket is "negligent" if it leaves a spilled, sticky liquid for twelve minutes in an aisle where a customer slips on it and breaks a bone. Answering that question requires a judgment which some might call a policy judgment. But the answer is not something one can deduce from data. It might be argued that one could verify the determination that a market was negligent when there was a collection of case results in which several courts unanimously concluded, on facts identical to those summarized above, that a market had or had not behaved below the appropriate standard of care in failing to clean up the spill. But in practice this set of identical circumstances will not occur frequently, if at all. And still the determination of negligence would be a judgment that is not a scientific conclusion. So scientists construct and prove propositions for their factual testability, but lawyers do not do that—at least not with propositions of law.

At the same time, we should note that both lawyers and scientists deal with problems of proof and that sometimes their professional processes overlap. Lawyers often use an adversary process to "prove" propositions, and sometimes those propositions are scientific in nature, in which case lawyers will employ scientists as "experts" for proof. In a roughly parallel way, it is not at all unusual for scientists to engage in what is basically an adversary process to argue about the appropriate "factual" or "scientific" conclusions from data. Those arguments may prove to be as contentious, and even as bitter, as arguments between lawyers in litigation.

1.2 Some Harmonizing Elements

We further observe that there are some harmonizing elements among the professional standards and approaches of lawyers and scientists. Both professions place a premium on analysis. Their professional education develops an ability to break a problem into its component parts. It instills a demand for relevance: for focusing on the data that count with reference to the problem at hand.

Both professions involve ongoing processes of discovery. This is elementally a part of scientific education. The method of falsification assumes that usually there are more truths to be discovered, so knowledge is always tentative.[1]

Lawyers, by comparison, may not consciously think about this kind of process as often as scientists, but it is in their bones also. The process of judge-made law is an ongoing one. The common law tradition, discussed in further detail in Chapter 3, involves an ongoing process of development that includes synthesis of precedents, sometimes culminating in landmark decisions. One of the most famous examples is the 1916 case of *MacPherson v. Buick Motor Co.*,[2] in which a judicial master, Benjamin Cardozo, strung together a series of nineteenth-century decisions, including English decisions, to arrive at the conclusion that an injured consumer could sue the manufacturer of a negligently made product. The prior law, using the concept of "privity of contract," had limited consumers to suits against only the entity from which they bought the product; for example, a retailer. Cardozo's conclusion was pithy and powerful: Against the idea that contract law defined the relation between the parties, he said, "We have put the source of the obligation where it ought to be. We have put its source in the law."[3] The process of common law reasoning does not proceed in straight lines and does not necessarily lead to expansions of the law. A pair of Texas decisions is illustrative. In one case, the state supreme court approved a claim for "negligent infliction of mental anguish."[4] Just six years later, a majority of the court rethought the prior decision and declared flatly that "there is no general duty in Texas not to negligently inflict emotional distress."[5]

Legislation, a very different form of law, is malleable in a very different way. One could hardly say that it reflects a constant search for truth, unless one speaks of political "truths." Each statute—the term for laws passed by legislatures—changes the landscape of rules by which we live. Just one example is the Occupational Safety and Health Act, discussed in Chapter 4, which firmly placed the federal government in a governing business it had not previously entered, at least not so directly—"to assure so far as possible every working man and woman in the Nation safe and healthful working conditions."[6] This statute created a new governmental agency—the Occupational Safety and Health Administration—and an entire new body of law, including many regulations and a new field of professional work for lawyers.

The professions of science and law share a problem of communication. This enigma is how to explain the technical aspects of their fields to a public that is uncomprehending and frequently skeptical. In science, a recurring problem in public perception arises from the use of statistics. There are at least four problems in this category. One is lies in arguments among experts about what the numbers are. Another is the broad ranges of some numbers. A good example of both is a much-cited study by the prestigious Institute of Medicine, which estimated that the range of "preventable" fatalities arising from the process of medical care was between 44,000 and 98,000.[7] Even more confusing to a layperson would have been a later estimate where the range for that number was between 210,000 and 400,000.[8] Dr. Ashish Jha of the Harvard School of Public Health told a subcommittee hearing chaired by Senator Bernie Sanders that "the IOM probably got it wrong."[9]

A related set of problems lies in the difficulty of distinguishing among causes of injury. Dr. Jha responded to Senator

Sanders's question about why the new statistics had not become front page news by saying that it is "very easy to confuse the fact that somebody might have died because of a fatal consequence of their disease, versus they died from a complication from a medical error." He said that it had "taken a lot to prove to all of us that many of these deaths are not a natural consequence of the underlying disease" but rather that "[t]hat they are purely failures of the system."[10]

An area of vigorous dispute arises at the very intersection of science and law. A good example is the question of whether a court can find that exposure to asbestos is a cause of colon cancer. This question divided judges in the New Jersey state courts and federal courts in New York. In the federal case, the trial court had refused to credit epidemiological studies that showed a standardized mortality ratio (SMR) of 1.14 to 1.47, saying that the minimum ratio it would accept was 1.50.[11] However, Judge Cabranes, speaking for the Second Circuit appellate court, rejected that bright-line ruling, referring to "a number of studies" that found SMRs from 1.14 to 1.47 were "statistically significant when taken together."[12] This holding, and a parallel reversal by the New Jersey Supreme Court of an appellate court that rejected epidemiological evidence with a relative risk of less than two,[13] illustrate the problem where the operational meaning of the law—in this instance in the case of medical causation—is the subject of controversy.

Like scientists, lawyers have difficulty communicating the technical aspect of their craft to laypersons. Many non-lawyer businesspersons are left glassy-eyed when attorneys try to explain to them why it is that courts will use rules of circumstantial evidence to impose liability on manufacturers whose relatively new products cause accidents—for example, the staple that unexpectedly shoots out of a staple gun.[14] And consumers may find it equally mysterious that a court would use other rules of circumstantial evidence to impose liability on the maker of a stock-picker machine when a worker was found unconscious on a warehouse floor next to the machine.[15]

Perhaps even more bewildering to a layreader would be a court's explanation of why it dismissed a New Jersey borough's claim against a railroad that stored butane on a siding in violation of the Hazardous Materials Transportation Act. The court justified its decision on the basis that the act, and its legislative history, did not "reveal any intent to protect a class that includes the plaintiffs, municipalities, among its members." Rather, the court said, "[a]ll residents of the United States are the HTMA's intended beneficiaries."[16] An elementary school child might wonder why a law intended to protect all Americans should be viewed as not including an American city.

1.3 Ideology and Neutrality

Can the law be ideologically neutral? The arguments surrounding this subject spin around decisions from the Supreme Court of the United States all the way down to the trial court level.

A great judge, Benjamin Cardozo, spoke of the many pressures, internal and external, that weigh on judges who strive for detachment from politics and personal prejudice. In an eloquent sentence, he spoke of the "forces which [judges] do not recognize and cannot name," that "have been tugging at them—inherited instincts, traditional beliefs, acquired convictions," with a "resultant" "outlook on life, a conception of social needs ... which, when reasons are nicely balanced, must determine where choice shall fall."[17]

There are several areas of the law where the deeply rooted intuitions of judges appear to control their decisions, sometimes when those intuitions are worn on their sleeves and at others when they must be discerned more subtly from their language. A good example is the doctrine that is sometimes called "assumption of the risk," a defense to injury actions which requires the defendant to show that the plaintiff voluntarily confronted a known risk, and which has been applied in cases of consumer products and various situations involving workplace injuries. An opinion on a consumer product, a power mower, makes no secret of the judge's worldview. Saying it was apparent when the plaintiff bought the mower that it had no safety devices, the court declared that "in a free market," the plaintiff "had the choice of buying a mower equipped with them, of buying the mower which he did, or of buying no mower at all."[18]

The same philosophy is apparent in a workplace case in which the plaintiff was using a bulldozer without a canopy while he was manipulating a fifty-foot-long oak tree that struck him in the chest. The court emphasized that the plaintiff had "full knowledge" of the bulldozer's characteristics and was "fully aware of the dangers ... in conducting operations without the canopy guard."[19] A countervailing point of view appears in a case involving injuries caused by a workplace machine in which the court stressed that the plaintiff felt she had "no realistic choice" but to follow her foreman's orders to work on the machine. The judge noted that the plaintiff theoretically could have quit her job but emphasized that she "lacked a trade or college degree and had to help support her family" and said that these facts "strongly rebut voluntariness in the ordinary sense of the word."[20]

The same kind of conflict between the ways different judges view the human condition—a conflict that mirrors the differing views of ordinary people—is evident in cases involving the tort doctrine called "intentional infliction of emotional distress." A century ago a great legal scholar, Roscoe Pound, discerned in ancient historical documents a trend in the law "to take account of purely subjective mental injuries to a certain extent and even to regard infringement of another's sensibilities."[21] Although that recognition appears in sources going back hundreds of years, it took until the second half of the twenty-century for American courts to employ a theory that became known as "intentional infliction of emotional distress." The leading summary of the elements of that tort action requires the plaintiff to prove that the defendant, with "outrageous" behavior, either intentionally or recklessly caused severe emotional distress to the plaintiff.[22]

The rise of Freudian psychology in the twentieth century confirmed what many people already knew intuitively—that there is no sharp boundary between injuries to body and mind. Yet, many courts continue to adhere to a wariness about imposing liability for emotional injuries unconnected to specific physical trauma. Thus, where virtually all courts recognize claims for intentional infliction of emotional distress, many have refused to extend liability when the defendant's conduct was negligent rather than intentional or reckless. The United States Supreme Court summarized some principal reasons for this reluctance in a case in which pipefitters sued for fear of cancer they attributed to their work in an asbestos-laden environment. In rejecting the claims of these "Snowmen of Grand Central," who worked in tunnels under the New York station, the Court referred to a "special difficulty for judges and juries" in separating valid claims from "trivial" ones, to the threat of "unlimited and unpredictable liability" and to the "potential for a flood of" of "trivial" claims.[23] Judicial opinions of this kind reflect judges' intuitions, rooted in their personal histories and personalities, that push them to resist claims for emotional injuries.

A special illustration of the tensions evident in this area of the law appears in the cases in which the plaintiff is a "bystander witness" who observes a physical injury to a third person. The plaintiffs in these cases typically have been family members of the person who suffered a physical injury. In a leading Wisconsin case, the court denied recovery to a mother who witnessed fatal injuries to her daughter caused by a negligently driven car. It said that injuries to a person like the mother, who was "out of the range of ordinary physical peril," were not so "unusual or extraordinary" that they could be said to subject her to "an unreasonable risk" of emotional injury.[24] However, some courts have imposed liability to bystanders. In one such case, a Maine court granted recovery to a five-year-old child who witnessed the death of her sister in a vehicle accident.[25] The struggles among judicial intuitions on the general question of liability for negligently caused emotional distress appear in cases of bystander witnesses—involving, for example, concerns about the difficulty of proving a compensable injury pitted against common sense recognition of the reality of emotional injuries to bystanders.

Struggles over whether to provide legal remedies become especially intense when the stakes are broader than those in cases involving individual plaintiffs suing individual defendants. A stark example is a case involving Inuit villagers threatened by a form of climate change. The village, called Kivalina, sat at "the tip of a six-mile barrier reef" in Alaska, about 70 miles beyond the Arctic Circle. The villagers sued more than twenty energy companies, alleging that erosion that threatened the survival of their village had been caused by greenhouse gas emissions attributable to the products of the companies. However, the Ninth Circuit affirmed a trial court decision for the companies against the villagers' claim for $400 million to pay for relocating their dwellings. The appellate court said that "[t]he solution to Kivalina's dire circumstance" "must rest in the hands of the legislative and executive branches of our government, not the federal common law" that is the province of the courts.[26] The decision is a good example of the way courts often divide judicial business from the realm of politics. A thousand and one scientists may assert the reality of climate change triggered by human activity, but this case is an illustration of how judges say that provision of a remedy lies beyond them in the rough-and-tumble of the democratic process.

The efforts to advance scientific research sometimes involve direct political action. A good example is the struggle over the effort of patients to obtain drugs that had not cleared the

FDA's investigational new drug (IND) process, an effort that came to a head over HIV/AIDS drugs. The agency, lining up with orthodox principles of drug testing, would not allow certain drugs on the market if they had not passed its IND criteria. Those criteria largely mandated testing under the "gold standard," which requires tests involving randomized groups of patients who took the drug at issue and those taking placebos. Under pressure from patients, including members of the HIV/AIDS community, in 1987 the agency issued "treatment IND" regulations designed to allow "desperately ill" patients to get drugs while the traditional process ground on. In its attempts to assure the role of "good science," the agency said that its rule "provide[d] for a standard of medical and scientific rationality on the basis of which experts could reasonably conclude that the drug may be effective in the intended patient population." It emphasized that there should be a requirement of "the absence of alternative therapy" for the granting of a treatment IND, although it acknowledged that "the mere fact that the disease in question has existing approved therapy does not mean that the approved treatments are satisfactory for all patients."[27]

This rule was not enough to mollify AIDS activists, who besieged FDA staff at its headquarters in Rockville, Maryland.[28] This led to an "interim rule" on treatment INDs. In this rule, the FDA stressed that placebo testing was "scientifically and ethically appropriate" "where no therapy has been shown to be effective," but said it would not require placebo controls where there was "known to be an effective therapy." This rule allowed protocols for treatment with drugs where the results of phase 2 IND testing—testing for effectiveness in a few hundred people—"appear[ed] promising." Indicating that it was ready to skip the large scale testing on [thousands] of people in Phase 3, the agency said that "[t]he treatment IND, as appropriate, would continue to serve as a bridge between phase 2 trials and the point of marketing approval."[29] In a further episode, AIDS activists were successful in their efforts to get approval for aerosolized pentamidine for use in preventing "acute cases of pneumonia," often associated with AIDS, for which a "gray market" had developed. After results of a successful community-based treatment trial, the FDA, after "countless meetings," concluded that the data from the trial had "proven efficacy in showing a dose response."[30]

The D.C. Circuit firmly held the line for the FDA in a wrenching case that began with the effort of Abigail Burroughs, a young woman with head and neck cancer, to purchase an experimental drug. Although Ms. Burroughs died after failing to get the drug, her father began the organization called the Abigail Alliance, which brought suit against the agency, opposing its resistance to allowing very sick patients to get drugs that had passed the first phase of IND trials but not Phase 2. The Alliance won the first round before a three-judge panel of the D.C. Circuit, with the panel majority saying that the due process clause of the Constitution afforded access to "potentially life-saving investigational new drugs" for "mentally competent, terminally ill, adult patients" when there were "no alternative government-approved treatment options." This opinion, by Judge Janice Rogers Brown, relied on "the longstanding tradition of the right of self-preservation."[31]

An eight-to-two decision of the full D.C. Circuit, however, overturned the decision of the panel majority. Judge Thomas Griffith said that it was "difficult to see" how a tort action based on "intentional interference with rescue" "would guarantee a constitutional right to override the collective judgment of the scientific and medical communities expressed through the FDA's clinical testing process."[32] He said that "the FDA's policy of limiting access to investigational drugs" was "rationally related to the legitimate state interest of protecting patients, including the terminally ill, from potentially unsafe drugs with unknown therapeutic effects."[33]

Beyond the legal controversies in which scientific research becomes embroiled, one finds land mines in the data themselves, which lead to results in which law, and public opinion, look over the shoulders of researchers. A prime example is the case of postmenopausal hormones. Two major long-term studies investigated the effects of these drugs on various aspects of women's health. In the mid-1990s there came a report from the Nurses' Health Study, begun in the early 1980s and which involved more than 50,000 women. After as much as "16 years of follow-up," it found a "marked decrease" in "the risk of major coronary disease ... among current users to estrogen and progestin, as well as among current users of estrogen alone."[34] However, a 14-year survey of nurses also reported a "significant elevation in the risk of breast cancer among women using conjugate estrogens alone ... estrogen plus progestin ... and progestins alone."[35] After this vast experiment had continued for another decade, a 2006 study indicated "a 30 percent lower risk" of coronary heart disease for "women using estrogen alone or combined HT [hormone therapy] compared with postmenopausal women who never used hormones."[36]

Contemporary research data from two other studies further complicated the picture, raising concerns among women taking hormones. In 1998, the Heart and Estrogen/Progestin Replacement Study (HERS) reported that there was no reduction in the "overall risk of nonfatal" heart attacks or deaths from coronary heart disease or "other cardiovascular outcomes" in women under 80 "with established coronary disease" who took estrogen plus progestin.[37] Four years later, two reports from the HERS researchers further built the case against hormone therapy. One of them found "no cardiovascular benefit" from hormone replacement therapy.[38] The other found increases in blood clots in the veins and of surgery on the tract that included the gall bladder.[39]

A week later, there came a first report from the Women's Health Initiative, which began a study involving almost ten times as many women as the HERS study who took either estrogen alone or a combination and who both had and did not have previous heart disease. Remarkably, these investigators said they had stopped their study on the combination products used in postmenopausal women. They had found an increase in breast cancer "along with evidence for some increase" in coronary heart disease, stroke, and pulmonary embolism that "outweighed the evidence of benefit for fractures and possible benefit for colon cancer." The data on the rate of stroke showed a 41 percent increase and a 29 percent increase in coronary heart disease events, most of them non-fatal heart attacks.[40]

Two years after that came another worrisome report, from the WHI, this time with a declaration that women with hysterectomies who participated in an estrogen-only study "stop taking their study pills."[41] A summary of this study said that estrogen "increases the risk of stroke"[42] and a statement from the WHI director said that "an increased risk of stroke is not acceptable in healthy women in a research study."[43]

Scientists may may take a combination of lessons from this story—lessons about the intersection of science, law, and public relations. In the background of all this was the role of the FDA, which hovered over the decisions of the investigators to stop their studies. It is clear that both scientists investigating products in the public spotlight and doctors who prescribe them must be prepared for expressions of deep concern, and sometimes litigation, from members of the public. Just illustratively, after the 2002 announcement of the ending of the study of postmenopausal estrogens, a Northwestern University doctor said that her patients were "miserable" and that "[t]heir quality of life isn't as good."[44] After the discontinuance of the second study in 2004, the NIH reacted to patients' concerns with attempts at bringing some calm to the market. It issued a statement that patients considering the use of hormone products "should discuss the risks and benefits with their physicians."[45] And the director of the WHI said that "[w]omen should not feel that this is some grand emergency for them."[46]

A kind of law quite distinct from the regulation exercised by the FDA is the private lawsuit, and the discontinuance of the first study brought an immediate reaction from lawyers who represent plaintiffs in injury cases. Just after that news became public, a newspaper article reported that plaintiffs' lawyers were "tripping over each other" to sue Wyeth, the seller of the combination product Prempro, which also made Premarin, an estrogen-only product.[47] These suits, fueled by lawyers' advertising, continue to the present day. One website tells readers that if they have "suffered serious side effects while taking HRT drugs such as Premarin, Provera, and Prempro" or "have been diagnosed with breast cancer" or are "experiencing symptoms associated with breast cancer," they "may have a claim against the manufacturer."[48]

This chapter exhibits the many differences, as well as areas of agreement, in the ways scientists and lawyers look at various aspects of life: at analysis and the process of argument over disputed hypotheses, at the weighing of evidence, at the continuous process of accumulation of new data, and at the role of personal choice with respect to encounters with risk.

Endnotes

1. A brief cited in the most important Supreme Court decision on scientific proof said that "scientists do not assert that they know what is immutably 'true'—they are committed to searching for new, temporary, theories to explain, as best they can, phenomena." Brief for Nicholas Bloembergen et al., cited in *Daubert v. Merrell Dow Pharmaceuticals*, 509 U.S. 579, 590 (1993).
2. 217 N.Y. 382 (1916).
3. Id. at 390.
4. *St. Elizabeth Hosp. v. Garrard*, 730 S.W.2d 649, 654 (Tex. 1987).
5. *Boyles v. Kerr*, 855 S.W.2d 593, 594 (Tex. 1993).
6. 29 U.S.C. §651(b).
7. *To Err is Human: Building a Safer Health System*, Nat'l Academies Press (1999).
8. J. C. Japes, A new, evidence-based estimate of patient harms associated with hospital care, 9, *J. Patient Safety* 122 (2013).
9. See Erin McCann, Deaths by medical mistakes hit records, *Health Care IT News*, July 18, 2014, printed from the Internet.

10. Id.

11. In re Joint E. & S. Dist. Asbestos Litig, 758 F. Supp. 199 (S.D.N.Y. 1991).

12. 52 F.3d 1124, 1134 (2d Cir. 1995).

13. *Landrigan v. Celotex Corp.*, 605 A.2d 1079 (N.J. 1992).

14. *Sanchez v. Stanley-Bostitch*, 2000 WL 968776 (S.D. N.Y. 2000).

15. *Wong v. Crown Equip. Corp.*, 676 So.2d 981 (Fla. Dist. Ct. App. 1996).

16. *Borough of Ridgefield v. New York S. & W.R. Co.*, 810 F.2d 57, 59 (3d Cir. 1987).

17. Benjamin N. Cardozo, *The Nature of the Judicial Process* 11–12, Yale Univ. Press (1921).

18. *Myers v. Montgomery Ward & Co.*, 252 A.2d 855, 864 (Md. 1969).

19. *Orfield v. Int'l Harvester Corp.*, 535 F.2d 595, 564 (6th Cir. 1976).

20. *Downs v. Gulf & W. Mfg. Co.*, 677 F. Supp. 661, 664-65 (D. Mass. 1987).

21. Roscoe Pound, Interests of Personality, 28 *Harv. L. Rev.* 343, 357 (1915).

22. Restatement of Torts (Second) §46 (1965).

23. *Metro-N. Commuter R. v. Buckley*, 521 U.S. 424, 443 (1997) (quoting precedent).

24. *Waube v. Warrington*, 258 N.W. 497, 501 (Wis. 1935).

25. *Carter v. Williams*, 792 A.2d 1093, 1099 (Me. 2002).

26. *Native Village of Kivalina v. ExxonMobil Corp.*, 696 F.3d 849, 858 (9th Cir. 2012).

27. 52 Fed. Reg. 19466, 19468 (1987).

28. See Larry Thomson, Experimental Treatments? Unapproved but Not Always Unavailable, *FDA Consumer*, Jan–Feb 2000.

29. 53 Fed. Reg. 41516, 41517–41520 (1988).

30. See A. Bruce Montgomery, How the Recent Changes in Expedited Drug Approval Procedures Affect the Work of a Clinical Investigator, 45 *Food Drug Cosmet. Law J.* 339, 339–343 (1990).

31. *Abigail Alliance for Better Access to Developmental Drugs v. Eschenbach*, 445 F.3d 470, 483–86 (D.C. Cir. 2006).

32. 495 F.3d 695, 709 (D.C. Cir. 2007).

33. Id. at 713.

34. Francine Grodstein et al., Postmenopausal Estrogen and Progestin Use and the Risk of Cardiovascular Disease, 335 *N. Eng. J. Med.* 453 (1996).

35. Graham A. Colditz et al., The Use of Estrogens and Progestins and the Risk of Breast Cancer in Postmenopausal Women, 332 *N. Eng. J. Med.* 1589 (1995).

36. Francine Grodstein et al., Hormone Therapy and Coronary Heart Disease: The Role of Time since Menopause and Age at Hormone Initiation, 15 *J. Women's Health* 35, 42 (2006).

37. Stephen Hulley et al., Randomized Trial of Estrogen Plus Progestin for Secondary Prevention of Coronary Heart Disease in Postmenopausal Women, 280 *JAMA* 605, 610 (1998).

38. Deborah Grady et al., Cardiovascular Disease Outcomes during 6.8 Years of Hormone Therapy: Heart and Estrogen/Progestin Replacement Study Follow-up (HERS II), 288 *JAMA* 49 (2002).

39. Stephen Hulley et al., Randomized Noncardiovascular Disease Outcome during 6.8 Years of Hormone Therapy, 288 *JAMA* 58 (Abstract).

40. Writing Group for the Women's Health Initiative Investigators, Risks and Benefits of Estrogen Plus Progestin in Health of Postmenopausal Women, 288 *JAMA* 321 (2002).

41. NIH, Statement from Barbara Alving, NIH Asks Participants in Women's Health Initiative Estrogen-Alone Study to Stop Study Pills, Begin Follow-up Phase (March 2, 2004).

42. Women's Health Initiative Steering Committee, Effects of Conjugated Equine Estrogen in Postmenopausal Women with Hysterectomy, 291 *JAMA* 1701 (2004).

43. NIH News, supra note 41.

44. See Judy Peres, Doubts Cast on Hormone Therapy, *Chi. Trib.*, July 12, 2002, at 1, 16.

45. NIH News, supra note 39.

46. Denise Grady, Estrogen Study Stopped Early Because of Slight Stroke Risk, *N.Y. Times*, March 3, 2004 (quoting Dr. Barbara Alving).

47. See Milo Geyelin, Wyeth's Prempro Problems Galvanize Plaintiffs' Lawyers, *Wall. St. J.*, July 16, 2002, at B1.

48. hrt-legal.com, consulted April 22, 2016.

Chapter 2

Various Approaches to Risk in the Legal System

A principal reason that scientists and healthcare professionals care about the workings of the legal system is due to the way that it deals with the risks created by their activities.

The world of ordinary individuals, including consumers of products and medical patients, often moves forward because providers of goods and services are willing to take risks. These people risk time and money to develop products and new ways of doing things. This taking of risks often brings to the market useful things such as drugs, medical devices, and lifesaving techniques, for example, methods of inserting medical devices into patients' bodies.

2.1 Effects of Law on Innovation

It is a truism that the law should encourage innovation, and it has been strongly argued that many legal rules—liability rules and regulatory rules—put brakes on desirable innovation. A case involving a medical product gives an example of the complexity of the subject, a complexity that includes the desirability of consumer choice. The defendant Baxter made two types of connectors for intravenous tubing. One of these, a Luer slip, or friction-fit, connector that required 5.5 pounds of force to disconnect it, had been on the market for 40 years. The other, a Luer-lock connector that had been sold for 20 years, employed a threaded collar and a threaded flange that screwed together. It cost a few cents more than the slip connector. The plaintiff in this case sued for the death of a surgery patient that occurred when IV tubing disconnected. An Illinois appellate court affirmed a large judgment for the plaintiff. A product manager for the defendant emphasized that "[y]ou have consumer preference," which was effectively revealed in the marketplace by hospitals buying the slip connector. However, the court noted that the slip connector "could and did come apart inadvertently, even when properly connected, despite compliance with industry standards" and that nurses sometimes "would, for convenience, loosely connect the luer slip," which it said the manufacturer "should have known."[1]

The Illinois Supreme Court affirmed the appellate court in a decision that tilted toward innovation as a boon to product safety. It noted that Baxter's patent application "stated that the Luer-lock was designed to overcome the problem of inadvertent disconnection that occurs with friction-fit connectors" and said that it was thus "reasonable to infer that Baxter" had "developed and marketed its product as a safety device." It also referred to the opinion of a witness for the plaintiff, a mechanical engineer with substantial experience in the IV field and "had personally designed and, in some cases, patented medical devices, including IV equipment," that "the friction-fit connectors became obsolete once the Luer-lock was invented." It agreed with the appellate court that the plaintiff had made a case on the theory that the slip connector had a design defect.[2]

A federal appellate decision that refused to impose liability on the designer of a trailer, which the plaintiff claimed had "badly designed" the rear underride guard, indicates the complicated nature of such decisions. In this case the complexity relates to the interaction of both federal and state rules on product design, including an Illinois decision tending to favor the defendant on underride guards. It also stems from the relationship of state liability rules to federal regulatory rules, in this case federal regulations on rear guards. Despite the existence of those regulations, the federal appellate court pointed out that the commentary accompanying them "counsels against judicial interference." It noted that "the regulations explicitly discuss the complicated tradeoff between excessively firm and excessively yielding rear guards, and they acknowledge that there is no perfect solution given the vast number of variables involved in any given accident."[3]

It is difficult to determine the effects of legal rules on innovation, for usually one cannot determine specifically which products would not have been developed or marketed, or which medical techniques would not have been used, because of risk-averseness of the part of manufacturers or healthcare providers. The data on these effects differ according to product areas, and frequently they do not answer the question of what useful innovations had been choked off by the law. We can quote, at a high level of generalization, the conclusion of a study on product injuries that products liability law gives "an extremely vague signal": "Be careful, or you will be sued."[4] One might assume, or at least speculate, that concern about potential litigation among product makers and those engaged in various forms of risky activity will lead to some lessening of innovation. In this connection, I note that—as I have pointed out in a previous book—all human activity includes experimentation, on ourselves and on others.

2.2 The Precautionary Principle

The assumption about the effects of law on innovation leads us to a discussion of a very risk-averse perspective. The overall label for this perspective is the term *the precautionary principle*. The term does not have the exactness that one would ideally desire as a scientist engaged in formal human experimentation, or as a doctor making on-the-spot judgments about whether to prescribe a medication. One quite broad statement of the concept is, "When an activity raises threats of harm to human health or the environment, precautionary measures should be taken even if some cause-and-effect relationships are not established scientifically."[5]

Two Supreme Court decisions in the 1980s featured strong arguments about how averse to the risk of disease regulators should be. In one of these cases, involving a limit placed by OSHA on airborne concentrations of benzene, Justice Stevens wrote for the Court in opposing the regulation that "'safe' is not the equivalent of 'risk-free'" and that "a workplace can hardly be considered 'unsafe' unless it threatens workers with a significant risk of harm."[6] Justice Marshall dissented, noting that "risks of harm are often uncertain," but that "inaction has considerable costs of its own." He said that "the agency must decide whether to take regulatory action against possibly substantial risks or to wait until more definitive information becomes available"—which he pointed out was "a judgment which by its very nature cannot be based solely on determinations of fact."[7]

Just a year later, the Court divided the other way in a case involving an OSHA regulation on permissible exposure levels for cotton dust, designed to minimize byssinosis—"brown lung"—in cotton mill workers, thousands of whom suffered from the disease. Here, Justice Brennan upheld the regulation, rejecting what he characterized as the position of the defendant American Textile Manufacturers that not only did OSHA have to "show a significant risk of material health impairment," but that it would have to show "that the reduction in risk of material health impairment is significant in light of the costs of attaining that reduction."[8] Justice Rehnquist, who had written a concurring opinion in the Petroleum Institute case, now dissented. He said that the words "to the extent feasible" in the OSHA statute represented an "abdicat[ion]" of Congress' "responsibility" to decide the "fundamental and most difficult policy choice" about weighing prevention costs against the "statistical possibility of future deaths."[9] A lesson from this pairing of conflicting opinions is that when questions of how regulators should respond to physical risk involve large conflicting forces, the answers cannot be neatly placed on a grid. Courts first look to the language of a statute but they then interpret that language, and their interpretation often reflects their policy preferences. Those preferences will entail a mixture of judgments about the need for economic production and the value of life and limb.

In civil cases, in which the basic rules of decision are governed by the common law or by common law-like statutory provisions, many courts have adopted a risk-averse view partial to injured persons. A good example is the quotation by many courts of a comment to Section 402A of the Restatement (Second) of Torts, an extensive compilation of rules summarizing what its drafters believed were the best rules across the broad body of tort law: That a product seller undertakes a "special responsibility toward any member of the consuming public who may be injured by it."

There are two sets of more or less competing approaches that courts have taken in injury cases. One of a pair of economics-focused tests weighs the risk of injury against the utility of the activity or product at issue. Another compares the costs of the product or activity with the benefits it provides. Another pair of approaches may roughly be labeled "justice" approaches. Both of these emphasize the vulnerability of persons who have been injured and the long-lasting consequences to them due to their injuries. One of these approaches, which stresses individualized justice, looks to the relatively disadvantaged power position of many injured persons—typically involving a defendant with more access to information about risk, often more wealth, and a better opportunity to acquire insurance than the injured person.

A different concept is that of social justice. The basic idea includes the disparities in social and economic power between groups. Examples are the differing amounts of expertise and information possessed by healthcare professionals and product manufacturers, on one hand, and, on the other hand, patients and consumers. Decisions in favor of parties in the more disadvantaged position seek to strike a balance of justice between groups. Courts deciding individual cases of injury are less likely to employ ideas of social justice than concepts of individual justice between the parties. A principal reason for this lies in the notion that issues involving what amounts to a redistribution of resources between groups are more appropriately resolved by legislatures than by courts, with legislatures being arenas where major choices of social policy are fought out politically. Notwithstanding that argument, however, the by-products of many judicial decisions are relatively broad social impacts.

Endnotes

1. *Hansen v. Baxter Healthcare Corp.*, 723 N.E.2d 302, 308, 313–14, (Ill. App. Ct. 1999), aff'd, 764 N.E.2d 35 (Ill. 2002).
2. *Hansen v. Baxter Healthcare Corp.*, 764 N.E.2d 35 (Ill. 2002).
3. *Rennert v. Great Dane Ltd. Partnership*, 543 F.3d 914, 918 (7th Cir. 2008).
4. G. Eads & P. Reuter, Designing Safer Products: Corporate Responses to Products Liability Law and Regulation viii (Rand, R3022-CJ, 1983).
5. Wingspread Statement on the Precautionary Principle (Racine, Wis., Jan 20, 1998), www.seh.oreg/wing.html.

6. *Industrial Union Department, AFL-CIO v. American Petroleum Inst.*, 448 U.S. 607, 642 (1980).
7. Id. at 722–23 (Marshall, J., dissenting).
8. *American Textile Manufacturers v. Donovan*, 452 U.S. 490, 506 (1981).
9. Id. at 547 (Rehnquist, J., dissenting).

Chapter 3

Institutional Background

3.1 Constitutions

Highest on the ladder of legal force are constitutions. The Constitution of the United States, indeed, declares that it, along with "the laws of the United States which shall be made in Pursuance thereof," and "all Treaties made, under the authority of the United States," is the "supreme Law of the Land." The reference to laws "made in Pursuance thereof" has been interpreted to signal that the courts shall determine whether laws are constitutional. When courts strike down statutes as unconstitutional, the area of law to which they pertain remains subject to judicial decisions interpreting the existing law—which may consist of judge-made law—and also subject to further attempts to draft a statute that will be held constitutional.

State constitutions are themselves viewed as having the highest force of law within their states. Some provisions in both the U.S. Constitution and state constitutions that are the center of legal arguments are those that require that individuals receive due process of law and that they have equal protection of the laws. Good examples of such clashes in an area involving medicine are statutes that impose dollar limits on the amount that plaintiffs in medical malpractice cases can recover for such "noneconomic loss" as pain and suffering. Many state constitutions include "open courts" provisions, with language that typically declares, as in the Texas constitution, that "[a]ll courts shall be open, and every person for an injury done him, in his lands, goods, person or reputation, shall have remedy by due course of law."

3.2 Legislation

Generally speaking, legislatures—Congress and state legislatures—are the primary makers of law in the form of statutes, although as we have noted, legislation is subject to constitutional review by courts and also often requires inter-pretation by courts. Arguments often erupt about "judicial law-making," when parties opposed to court decisions complain that judges have taken over "lawmaking" functions that are the province of legislatures. These arguments are made from era to era by people on every segment of political divides. Yet the basic theory is fairly firm: Legislatures are the place where contending forces fight out questions with a high policy valence. Although courts may make decisions with political impact, they are supposed to bow to policy decisions embod-ied in statutes—again subject to constitutional limitations.

Legislatures are representative democracy, but there is a form of direct democracy in which people vote directly. This is the referendum, which may result in a provision in a state constitution.

3.3 Courts

The basic purpose of courts is to resolve particular disputes. There are two principal sets of courts in the United States— federal courts and state courts. The first level of federal courts, where trials occur, is the federal district courts, which rule in the first instance on matters concerning the U.S. Constitution and federal statutes and disputes involving citizens of different states—the so-called "diversity jurisdiction." Above the district courts are the federal courts of appeal. These courts tend to focus on questions of law, but they also review findings of fact to determine whether the fact finders, often juries, have made decisions that do not agree with the evidence presented in trials.

The highest court in the federal system is the Supreme Court of the United States. There are a few types of cases in which parties might take a direct appeal to the Supreme Court. However, most cases in the lower courts get a hearing in the Supreme Court only if the justices agree to take the case. They exercise this discretionary jurisdiction in such cases as those involving matters of great public interest or those in which at least two federal appellate courts disagree on questions of law.

The state courts also have hierarchies that begin with trial courts. Most states have intermediate appellate courts and all have a highest court. Those courts having different names—for example, the New York Court of Appeals and the Massachusetts Supreme Judicial Court. The highest state courts will exercise discretion over which appeals they accept. As with the federal courts, when a case goes above the trial court level the focus of the court's review will be more on questions of law rather than questions of fact, although again the state appellate courts decide whether trial court decisions are rationally related to the evidence—or whether they are so arbitrary that they are a violation of due process.

In cases where federal courts properly have jurisdiction, they often apply state law. Many of these cases involve the "diversity jurisdiction" in which the litigants are citizens of different states. Illustratively, a federal court must determine whether state law allows actions for invasion of privacy. Just an example of the room for legal competition here is the possibility that in a state with more than one federal district, judges in two federal district courts may disagree on the interpretation of state law.

A growing area of complexity arises when there are potential collisions between federal and state law. A specialized set of problems has to do with the question of whether a federal statute—for example a health or safety statute—"pre-empts" state law in the areas covered by the federal statute. Just one example, which is representative of disputes involving federal safety statutes, is the occasion where state courts have decided cases involving injuries attributed to medical products, particularly prescription drugs and devices. In several product areas, cases of this kind have gone all the way to the Supreme Court. In some of these cases, the Court has held that the federal legislation "occupies the field" and leaves no room for individual suits for personal injury. In others, the Court has concluded that the federal laws are not "pre-empted" and has allowed suit in state courts or in federal courts under the diversity jurisdiction. These decisions by the Supreme Court have spawned many decisions by the lower federal courts. To complicate matters further, the lower courts sometimes engage in interpretation of language in Supreme Court decisions—which in turn has interpreted the language of the federal statute.

3.4 The Process

3.4.1 Common Law: Judge-Made Law

Several aspects of the judicial process are integral to the way judges decide cases. A significant part of that process is that it is common law, judge-made law, which contrasts with the law made by legislatures. An important aspect of the common law is that it develops incrementally, case by case. Law students are familiar with progressions of cases in which the court begins with a single rule or principle and then expands it to cover other kinds of situations. One example is the evolution of the tort called "intentional infliction of emotional distress," a term that courts did not even use before the 1940s. A court might first decide that one person's threats to the family of another person qualified for that label. In the next case, it might use the reasoning in the threat case to extend the tort to cases of sexual harassment. After that, it might extend its reasoning to cover cases of racial insult.

Each of these steps takes place after argument before courts about the legal limits that are appropriate for the tort doctrine of issue. Importantly, the development is case by case, with courts defining the reach of the doctrine. In that process, judicial choice of legal terms is relatively plastic, rather than confined to the particular words of a statute passed by a legislature—although courts may develop gradated sets of meanings when they interpret legislatively enacted laws.

3.4.2 Reasoning by Analogy

A technique that all lawyers learn is reasoning by analogy. No two cases are exactly alike on their facts, but often they share elements that may be said to parallel each other closely. When courts see close parallels, they may say that the case before them is enough like a prior case that it should use the legal principle for which the prior case stands.

3.4.3 Precedent

Reasoning by analogy is part and parcel of another element of common law decision-making: the importance of precedent. Litigating lawyers are always on the lookout for past decisions that support the rule or principle for which they are contending. An example comes from the idea of "informed consent" in medical malpractice cases. Physicians may find it interesting that this phrase only came into use in three judicial decisions in the early 1980s. It was from that platform that courts began to articulate relatively specific principles to govern particular cases, but courts have not always agreed on the elements of the informed consent doctrine. One question is how to define the materiality of the kinds of risk that doctors must disclose. This may depend on the statistical frequency and the severity of the risk at issue. An illustration involves two cases decided by the federal appeals court for the District of Columbia. In one case, it held that a 0.001 percent risk of local paresthesia in the face of a patient having his wisdom teeth removed was not material.[1] But a few years later, the same court concluded that a 0.1 to 0.3 percent risk that a cauterization operation would fail could be material to a woman whose medical history included significant problems from prior pregnancies, when there was evidence that her doctor knew that she was "extremely upset" and "very agitated" about the prospect of becoming pregnant again.[2]

3.5 Distinguishing Cases

Our description of these cases leads us to another element of the common law way of deciding cases, a kind of opposite to reasoning by analogy. This is the method of distinguishing cases. A court using this method finds distinctions between the case before it and the facts of precedents that it finds persuasive against the application of the precedent. A classic set of examples involves injuries to vehicle drivers on railroad tracks who were hit by locomotives. In an austere decision holding for the railroad in a case in which the driver died, Justice Holmes—who was famous for the conciseness of his pronouncements—said that "[w]hen a man goes upon a railroad track he knows that he goes to a place where he will be killed if a train comes upon him before he is clear of the track."[3] By comparison, in a decision just seven years later, Justice Cardozo said that Holmes' declaration did not automatically bar the driver's claim against the railroad. This case had some specific facts that could be said to have limited the plaintiff driver's vision of train tracks in an urban setting in a way that could be distinguished from the driver's span of vision in the prior case, arguably making it impossible for the plaintiff to see the oncoming engine. Justice Cardozo said that the case before him was one that bore "witness to the need for caution in framing standards that amount to rules of law."[4]

It is worth remarking on two features of these cases that are instructive. One is simply that opinions of two great Justices of our highest court, just seven years apart, involved distinctions between two cases that on the surface appeared to be quite similar—injuries to truck drivers hit by trains.

The other feature of these cases involves a very broad legal distinction—the difference between questions of law and questions of fact. The line between these two categories can be very blurry. Justice Holmes saw his case as turning on an exact legal standard, to be applied to any driver whose vehicle is hit by a train. Justice Cardozo in effect viewed the question of whether the driver had behaved reasonably as a question of fact, which ordinarily would be determined by a jury. Acknowledging that "[s]tandards of prudent conduct are declared at times by courts," he insisted that "they are often taken over by the facts of life."

3.6 Adversary Procedure

Litigation is by definition an adversary procedure. It relies on lawyers to find and present evidence on behalf of their clients and to make arguments for them based on many kinds of law, such as statutes, judicial precedents, and government regulations. Other legal systems employ different procedures to achieve justice. Some continental countries, for example, use an "inquisitorial" system, in which judges investigate facts. However, the adversary method is firmly established in the United States, with juries—or judges acting as fact finders— weighing evidence, and courts ruling on questions of law, although as we have explained the boundary between fact and law can be a blurry one.

3.7 What Is "Truth" for Lawyers?

Professionals trained as scientists or physicians tend to view truth as conclusions based on objective assessment of evidence. Two decisions from Texas appellate courts present dramatically different views of this idea. The issue was whether the drug Bendectin could cause birth defects in children whose mothers had ingested the drug. In a rather extreme pronouncement upholding the plaintiff's jury verdict against the manufacturer of the product, the intermediate appeals court said, "We say we are engaged in a search for truth, and we accept the jury's verdict as true except in very limited circumstances," characterizing the jury's verdict as "the bedrock of our jurisprudence, however wrong its conclusion is in the eye of God or objective reality." The court declared that "[t]he purpose of the trial is to resolve the dispute, not to find universal truths."[5]

However, the Texas Supreme Court read a stern lesson in law and science to the appellate court, which it reversed. It focused on a "concept deeply embedded in our jurisprudence that a defendant cannot be found liable for an injury unless the preponderance of the evidence supports cause in fact."[6] It noted that there had been "over thirty published, peer-reviewed epidemiological studies on the relationship between Bendectin and birth defects," none of which had found "an increased risk of limb reduction birth effects." By contrast, it pointed out that "[n]one of the findings offered by the [plaintiffs'] five experts … have been published, studied, or replicated by the scientific community." Reiterating the general requirement that "claimants prove their cases by a preponderance of the evidence," the supreme court declared that "[i]n keeping with this sound proposition at the heart of our jurisprudence, the law should not be so hasty to impose liability when scientifically reliable evidence is not available."[7] The language of these two decisions is just an example of how lawyers' arguments can be entirely at odds—the appellate court resting its decision on the "bedrock of our jurisprudence" and the supreme court countering with a "proposition at the heart of our jurisprudence."

With the understanding that questions of scientific causation may involve many complexities, we can summarize the goal of the law as finding what one observer described as "what we are willing to regard as truth."

3.8 The Role of Experts

An important practical aspect of litigation is its reliance on experts, a topic with many subissues.

One may generalize that claimants in most cases involving medical and scientific matters must produce experts to testify about such matters as standard of care and causation. One important exception to this rule is that experts are not required when the "common knowledge" of jurors renders them competent to make judgments on such issues. An obvious potential application of the exception, although one that did not bring a victory for the plaintiff, was a case in which a second abdominal operation revealed a towel with the words "Medical Department U.S. Army" embedded in the plaintiff's stomach.[8] The trial court implicitly accepted that it was not necessary to present expert testimony on surgical negligence, although the plaintiff lost the case because of a rule that barred actions by service personnel for injuries "incident to service."

A products liability case in which experts were not necessary involved a simple product design, that of shoelaces on running shoes. Suing Nike, the plaintiff argued that the laces on her shoe were "too long" and that another problem that caused her to fall while she was running was the "rigid 'pull-tab' near the top of the heel." The court said that expert testimony was "not needed for a jury to find that a sneaker with excessively long shoelaces which could become caught in the pull-tab is defectively designed."[9] One may note two ancillary points. First, physicians may sympathize with this runner plaintiff, an orthopod who claimed that the injuries from her fall kept her from getting a position as a surgeon. Another point—my speculation—is that this decision explains why the laces on my own running shoes have become significantly shorter—which I conjecture provides an example of how judicial rulings have an impact on conduct.

A contrasting result in a medical case involved a surgeon who removed bulging material from the plaintiff's spine, having concluded by touch that he "had located the … interspace between" the lowest lumbar vertebra and the first sacral vertebra, which his expert witnesses said followed "accepted medical practice." However, the plaintiff's spine had the unusual condition of lumbarization, in which there was movability in the sacral vertebrae. The court rejected the plaintiff's argument that without expert testimony, lay jurors could conclude that the surgeon had malpracticed. It said that the procedure for locating the vertebrae was "the standard method" and that neither the procedures in such surgery nor "the normal anatomical considerations that underlie them are within the common knowledge of ordinary lay persons."[10]

An important element of expert testimony is the qualifications of experts. This subject features arguments about how specialized an expert must be. I have written elsewhere that in "highly developed professions like medicine," expertise may be seen as "a series of concentric circles, with the outer circles involving relatively general bodies of knowledge and the innermost circles representing the most intense kind of specialization."[11]

A good example of how courts refine the expertise category is a case in which the court allowed the testimony of a treating physician that it was mesothelioma that was the disease suffered by a man who had served on a ship during a nuclear testing operation. The appellate court rejected the trial court's exclusion of testimony of the witness, an internist, on grounds that he was not "an oncologist or a specialist in ... *definitive* cancer diagnosis." The appellate court thought it wrong to "exclude testimony by the treating physician who ordered the report and relied on it for life-and-death decisions about the patient's treatment." It also disagreed with the trial judge's exclusion of testimony about radiation as a cause of mesothelioma from a doctor who was board-certified in internal and pulmonary medicine. The trial court had said this witness "was not 'qualified as a radiation expert'" with respect to cancer because "[h]e's not an oncologist." The appellate court said it was wrong to require that "the expert have specialization in cancer and radiation, despite his expertise in lung diseases, including mesothelioma."[12]

A case involving the failure of a hemi-walker drew an opinion that included references to two great figures in science history. The plaintiff offered three witnesses with a variety of degrees, ranging from a bachelor's degree to a doctorate in mechanical engineering, including one who had taught mechanical engineering in universities and another who had been a professor in a department of mechanical engineering. The court rejected the defense argument that none of these witnesses had "demonstrated a particular expertise with hemi-walker devices." Caustically, it declared that, under the defendant's view, "Sir Isaac Newton should not have been permitted to offer his theory of gravity after watching an apple fall from a tree until he first demonstrated a special expertise in the field of horticulture, and Benjamin Franklin should have been precluded from discussing his experiments with electricity unless he supported his theories with a documented aptitude for championship caliber kite flying."[13] If these examples were not precisely analogous to the issue in the case, the court's opinion does capture the inclination of some courts to widen the permissible scope of witness expertise.

Yet, there are many illustrations of judicial reluctance to broaden that scope. An example of a case in which a witness was held unqualified, in part because of a lack of preparation on the specifics of the case, focused on a 250,000 BTU commercial space heater. The plaintiff sued for burns he suffered when his work pants "suddenly caught fire" as he walked by the heater. The court was unimpressed by testimony of a witness that the plaintiff argued "reinforce[d] the laymen's understanding that high heat may ignite cotton material," a conclusion it said "appear[ed] not to be based upon his training and education but rather on 'common knowledge.'" It also noted that the witness had never designed nor operated such a product, that he "did not interview the plaintiff or review the plaintiff's deposition testimony," and that he "did not ascertain the plaintiff's speed" as he walked by the heater, his proximity to it, or the time he spent in front of it.[14]

One way that courts can be persuaded to allow challenged testimony on scientific matters is a direct result of the adversary system. An illustration is a suit against cigarette makers for peripheral vascular disease (PVD). The defendants argued that several experts for the plaintiff had insufficient specialization on PVD, but—in language similar to that in many decisions—the court said that any gaps in the qualifications of one of the proffered witnesses "goes to the weight of his expert testimony and can adequately be addressed by cross-examination," echoing this idea with respect to other witnesses.[15]

Endnotes

1. *Henderson v. Milobsky*, 595 F.2d 654, 659 (D.C. Cir. 1978).
2. *Hartke v. McKelway*, 707 F.2d 1544, 1549–51 (D.C. Cir. 1983).
3. *Baltimore & O. R. Co. v. Goodman*, 275 U.S. 66, 69 (1927).
4. *Pokora v. Wabash Ry. Co.*, 292 U.S. 98, 103 (1934).
5. *Merrell Dow Pharms, Inc. v. Havner*, 907 S.W.3d 535, 553–54 (Tex. Ct. App. 1995).
6. *Merrell Dow Pharms. Inc. v. Havner*, 953 S.W.2d 706, 726, 728 (Tex. 1997).
7. Id. at 726–28.

8. *Jefferson v. United States* 77 F. Supp. 706 (D. Md. 1949), aff'd, 178 F.2d 518 (4th Cir. 1949), aff'd 340 U.S. 135, 146 (1950).

9. *Faryniarz v. Nike, Inc.*, 2002 WL 530997, at 2 (S.D.N.Y. April 8, 2002).

10. *Sitts v. United States*, 811 F.2d 736, 741 (2d Cir. 1987).

11. Marshall S. Shapo, *The Law of Products Liability* ¶23.07[A][2] (7th ed. 2017).

12. *Holbrook v. Lykes Bros. SS. Co.*, 80 F.3d 777, 782–83 (3d Cir. 1996).

13. *Gibson v. Invacare Corp.*, 2011 WL 2262933, at 4 (S.D. Miss. June 7, 2011).

14. *Bland v. HC Beck & Rental Svc. Corp.*, 2007 WL 748461, at 2, 4 (E.D. Mo. March 7, 2007).

15. See *Burton v. R.J. Reynolds Tobacco Co.*, 183 F. Supp.2d 1308, 1312–17 (D. Kan. 2002).

Chapter 4

Regulation

4.1 The Institutional Background

Regulatory law is very different from law that originates with judicial decisions. The basis for regulation is legislation, statutes passed by Congress and state legislatures and often spelled out by administrative agencies that are creatures of the legislation. It bears repeating that legislation, although it is subject to constitutional challenges, is superior in legal effect to judicial decisions. Two other things are worth noting. One is that courts often determine whether regulations passed by agencies are proper use of the language of statutes. Another is that court decisions on the common law may themselves have regulatory effects.

4.2 Examples of Regulatory Statutes

A principal rationale for statutes that regulate safety is protection of vulnerable groups of people. Among the clearest examples are the statutes that make it an offense to employ children under a certain age in dangerous work. These statutes may carry criminal-type penalties and fines but also can have effects in civil litigation. For example, when an underage child is injured riding a tractor, the court will not even ask whether the employer was factually careless in using the child in that job, but effectively will determine as a matter of law that the employer fell below the proper standard of care. Another example comes from a case in which a statute required school bus drivers to flash their signal lights until children crossing a highway reached the other side. The court imposed an absolute form of liability on a school district when a student was fatally struck by a car as he followed a friend across the road, without inquiry into whether the deceased student was contributorily negligent.

Many federal safety statutes respond to the inability of classes of people to protect themselves against injuries that could be avoided by others, for example, employers and manufacturers. A law of this kind with far-reaching effect is the Occupational Safety and Health Act, under which the Occupational Safety and Health Administration and the Secretary of Labor may take action against employers who violate regulations. The language of the act is broad, going beyond basic ideas of the "unreasonable conduct" that supports civil actions under the common law of negligence. It defines a commitment to "assure so far as possible every working man and woman in the Nation safe and healthful working conditions."[1] And in its so-called "general duty" clause, the act requires an employer to "furnish to each of his employees employment and a place of employment which are free from recognized hazards that are causing or are likely to cause death or serious physical harm to his employees."[2]

Another statute that protects an especially vulnerable class of persons is the Poison Prevention Packaging Act,[3] regulations under which are the reason that adults must sometimes struggle to get the top off a pill bottle. The PPPA principally targeted deaths and injuries of children who ingested pills from bottles that were easy to open. The regulations under this law require testing on groups of young children of the closures on pill containers, with statistical parameters for the determination of which closures can be considered safe.[4]

A statute that rather unusually includes one set of quantitative definitions in its legal standards is the Federal Hazardous Substances Act. This legislation in effect requires warnings with "the signal word 'DANGER'" on substances "which are extremely flammable, corrosive, or highly toxic."[5] It defines "highly toxic" according to testing on laboratory white rats that produces death in various categories. These include for example, deaths "within fourteen days in half or more than half of ten or more" animals "each weighing between two hundred and three hundred grams, at a single dose of fifty milligrams or less per kilogram of body weight, when orally administered."[6] Other definitions are somewhat more abstract. For example, the category "hazardous substance" includes "an irritant," which is defined as "any substance not corrosive"—itself a term defined in the act—"which on immediate, prolonged, or repeated contact with normal living tissue will induce a local inflammatory reaction."[7]

A separate category includes "mechanical hazard[s]." It has nine separate subcategories of products that "in normal use or when subjected to reasonably foreseeable damage or abuse" present "an unreasonable risk of personal injury or illness" from such events as "fracture, fragmentation, or disassembly of the article," "propulsion" of it, or "from moving parts."[8]

Motor vehicles of all kinds are subject to the National Traffic and Motor Vehicle Safety Act, which gives the National Highway Traffic Safety Administration (NHTSA) the power to set standards to protect the public "against unreasonable risk of accidents occurring because of the design, construction, or performance of a motor vehicle" and against "unreasonable risk of death or injury to persons in an accident."[9] This pairing of injury-causing events includes both the initial occurrence of an accident and the kind of injury that happens in the so-called "second collision," in which, for example, a passenger is hurt by elements of a vehicle in the seconds after its first impact with another vehicle or some other object.

A law with reach across a broad range of products is the Consumer Product Safety Act, under which the Consumer Product Safety Commission can establish "consumer product safety standards" that are "reasonably necessary to prevent or reduce an unreasonable risk of injury."[10] In some cases the agency may ban or even seize especially dangerous products, with the remedy of seizure applicable to products that present "imminent and unreasonable risk of death, serious illness, or severe personal injury."[11]

We should note that in most of these statutes, the standard for regulation is not quantitative, as it is for "highly toxic" products in the Hazardous Substances Act. Rather, it is in relatively general terms such as "unreasonable risk." This kind of law provides room for the exercise of discretion by administrative agencies—judgments that may be kicked up to courts by persons dissatisfied with the interpretation of an agency.

Of special interest to physicians and medical scientists is the legislation now titled the Food Drug and Cosmetic Act, which applies to those products and also to medical devices. The FDA and courts have elaborated on the definition of "drugs" and "devices." The FDA's general definition of "drug" speaks of "articles intended for use in the diagnosis, cure, mitigation, treatment, or prevention of disease in man or other animals."[12] The law defines a "device" to include "an instrument, apparatus, implement, machine, contrivance, implant, in vitro reagent, or other similar or related article, including a component part, or accessory, which is ... intended to affect the structure or any function of the body of man or other animals," specifically saying that the object "does not achieve its primary intended purposes through chemical action within or on the body of man or other animals," and that "the object is not dependent upon being metabolized for the achievement of any of its primary intended purposes."[13]

New drugs in particular, as doctors and medical scientists know, must jump a series of hurdles on the way to the market. The first in the Investigational New Drug (IND) process, which

goes through three stages of tests on human beings—the
first as what I have termed "biochemical black boxes"—and
the next two, involving increasing numbers of subjects, moving to effectiveness and safety.[14] These two concepts, safety
and effectiveness, are crucial to the approval of a new drug
application (NDA).[15] Again, the agency—and occasionally,
courts—must make judgments about concepts with degrees of
relativity.

Politics intrudes into this overall framework of law. An
important recent example is the so-called "compassionate
IND," which under the statute tells the Secretary of Health
and Human Services to "encourage" drug makers "to design
protocols for clinical investigations" of a drug "to permit the
addition to the investigations of persons with the disease or
condition who need the drug to treat the disease or condition
and who cannot be satisfactorily treated by available alternative drugs."[16] We noted in Chapter 1 a historical event in the
near background of this law, the occasion on which a thou-
sand AIDS activists pressed the agency with a demonstration
that effectively trapped its officials in their own headquarters.

After a struggle on the question of access to drugs in early
stages of approval, Congress passed the FDA Modernization
Act in 1997. This law allowed the Secretary to authorize the
shipment of investigational devices and drugs for "emergency
situations," allowing individual patients access to products
when a physician determined that a patient had "no comparable or satisfactory alternative therapy" and the "probable
risk" of the investigational product was not "greater than the
probable risk from the disease or condition" of the patient.
A balancing provision bowed to the need to maintain traditional science, including double-blind randomized trials: The
Secretary must decide that providing the investigational product would "not interfere with ... clinical investigations."[17]

Readers will appreciate the tensions—politics veiled, so to
speak—in the bitterly contested Abigail Alliance court case
we summarized in Chapter 1 that began with the effort of a

patient to get access to an experimental drug. In the opinion favoring the FDA that eventually prevailed in the United States Court of Appeals for the District of Columbia, Judge Griffith said that the drugs at issue were "experimental and had not shown to be safe, let alone effective (or 'necessary' for) prolonging life."[18] The dissenting judge brought medical practice into the argument, mentioning the fact that many physicians prescribe drugs "off label," with the result that "[e]ven today, a patient may use a drug for unapproved purposes where the drug may be unsafe or ineffective for the off-label purpose." She concluded that "encumbrances on the right of a patient and her physician lack the historical pedigree of the rights that the Alliance seeks to vindicate."[19]

This clash of views underscores a lesson that may clash with the intuitions of scientific professionals that there surely must be a single answer the law can provide to questions as sharply focused as that in the Abigail Alliance case. But anyone familiar with the divisions in the Supreme Court on questions with high political content will understand that judges at all levels of courts often will disagree on the answers when opposing lawyers have fought a case beyond settlement.

This review of a few regulatory statutes dealing with safety is purely illustrative. Here is a list of other statutes and subject matters, also only illustrative, that have been the subjects of litigation: Cigarettes, flammable fabrics, meat inspection, boat safety, food additives, and agricultural chemicals.

4.3 Rationales for Regulation

A leading theoretical basis for our economy is the idea of efficient markets, which, in theory, provide the best kind of result for consumers. The basic idea is that if consumers possess good information about the benefits and costs of products and services, they will make the choices that best achieve the satisfactions they seek from those goods. Problems arise, however, when there are breakdowns in this nicely structured model. Those breakdowns may occur when consumers have insufficient information about risks and benefits—in part, because of the costs of transmitting that information. This is not ordinarily a big problem when there is face-to-face bargaining between consumers and suppliers. The problem becomes significant when suppliers cannot effectively communicate with large groups of people, or information is complex and difficult to understand.

Another angle on the problem of inefficient markets appears in the concept of negative "externalities"—that is, injuries that occur as a result of the dangers of activities and products. Simple examples of externalities in the medical field include prescription of the wrong drugs by doctors and unwanted side effects caused by drugs, and failures to prevent preventable infections in hospitals. In other areas of products used by workers and consumers, one finds industrial machines with inadequate safety guards and automobile components designed without sufficient consideration of the possibility that they will explode after periods of use in certain climates.

One after-the-fact remedy for negative externalities is to require suppliers and producers to pay for the injuries caused by their services and products. The theory is that making them pay compensation will "internalize the externalities," often with the effect that those parties will change their behavior in ways that minimize injuries. A particular set of problems for law lies in the impact that injuries have on people who do not directly sustain those injuries.

Examples of indirect but often substantial externalities appear in the burdens that injuries cause to families. This includes families who lose their principal earners due to injuries. It also includes the toll in caretaking energy and in emotions that injuries take on family members—costs that will ordinarily not be chalked up in tort damage awards. And physical consequences may indeed affect third persons—for example, family members of people who work with asbestos

and bring the dust from those products home, causing mesothelioma in spouses or children. A special kind of externality,
also not often tallied in tort judgments, is the emotional shock
to those who witness injuries to others.

A challenging set of problems lies in an area that mixes economic theory and moral philosophy. These are problems arising
from injuries, which can be physical or economic, to consumers who are disadvantaged in some way, for example by lack
of education and sophistication. Several judicial statements in
various branches of the law, not focused on regulatory statistics
but with effects on conduct, have indicated a sympathy for such
consumers. A statement in a 1910 trademark case, which was
quoted in decisions involving direct deception of consumers,
declares that the law was made for "that vast multitude which
includes the ignorant, the unthinking and the credulous who, in
making purchases, do not stop to analyze, but are governed by
appearances and general impressions."[20] An opinion in a 1960
Georgia appellate case displayed the same kind of sympathy
for an illiterate consumer who was deceived by a high-pressure
salesman of stainless steel cookware. The court found sufficient
evidence to impose liability on the seller on the basis that its
salesman had created "immediate fear in the plaintiff for her
own health and that of her family" "by the use of 'scheme, arti-
fice, or method,'" knowing that "the plaintiff was laboring under
a misapprehension … that food cooked in aluminum cookware
becomes impregnated with a cancer-producing substance."[21]

A remark by an employee relations manager about a worker's ignorance of a risk put a weight in the scale against the
maker of a salt bath furnace, into which the worker slipped or
misstepped, sustaining burns that required the amputation of a
leg below the knee. The manager said that the employee was "a
great person but it's hard to guard against ignorance." In reversing a judgment in favor of the manufacturer, that court said that
"in the case of a dangerously designed salt bath furnace with
a defect which may not be obvious to the plaintiff, this is … [a]
factual question that is properly before the jury."[22]

A foundry worker overcame what is sometimes called the "sophisticated user" defense in a suit for silicosis. The Minnesota Supreme Court reversed a judgment for a supplier of silica, saying that the plaintiff, the "end user," had not been shown to be "familiar with industry or government publications on the dangers of silicosis" and that "[h]is general knowledge of the risk was little more than the intuitive sense of danger from experiencing dust in the foundry environment."[23]

A case involving a medical product, silicone gel breast implants, reached higher into the realm of sophisticated users. This case arose from the bankruptcy of Dow Corning, which argued that two makers of implants were sophisticated purchasers. Rejecting this as at least an outright defense, the court said that even though the implant makers "may have been sophisticated buyers," there was a question of fact as to whether the makers of the implants "relied on Dow Corning's superior knowledge, as advertised by Dow Corning, regarding the safety of the silicone fluids."[24]

Thus, even corporations with some expertise in a product arena may be found at a legal disadvantage to firms with even more expertise. The general impression of superior knowledge may weigh against those who possess it. As a great state court judge wrote in a case involving injuries caused by a power saw, "It should not be controlling whether the plaintiff selected the machine because of the statements in the brochure, or because of the machine's own appearance of excellence that belied the defect lurking beneath the surface, or because he merely assumed that it would safely do the jobs it was built to do."[25] Generally, good advice for doctors and product sellers.

4.4 Some Background on Representative Statutes

The major safety statutes have varied histories. The 19th-century background of the present Food Drug and Cosmetic Act is fascinating. Cocaine is now a Schedule II drug under

the Controlled Substances Act, a category which the Drug
Enforcement Administration defines as "drugs with a high
potential for abuse," with use potentially leading to "severe
psychological or physical dependence." But cocaine was a free
market drug into the early 20th century, a leading exponent
having been no less a physician than Sigmund Freud, who
said that for users, "[l]ong-lasting mental or physical work can
be performed without fatigue" and that, indeed, it "completely
banished the need for sleep."[26] Recommended uses included
"hay fever, asthma, sciatica, tuberculosis, even … the common
cold,"[27] with the journal *Lancet* suggesting it in 1891 as an
ingredient in a nasal spray for colds.[28] Cocaine combined with
caffeine in a "soft drink" named Coca-Cola was a usage that
persisted until 1903 and at least until that year was so available
in a Philadelphia drugstore that customers would hold up the
number of fingers that corresponded with the amount of the
"five-cent powder" that they desired.[29]

It was only the passage of the Pure Food and Drug Act of
1906 that began to put restrictions on cocaine, calling drugs
and food items misbranded if their labels did not disclose the
"quantity or proportion" of a group of eleven substances that
included cocaine as well as heroin and alcohol, and restricting
its importation. It took until 1914, by which time most states
regulated distribution of cocaine, that the Harrison Act set up
a registration system for its distribution.[30]

The 1906 act did regulate drugs, to the extent that "in
accordance with the standards of strength, quality, and
purity in the *United States Pharmacopoeia* and the *National
Formulary*," they "could not be sold in any other condition
unless the specific variations from the applicable standards
were plainly stated on the label."

In fact, though, the major inciting cause for the legislation was the conditions existing in the meatpacking industry,
captured by Upton Sinclair in his novel *The Jungle*. Harvey
Wiley, who had been the chief chemist of the Department
of Agriculture, became known as the father of the act, and

oversaw its administration. He centered his emphasis "on foods, which he believed posed a greater public health problem than adulterated or misbranded drugs."[31]

Impetus for safety legislation often comes from clusters of injuries, some in short periods of time and some that occur over decades. A condensed cluster of injuries led to the second major piece of food and drug legislation, in 1938. This was the 100 or so deaths caused by the drug elixir sulfanilamide, which was used to treat streptococcal infections, but had not been tested for toxicity and for which no pharmacological studies had been done. Outrage over these events was a principal factor in the passage of the legislation, which provided for the FDA to require evidence of safety for new drugs and to set food standards, including quality and identity standards.

Another, larger cluster of injuries, this one centered abroad—from European nations to Australia—led to the passage of another major statute, the Drug Amendments of 1962. The trigger for this legislation was the birth of thousands of children with limb defects, occurring after their pregnant mothers had taken the drug thalidomide for morning sickness. An American heroine in this story, the FDA medical officer Dr. Frances Kelsey, refused to approve the drug. The ensuing public outcry led to the 1962 amendments, which combined requirements that drug manufacturers prove their products were effective before they were marketed and that they provide reports of adverse effects that occurred after marketing.

The administration of another important statute began to change with the story of another safety heroine, Rachel Carson. Carson's 1962 book *Silent Spring* centered on pesticides, generated public awareness of the dangers of chemicals used in the environment. The statute, initially passed in 1947, is the Federal Insecticide, Fungicide and Rodenticide Act (FIFRA), which originally focused on the labeling of such products. A 1972 amendment, the Federal Environmental Pesticide Control Act, centering on the dangers of pesticides used in agriculture, established requirements for manufacturers to register their products with the Environmental Protection Agency, which had to approve the labels with instructions for safe use. These provisions are firmly in place, although there has been considerable litigation on the question of whether the statute prevents civil suits by persons injured by products covered by the legislation.

The decisions in this area, which include a major Supreme Court decision, sometimes deal with the interpretation of the statute with reference to specific legal doctrines under the common law including express warranty, defective design, and defective manufacture of products. The basic language of the statute is simple enough, aiming to prevent sale of products that have "unreasonable adverse effects on the environment." However, the gremlin in the statutory details is language that bars states from "impos[ing]or continu[ing] in effect any requirements for labeling or packaging in addition to or different from those required under" the law. It is this language that has required the courts to deal with claims based on specific theories of liability like the ones I have mentioned.

Another individual—a hero to some but not to others— was the moving force behind the legislation that became the National Traffic and Motor Vehicle Safety Act. This was Ralph Nader, whose 1965 book *Unsafe at Any Speed* was a principal stimulant for the law. This book brought to public consciousness the toll taken on vehicle passengers by the design of the vehicles themselves, including exposure of passengers to injuries caused by the "second collision." It is under that law that the National Highway Traffic Safety Administration has adopted regulations on such elements of vehicles as passenger restraints, airbags, side strength of cars, resistance of vehicle roofs to crushing, and energy-absorbing steering columns.

The Occupational Safety and Health Act was the product of concerns with health and safety that grew through the 1960s.[32] The one case focusing on OSHA regulations that has come to the Supreme Court captures the profile of law that confronts those who design and oversee industrial workplaces. The case began with the refusal of two workers at a Whirlpool manufacturing plant in Marion, Ohio, to carry out orders of a foreman to perform maintenance on a guard screen from which an employee had fallen to his death. A detailed agency regulation provided a process under which employees could refuse to work when facing "a real danger of death or serious injury" that was sufficiently urgent that it could not be remedied through "regular statutory enforcement channels." The Supreme Court upheld this regulation, affirming a judgment by a court of appeals that reversed a decision by the federal district court. The court said that the regulation "appears to further the overriding purpose of the Act."[33] It quoted a sponsor of the Senate bill that became the act as saying that "We are talking about people's lives, not the indifference of some cost accountants."[34] The case is an interesting study in how a problem for two ordinary people worked its way through a complicated system—beginning with an agency regulation and going through three levels of federal courts—to achieve a result that fashions a small wedge of law, specifically, the validity of a regulation.

Many of the laws we have discussed here were the product of growing consumer concern about safety in the 1960s, with the Occupational Safety and Health Act being passed in 1970. A National Commission on Product Safety in that year laid the foundation for another statute with its declaration that "[f]ederal products safety legislation consists of a series of isolated acts treating specific hazards in narrow product categories." There was "[n]o government agency" with "general authority" to enforce safety in consume products generally, which one Senator called a "wholly inadequate" "piecemeal approach to product safety."[35] This situation led to the passage of the Consumer Product Safety Act in 1972. The Consumer Product Safety Commission, which enforces the statute, has forced recalls on products ranging from toys to lawn and garden tractors and from football helmets to swivel patio chairs.

In concluding this summary of safety regulation statutes, we mention the Ryan White Comprehensive AIDS Resources Emergency Act, a striking example of federal legislation that responds to medical needs arising from a safety hazard. The spark for this statute was the plight of a single individual, an Indiana teenager who contracted HIV from a blood transfusion. The Department of Health and Human Services summarizes the Ryan White HIV/AIDS Program as the "largest Federal program focused specifically on providing HIV care and treatment services to people living with HIV."

What is notable about this catalog of statutes is the diversity not only of their subject matter but of their historical wellsprings. Since they are statutes, they represent political consensus on their subject matter, and often they bespeak legislators stirred by sympathetic stories—of both individuals and groups of people who are victims of injury or illness. It is especially interesting that the Occupational Safety and Health Act and the Poison Prevention Packaging Act, passed in 1970, and the Consumer Product Safety Act, enacted in 1972, were all signed into law by President Nixon. One way or another, politics is the basis for legislation, and for that Republican chief executive, the time had come for these statutes. Those who provide health care and those who design and sell products should keep in mind how adverse consequences of their activities and goods may affect the public sentiment that drives the passage of such laws.

4.5 Recurring Issues for Safety Regulation

There are a number of issues that cut across the many controversies that arise concerning safety regulation. A constant is the need to compare the tradeoffs between the risks and benefits of the activities and products regulated. A very good set of examples appears in the sagas which we summarized in Chapter 1 involving the regulation of estrogen products.

The twists and turns of these sagas, which have gone on for more than half a century, typify problems that exist when medical patients lack the knowledge of scientists, let alone knowledge of what scientists do not know.

The decision of the Women's Health Initiative to end its study of combination hormone products, with its statement that "health risks exceeded health benefits over an average follow-up of 5.2 years"[36] is emblematic of the kind of risk–benefit tradeoff that challenges research professionals and frequently befuddles consumers. It also symbolizes the blurriness of the boundary lines among regulators, researchers, and producers such as makers of hormonal products.

A related set of issues arises from the different applications of the term "good science." This phrase is thrown back and forth in discussions about the data on medical products. The so-called "gold standard" for clinical investigations of such products is the randomized, double-blind study. During the controversy over the Abigail Alliance case, decisions on which are summarized previously in this chapter and in Chapter 1, Ezekiel Emanuel scathingly criticized the panel decision of the court of appeals that favored the Alliance. He noted the suffering that bone marrow transplants outside of the FDA process had imposed on thousands of women with metastatic breast cancer. He estimated the dollar costs of those treatments as "millions, if not billions" for what turned out to be a "substandard treatment." He said that the panel decision would have brought "access to unproven experimental agents for a few patients at the expense of more, faster research and access to proven treatment for every patient."[37]

Further instructive is the controversy over the cardiovascular effects of the diabetes drug Avandia, discussed more fully in Chapter 9. After the first alarms were sounded on the drug, the *Medical Letter* pointed out that there had been "no prospective double-blind trial comparing the cardiovascular safety" of Avandia and the competing drug Actos. The complicating factor of public perceptions and public desires was evident in the statement of a member of an FDA panel on Avandia who had treated diabetes patients that doctors should have "as many choices of drugs as possible." Dr. Clifford Rosen, the chair of a joint FDA advisory committee that addressed the Avandia controversy, lamented that "very little" had been said in a hearing "about the balance of risks and benefits," pointing out that "though the risks were apparent from the data presentations, there was virtually no discussion of any unique benefits" of Avandia.[38] These examples simply illustrate the difficulties that arise when regulation encounters scientific disagreement—a disagreement that was so fierce in the case of Avandia that Dr. Rosen noted that the FDA's joint advisory committee had "met for 20 hours over 2 days."[39]

All of this, including the disputes among scientists about data and the strong desires of patients for access to medications that have not met the "gold standard," implies the problems inherent in "direct-to-consumer" advertising of prescription products to consumers. The writer's own internist, weary of patients who want a drug they saw promoted on cable television, has emphatically indicated his vexation at this kind of advertising.

Part of the background of government regulation of medical products is the vastness of the research enterprise and the competition within it. Discussions of the death of a research subject at Johns Hopkins in 2001 manifested how big science becomes big business. Investigators at Hopkins, then the recipient of the most federal research money, were conducting 2,800 clinical trials, with over $300 million in funding.[40]

With stakes this high, federal research becomes a kind of ongoing scientific Olympics, with winners and losers. The competition obviously has produced both. Scientist winners are those who receive grants, and winners among patients are those who benefit from discoveries that alleviate or cure illness. Losers are investigators who do not get grants and patients who suffer ill effects from experimental products such as drugs and medical devices. Some of these products may be insufficiently investigated in the rush for professional recognition. Others, after tryouts on the mass market, simply prove to be on the wrong side of risk–benefit accounting.

A particular facet of this competition appears in the requirement by medical journals that authors of articles reveal potential conflicts of interest (COIs). A statement by an association of editors of journals presents a long list of possible "competing interests." These include, most obviously, authors who have "received or expect[] to receive money (or other financial benefits such as patents or stocks), gifts, or services that may influence work related to a specific publication." The statement says that "[c]ommercial sources of funding, by companies that sell drugs or medical devices, are generally seen as the most concerning." The list includes clinicians, said to "have a financial competing interest if they are paid for services related to their research—for example, if they write, review, or edit an article about the comparative advantage of a procedure that they themselves provide for income." Even editors of journals are subject to conflicts—for example, if "they have or a close family member has a COI (financial or otherwise) in a particular manuscript submitted to their journal."[41]

All of the considerations we have discussed—economic and political—lie in the background of regulation of medicine and medical research. Many of them are unknown to the population of patients that regulators serve.

We turn now to a different body of law that is of considerable interest to a variety of entrepreneurs and professionals. This is the private law called *tort law* that governs civil litigation on injuries between individuals and other individuals or business entities. Judicial decisions in these cases resolve those specific conflicts. But it is worth noting, at the end of this chapter on regulation, that decisions in particular cases under this body of private law often may have regulatory effects—effects beyond the resolution of individual disputes.

Endnotes

1. 29 U.S.C. § 651(b).
2. 29 U.S.C. § 654(a).
3. 15 U.S.C.A. § 1471.
4. 16 C.F.R §§ 1700.15, 1700.20.
5. 15 U.S.C.A. § 1211 (p) (1).
6. 15 U.S.C.A. §1261(h)(1).
7. Id. §1261(j).
8. Id. §1261(s).
9. 49 U.S.C.A. § 30102(9).
10. 15 U.S.C.A.§ 2056.
11. Id. §§ 2057, 2061(a).
12. 21 U.S.C.A. § 321(g).
13. 21 U.S.C.A. § 321(h).
14. 21 CFR §321.21.
15. 21 U.S.C.A. §355.
16. 21 U.S.C. § 360dd.
17. 21 U.S.C. §360bbb.
18. Abigail Alliance for Better Access to Developmental Drugs, 495 F.3d 695, 708 (D.C. Cir. 2007).
19. Id. at 726 (Rogers, J. dissenting).
20. *Florence Mfg. Co. v. J.C. Dowd & Co.*, 178 F. 73, 75 (2d Cir. 1910).
21. *King v. Towns*, 118 S.E.2d 121, 126 (Ga. Ct. App. 1960).
22. *Pargo v. Elec. Furnace Co.*, 498 So.2d 833, 834–36 (Miss. 1986).
23. *Gray v. Badger Mining Corp.*, 676, 126 N.W.2d 268, 276–77 (Minn. 2004).
24. In re: Dow Corning, 2008 WL 4585249, at 8–9 (E.D. Mich. 2008).
25. *Greenman v. Yuba Power Prods Co.*, 377 P.2d 897, 901 (Cal. 1963).
26. E. M. Thornton, *The Freudian Fallacy: An Alternative View of Freudian Theory*, 22 (1984).
27. Id. at 130.
28. Id. at 137.
29. See Richard Ashley, *Cocaine: Its History, Uses and Effects*, 59–60 (1975).
30. For a summary of these developments, citing sources, see Shapo, Freud, Cocaine, and Products Liability 77 *B.U. L. Rev.* 421, 424 (1997).

31. FDA, FDA History, Part I, http://www.fda.gov/AboutFDA
/WhatWeDo/History/Origin/ucm054819.htm.

32. For a brief summary, see Congressman Lloyd Meeds, The
Legislative History of OSHA, 9 *Gonz. L. Rev.* 327, 329 (1974).

33. *Whirlpool Corp. v. Marshall*, 445 U.S. 1,13 (1980).

34. Id. at 12 n.16.

35. Nat'l Comm'n on Product Safety 2 (1970).

36. Writing Group for the Women's Health Initiative Investigators,
Risks and Benefits of Estrogen Plus Progestin in Healthy
Postmenopausal Women, 28 *JAMA* 321 (2002). See also the
discussion of the WHI investigations in Chapter 1, text accompanying notes 40–43.

37. Ezekiel Emanuel, Drug Addiction, *New Republic*, July 3, 2006,
at 9–10.

38. Gardiner Harris, Panel Suggests Limit on Drug for Diabetes,
N.Y. Times, July 15, 2010, at A1 and A23; Clifford Rosen,
Revisiting The Rosiglitazone Stor—Lessons Learned, 363 *N. Eng.
J. Med.* 303 (2010).

39. Id. I have summarized these events and arguments in Marshall
S. Shapo, *The Experimental Society*, 70–77 (Transaction
Publishers 2016).

40. See Susan Levine, FDA Faults Clinical Research at Hopkins,
Wash. Post, Sept. 8, 2001.

41. WAME, Conflict of Interest in Peer-Reviewed Medical Journals
(2009). http://www.wame.org/about/conflict-of-interest-in-peer
-reviewed-medical.

Chapter 5

Tort Law Generally

Tort law is a body of law that looms large in the minds of medical professionals, others engaged in risky activities, and makers and sellers of products that present some degree of danger to consumers and others who may encounter those products.

5.1 Defining Tort

Tort can be defined with varying degrees of abstractness. Tort law is the body of law that governs actions for injuries claimed to be caused by behavior that is wrongful or otherwise regarded as unjust if it causes injury. Torts involve invasions of personal physical and mental security, interests in property, and some other kinds of economic interests. A convenient dividing line in law is the one between tort—which signifies injuries that occur when a claimant has had no opportunity to bargain on exposure to risk—and contract, where the parties make an agreement that at least in some sense covers risks. These two compartments are not airtight—sometimes tort law applies to cases that are partly covered by some kind of contract.

When I say that text covers behavior that is "wrongful or otherwise regarded as unjust," I note that there is a spectrum of liability theories that span a range of culpability and can even include liability without fault. At the most culpable end of this spectrum are "intentional" torts, a category that has been expanded to include not only conduct that has a desire or purpose to injure but in which the defendant is shown to have "knowledge of substantial certainty" that the injurious result will occur. Next down the spectrum are categories labeled "willful and wanton" conduct or reckless behavior. A shade less culpable is "gross negligence." The most quantitatively important tort category is negligence. This tort has been defined in a dozen or more ways. The simplest kinds of definitions are those that speak of exposing "others to an unreasonable risk of harm" or a "failure to exercise reasonable care under the circumstances." At the other end of the spectrum are doctrines of strict liability, which have been employed to impose liability in two major categories: Activities that are "abnormally dangerous" and products that are sold in "a defective condition unreasonably dangerous to the user."

There are frequent references to the "tort liability system," which includes both rules of tort law, especially rooted in reported decisions of courts, and the process of litigation, which decides disputes. Later we will discuss controversies about systemic features of tort law, including some of the most basic aspects of legal doctrine and, in Chapter 10, some very specific rules that affect access to the system.

5.2 Rationales of Tort Law

The principal remedy for injuries claimed to be torts is money damages, although courts may also give orders regulating conduct—for example, orders not to do things like putting certain substances into the environment—that carry a risk of injury. One way or the other, judicial imposition of remedies for torts will impose financial costs on the alleged injurer—the "tortfeasor." It is therefore important to identify the rationales that have been advanced to justify judgments which transfer wealth from tortfeasors to those claiming they have been injured by torts.

A gritty threshold justification for tort law is that its very existence affords to persons who believe they were wrongfully injured a method of redress so that they will not engage in "self-help"—as one great scholar phrased it in describing the roots of tort in ancient law, "private vengeance and private war."[1]

A shorthand of a principal rationale for imposing tort liability is "deterrence"—that is, controlling behavior by imposing money costs on those who engage in risky activities. The simple economic proposition is that if you make a certain kind of conduct more expensive, you will get less of it. There is more than one flavor of deterrence. Economic theorists seek an "optimal" level of deterrence—one in which risk levels are efficient in the sense that consumers purchase packages of risks and benefits at prices that are acceptable to them. Thus, they may choose to buy a machine tool without guards because its price is less than one with guards, thus accepting the added risk of injury to get the lower price. A cousin to this idea of efficiency is the notion that tort law should impose liability only when the costs of accidents exceed the costs of preventing them.

Yet another set of economic cousins to these approaches are various forms of cost–benefit analysis. Physicians in particular can relate to the question of the average length of an office visit. Thirty-minute visits may minimize the chances of misdiagnoses; twenty-minute visits may increase them. An astringent view of the issue may lead one to ask whether the cost to patients of misdiagnoses in the shorter visit outweigh the economic benefits achieved by correct diagnoses of more patients during shorter visits.

Yet another efficiency-oriented idea is that the burden of accidents should be placed on the "cheapest cost avoider," who may be the injury victim as well as the risky actor. Illustratively, in the setting of dangerous workplace machines, the user of the machine may be able to avoid an accident at lower cost than the designer of the machine. Of course, as is the case with much economic analysis, it may be difficult to quantify the cost to the worker—and his or her employer—of the worker taking more care in the pressured circumstances of a job where the time for completing tasks is important. One result of this form of reasoning is that from an economic point of view, there can be too few accidents as well as too many accidents. In colloquial terms, one can be too careful. A complicating factor is that many injuries that could be held to be torts are never the subject of lawsuits, so that the costs of those injuries never enter into social accounting. The authors of a 1978 study of medical injuries wrote that "the number of suits, even though it is burgeoning, remains far below the theoretical level required to signal [to medical providers] the expected loss ... resulting from negligence."[2]

A rather different view of deterrence goes beyond economic efficiency to a moral emphasis. This type of deterrence stresses that what are regarded as morally unacceptable types or levels of accidents should be reduced, even if reducing them would fall below the economically efficient level. An opinion in a products liability case involving a rental car simply spoke of achieving "maximum protection for the victims of defective rentals."[3] To be sure, there are points at which efficiency and morality overlap, if not becoming fused. Imposing liability on sellers of products that cause injury may reflect a recognition that there is an imbalance of information about risk between product sellers and consumers. Recognition of the imbalance may have components of both economic rationality and fairness.

A separate, but related, idea is that tort judgments send a moral message both to defendants against who they are rendered, and to the community at large. The simplest form of the message is one of right and wrong: The defendant should not have acted as it did. This is surely the lesson in cases where the defendant has acted negligently, or even more culpably. The message is less powerful when the court imposes strict liability on the defendant, although some strict liability cases turn out to have a whiff of negligence about them.

Paralleling these issues is the question of how one defines consumer welfare. Sometimes consumer preferences clash with the weight of scientific evidence on the hazards of a product. Illustrative is the case of the heavily marketed painkiller Vioxx, which Merck, under pressure, withdrew from the market only after data indicated substantial increases in heart attacks and strokes in patients taking the drug. Yet a colleague of this author said she found the drug so effective that she would risk taking it to alleviate her pain. Illustrative of the financial risk to companies that make the wrong estimate of risk was Merck's $4.85 billion settlement of 27,000 Vioxx lawsuits.

A powerful pair of rationales for tort law are compensation and individual justice. Damage awards provide funds to injury victims that make up, to a certain extent, the cost of medical bills and lost wages, and provide a representation in dollars of such non-economic losses as pain and suffering. It should be noted that tort awards are a relatively small slice of compensation received by injury victims, who get much more money from such sources as health insurance, various types of disability insurance, and workers' compensation—the latter to be discussed later. However, there is a symbolic element to tort compensation which may be summarized in the term "corrective justice"—a direct, one-on-one outcome between an injurer and an injury victim. One writer has described an allied version of this idea by saying that "'acting against' another in response to wrongdoing is a distinctive form of 'moral address.'"[4] We should add, though, that this form of direct justice is attenuated when tort judgments are paid—as usually they are—from liability insurance held by the defendant.

Tied in with these rationales is the idea that tort judgments vindicate personal rights. Arrived at in a public setting, they do so in favor of individual victims of injury and provide that vindication symbolically for society at large. Yet another facet of these rationales is that tort judgments embody the concept of personal responsibility. That idea applies not only to those who engage in activities risky to others, but also to injury victims. Various tort doctrines place responsibility—sometimes complete responsibility—on claimants who have been careless or have behaved in ways that may be said to "assume the risk" of injury. A defense that overlaps with these is the defense of "misuse" of products, which sometimes may involve consumer carelessness and sometimes simply focuses on product sellers' arguments that a consumer's use of their goods was simply not an intended use.

An important, controversial, rationale for tort liability is that of risk-spreading, or loss-spreading, sometimes described as *loss distribution*. A simplest form of this rationale assumes a single individual who is injured by, say, a product, with a cost to him or her of $1,000,000, but with no other persons being injured by that product. Assume further that 10 million people buy the product. The cost of the injury is passed through to those customers in the form of increased prices—a dime per unit of the product on the market. Although that result itself includes an assumption that does not always work out in practice, theoretically the injured person's cost is "spread" among those who have benefited from the product.

5.3 Products Liability

5.3.1 Theories of Liability

There are several legal theories on which a person injured by a product may sue. Some of them are directly represen-tational, with a spectrum of culpability that parallels the general one described above. Tort theories of liability for misrepresentations begin with the most culpable—fraud, or untrue statements made recklessly of their truth or falsity. The spectrum then runs through negligent misrepresentations to innocent misrepresentations, which in some states may be the basis for a tort action against sellers including manufacturers, especially for advertising representations that turn out to be untrue. An analogous theory based on contract law which has been codified in the Uniform Commercial Code, now adopted in all the states, is express warranty—an "affirmation of fact or promise … which relates to the goods and becomes part of the basis of the bargain." This is a non-fault theory of liability— basically, all that is necessary is that the statement be an "affirmation of fact or promise" that events show was not correct. Another theory with representational overtones is the implied warranty of fitness for a particular purpose, which arises when the seller has "reason to know" the buyer's purpose for the product and that the buyer "is relying on the seller's skill and judgment."

There are also a number of theories of tort liability for products that do not require a showing of a specific representation. An all-purpose vehicle here is negligence— unreasonable conduct in the design, manufacture, or sale of goods that cause injury. Many courts also use a theory of strict liability for products with defects that make them unreasonably dangerous. A contract-based theory that parallels that tort doctrine is the implied warranty of merchantability, which requires a showing that goods are "fit for the ordinary purposes for which such goods are used." This is a non-fault theory, which applies to items that are "fungible"—that is, interchangeable with other identical items. A simple, graphic example appears in Judge Cardozo's concise statement that loaves of bread "baked with pins in them are not of merchantable quality."

In many cases, there may be representational backgrounds that bolster judgments for consumers based on theories, like negligence and strict liability, that are not based on specific representations. Those backgrounds include various kinds of product promotion such as advertising.

5.3.2 *The Concept of Defect*

Generally speaking, a consumer disappointed by a product must show, in one way or another, that it had a defect. This requirement is implicit for some theories and explicit for others, especially the theory of strict products liability. A standard used by many courts for a finding of defect under strict liability requires that a product be "unreasonably dangerous"— a test applied to the level of danger of the product as it is viewed at the time of trial.

There are two principal kinds of defect—the manufacturing defect and the design defect, with some courts employing the term "warnings defect," which consists of a failure to warn of the hazards of a product. A manufacturing defect is, to use a simple nontechnical term, a "flaw" in a product. There is general agreement that a unit of a product that departs from the manufacturer's design is a manufacturing defect to which strict liability applies. Representative cases are hairline fractures in very different kinds of products, ranging from connecting rods in automobiles to glass in old-fashioned soda bottles. Even if the manufacturer lived up to industry standards in making the product, its liability is still strict. A principal rationale is that as compared with a totally innocent consumer, the manufacturer is in the best position to spread the risk of injury.

There is much controversy about the concept of design defect, in cases where the consumer in effect argues that the very blueprint of the product makes it unreasonably dangerous. This theory is different from that of manufacturing defect, although there may be some products where it is difficult to make the distinction. With a design defect there is no "flaw" in the product; it comes to market in the same condition that the manufacturer intended. The discussion that follows does not sharply differentiate the concepts, but it largely applies to cases where the product on which suit is brought is the product that the manufacturer designed and intended to market.

Of particular interest to scientists and physicians is the concept of the "unavoidably unsafe" product. That term has been used to describe medical products like drugs, vaccines, and devices, which, as a leading source puts it, "in the present state of human knowledge, are quite incapable of being made safe for their intended and ordinary use."[5] One decision employing this test said that it "vindicate[d] the public's interests in the availability and affordability of prescription drugs."[6] A contrasting decision involving a vaccine saw "no public policy need for ... shifting from the drug manufacturers to the consumer/victim the responsibility for all of the 'unfortunate consequences'" suffered by injured patients.[7]

The particular case of vaccines demonstrates a parallel between common law decision-making and legislation. Responding to the costs of vaccine injuries, Congress in 1986 enacted the National Childhood Vaccine Injury Act, which set up a no-fault compensation system under which persons injured by vaccines could file petitions. An alternative for those unsatisfied with the decision of a special master for the Secretary of Health and Human Services was to file a regular tort action.

Another controversial set of concepts under the defect heading includes what could be called the dangerous "good" products. These are products that are legally sold, not adulterated, and in common use. One formulation has referred to such products as "good whiskey," "good tobacco," and "good butter"—all products concerning which there is a certain amount of public knowledge about their risks.[8]

The thrust of the case law on alcoholic beverages has decidedly been to immunize sellers from consumer suits. In one case, involving an 18-year-old driver who had a collision while drunk, the court quoted a statement that there was no duty to warn about products that are "only dangerous, or potentially so, when consumed in excessive quantity, or over a long period of time, when the danger, or potentiality of danger, is *generally known and recognized*."[9] However, some decisions have recognized liability against makers of alcoholic drinks. A remarkable case focused on the death from pancreatitis of a 26-year-old man who had consumed two or three cans of the defendant's beer four nights a week. The court said, among other things, that consumers were "unaware of the risk created by the consumption of beer in the way that the decedent had consumed it," and concluded that there was a "material dispute as to whether Stroh's beer without a warning is safe for its intended use."[10] Another decision, although eventually reversed in favor of the defendant, initially refused to bar a suit for the death of a college freshman who engaged in a bout of drinking straight shots of tequila.[11]

The legal battle about the liability of cigarette makers has been fiercer and more complicated. One court that denied a claim drew on the lack of adulteration of the defendant's products—saying that there was "no proof that these cigarettes were 'improperly manufactured' or contained 'dangerous impurities.'"[12] Other courts stressed that plaintiffs had not shown there was an alternative design for cigarettes.[13] Even some legislatures adopted statutes that immunize cigarette makers. A Texas law barred suits for products that were "inherently unsafe and ... known to be unsafe by the ordinary consumer who consumes the product with the ordinary knowledge common to the community." Borrowing from the language of the general formulation quoted above, this statute referred to "common consumer product[s] intended for personal consumption, such as sugar, castor oil, alcohol, tobacco, and butter."[14]

A contrasting set of opinions emphasized both lack of consumer knowledge and the particular feature of the addictive properties of cigarettes. One court, confronted with a plaintiff who smoked between 1950 and 1965, said that for that period, a "rational jury could find the absence of 'common knowledge' of the nature of the link between smoking and lung cancer." It cited an expert's quotation of "extensive data" to support her conclusion that "so far as I know, people thought cigarette smoke was simply as dangerous as breathing city air." The court also mentioned legislation on cigarette labeling as indicating that Congress "may have implicitly recognized that the link between smoking and lung cancer was not 'common knowledge.'"[15] With respect to the element of addictiveness, another court said there was "no basis" for it to take judicial notice of the knowledge of that fact by ordinary consumers when the plaintiff before it began smoking.[16] Some courts even challenged the "pure tobacco" idea, with one noting allegations that the flue curing of tobacco and the addition of as many of as 110 or 115 additives made the defendant's cigarettes "more inhalable and more dangerous."[17] Another cited allegations that a company had "manipulated nicotine levels and rejected safer alternative cigarette designs."[18] This spectrum of decisions captures the importance of facts in litigation concerning risks that might be thought to be well known.

Arguments continue about what the general standard is for determining whether a product has a defect. With law professors loving concepts—and variations on concepts—as they do, there have been several formulations of the elements of the defect concept. They range from a list of five to a list of fifteen. One of the most cited lists includes such elements as "the usefulness and desirability of the product," the availability of practical substitutes, "the manufacturer's ability to eliminate the unsafe character of the product without impairing its usefulness or making it too expensive to maintain its utility," and "the user's anticipated awareness of the dangers inherent in the product."

A particularly fierce set of arguments concerns two standards, one stressing the expectations of ordinary consumers and the other a comparison of the "utility of the product" and "the risk it creates." These standards have been embedded in competing versions of the Restatement of Torts, an ongoing project of the American Law Institute, a private organization that attempts to state the general principles governing many kinds of laws.

With respect to the controversial issue of whether a product has a design defect, those who support risk-utility analysis argue, in part, that it creates "incentives for manufacturers to achieve optimal levels of safety in designing and marketing products." They suggest that a consumer expectations standard is too vague and may leave too much decision-making power to judges, and to juries, when the focus should be on the balancing of risks. A standard that has been melded with risk-utility analysis would require that plaintiffs in design defect cases prove that there is a reasonable alternative design for the product at issue. The complexity of these arguments is evident in the facts that some courts have adopted combinations of the two standards and that even proponents of the risk-utility standard and the requirement of a reasonable alternative design recognize exceptions, for example, an exception for products with "manifestly unreasonable design."

The area of design defects reveals tensions in the roles of judges and juries. One judge focused on this tension when he contrasted the "basically factual question" of "what reasonable consumers do expect from the product" with the question of "how strong products should be," which he said courts had decided was "strong enough to perform as the ordinary consumer expects."[19] It usually would be practically impossible to do the opinion polling to determine exactly what consumers expect from a product, and so the question may be viewed as requiring a judgment by the court that embraces consumer perceptions.

The question of whether products are defective partakes not only of consumer expectations and a comparison of risk and utility but of the prices of products and their variety. Often there is continuum of product models that offer different risks and utilities. A good example is a case in which a state trooper was wearing a protective vest, "one of several different styles then on the market," which did not have as much protection as another, "wrap-around" vest. The vest he was wearing did repel some bullets fired by an assailant but six bullets struck him in parts of his body not protected by the vest. The trooper's widow won a substantial jury verdict, but a federal appellate court reversed the judgment, saying it was "not the place of courts or juries to set specifications as to the parts of the body a bullet-resistant garment must cover." It essentially adopted a continuum argument, saying that "[a] manufacturer is not obliged to market only one version of a product, that being the safest design possible."[20]

An interesting question in this area is whether lawsuits should be allowed for injuries occurring to motorists and passengers because their vehicles did not protect them against the consequences of crashes. Two federal courts initially gave very different responses to that question. In one of these cases, the court refused to impose liability on a car manufacturer, saying that "the intended purpose of an automobile does not include its participation in collisions with other objects, despite the manufacturer's ability to foresee the possibility that such collisions may occur."[21]

The other court of appeals showed the other face of the topic, saying that "[w]hile automobiles are not made for the purpose of colliding with each other," collisions were "a frequent and inevitable contingency of normal automobile use." Given that agreement on the basic facts, the second court found "no rational basis" "for limiting recovery to situations where the defect in design or manufacture was the causative factor of the accident."[22] That decision led to the development of a small industry for lawyers, those representing plaintiffs injured in collisions and those defending car makers in what have come to be called "crashworthiness" cases. Illustrative of the force of the doctrine was a case in which the highest court of New York allowed a crashworthiness suit by a driver whose intoxication caused him to crash into a utility pole. The court concluded that the car maker had breached its duty to provide collision protection to "any driver ... involved in a crash regardless of the initial cause." It said that the plaintiff was asking "only that [the defendant] honor its well-recognized duty to produce a product that does not unreasonably enhance or aggravate a user's injuries."[23] Some courts have taken the crashworthiness doctrine beyond automobiles, for example to a tractor, a forklift, and a riding mower.

A basic lesson for product designers is that they must pay special attention to the environments in which products will be used. An example is a case in which the plaintiff slipped on the muddy step of a tractor. The court mentioned testimony by an engineer for the defendant that "debris and mud would fall upon and adhere to the access step," and that operators of the tractor would "kind of ... make a little hole, digging your foot in, and kicking your foot against the side of the muddy area." Noting evidence that the access step did not have non-skid material, the court concluded that there was "more than a scintilla of evidence for [a] jury finding that the step ... was negligently designed."[24]

"State of the art" is a phrase familiar to both product sellers and physicians. Readers probably have their own personal definitions of the phrase, but one should understand that even legal specialists have remarked on its ambiguity. One definition that has been offered, which itself has two branches, is that the phrase "may include industry custom or the most scientifically advanced developments in the field." A different definition offers a defense to product makers when particular concerns about safety "are not generally recognized as reflecting the best data reasonably available at the time." Yet another refers to "the aggregate of product-related knowledge which may feasibly be incorporated into a product." And a variation, especially favorable to plaintiffs, is "the aggregate of product-related knowledge existing at any given point in time."

There is a link between state-of-the art-defenses and consumer expectations. In a case in which the plaintiff argued that a motorcycle helmet had inadequate shock absorption, the plaintiffs' witness testified that a prototype helmet he built showed that available technology would have enabled a safer design. However, the court rejected the suit on the ground that "[a] product can only be defective if it is imperfect when measured against a standard existing at the time of sale or against reasonable consumer expectations held at the time of sale."[25]

Two cases involving mowing machines demonstrate the room for factual argument about state of the art. In one case, the court turned down the suit when safety devices on a mower mentioned by the plaintiff's lawyer "had not been developed at the time of manufacture."[26] In the other case, though, the court concluded that a jury could reasonably have found for the plaintiff when an expert said he had installed a dead man control with a shortened stopping capability on a mower of that manufacturer three years before the model on which the plaintiff was injured was made.[27] Some nuances appear in another decision in a helicopter case. The court said that it was not requiring a manufacturer "to design the safest possible product, or one as safe as others make, or a safer product than the one it has designed." However, it declared that once a firm "produced a design which was known to be safer," it "owed a duty" "to refrain" from using the older system.[28]

A small but interesting group of cases includes people who have uncomfortable reactions to products, variously described as involve "allergies," "hypersensitivities," and "abreactions." Characterizations of these types of cases by two distinguished attorneys exhibit the importance of putting verbal labels on things. One, a plaintiff's lawyer, said that the question was one of reasonable consumer expectations. The other, a defense lawyer, insisted that any defect was not in the product that caused the reaction, but rather "a defect in the person."

A Wisconsin decision involving a suit by a CT scan technologist links a product to its use in the process of health care. The product, latex gloves, had been shown to "cause allergic reactions in 5 to 17 percent of ... consumers." With a plaintiff who used up to 40 pairs of gloves per shift, the Wisconsin Supreme Court concluded that a jury could have found that the gloves were defective and unreasonably dangerous. It established a standard that required plaintiffs to show that a product contained "an ingredient that can cause allergic reactions in a substantial number of consumers" and that the "ordinary consumer does not know that the ingredient can cause allergic reactions in a substantial number of consumers."[29]

Other products used in healthcare have links to the idea of product continuums discussed previously. A graphic example, summarized in Chapter 2, is a case focusing on IV connectors. There were two basic models of these connectors—a Luer slip corrector and a Luer lock connector. The slip connector, which had been used for 40 years, required only 5.5 pounds of separation force to disconnect. The more secure lock connector, which "cost only pennies more" and had been in use for 20 years, had a threaded collar and a threaded flange. A manager for the manufacturer cited "consumer preference" for the choice between the two models: "They're both safe products, so you offer them what they want ... what they decide they need." In a suit for the death of a patient ascribed to the disconnection of a slip connector, which was said to have "come apart inadvertently," the court affirmed a large judgment for the plaintiff despite the existence of a market for slip connectors. [30]

Another case, involving a hormone product, exhibited a countervailing argument that itself shows how lawyers can use characterization. The product was Prempro, which combined estrogen and progestin. The plaintiff, alleging that it caused her breast cancer, argued that an estrogen-only product was safer and that the combination product made "hormone therapy unreasonably dangerous by substantially increasing the risk of breast cancer." The court rejected the claim, saying that "[i]n essence," the plaintiff was arguing that "the product Prempro should have been a different product," which it said was a "categorical attack on a product" that state law did not recognize.[31]

5.3.3 Damages

The place where the rubber meets the road in tort litigation is damages. It is damages awards that provide one of the principal reasons for imposing tort liability: Compensation. The potential amounts of these awards also provide an incentive for lawyers to bring tort actions, which are usually litigated on contingency fees, which we briefly discuss in Chapter 10. We discuss here three kinds of tort damages. Two of these are classified as compensatory: economic losses and noneconomic losses. The other is punitive damages.

Several categories of economic loss are relatively straightforward, but even these have nuances. One, medical expenses, includes doctors' bills and hospital costs, which can be nailed down by printouts. The nuances begin with the category of lost earnings. Among the many questions that arise here are questions of how to prove a disability and what kinds of employment may be available to someone whose injury has cost him the ability to do the job he held before the injury. How stable was the industry in which he was working? How transferable are the abilities that enabled him to do the pre-injury job?

Typically damages are awarded, at least initially, on a lump sum basis. This brings into play the plaintiff's life expectancy, which may require expert testimony, and perhaps might include evidence about possible chances for increased earnings after job promotions. A collateral question is whether a plaintiff should be able to recover for a decrease in life expectancy itself.

A separate question is how to compensate for the value of household services. This often raises a gender problem because statistically a disproportionate amount of household work is the province of women, who may hold jobs outside the home but also are the principal "homemaker," services which tort law tends to quantify as low value.

The major legal battles over compensatory damages occur in the area of what has been labeled "noneconomic loss." The biggest item in this category is pain and suffering. Pain itself has several subcategories, measured for litigation purposes—insofar as that can be done—by such factors as intensity and length of time. Distinctions have been drawn between "chronic pain" and chronic pain syndrome (CPS). Suffering has been classified as situations in which people "perceive pain as a threat to their continued existence." The problem for the legal system in these categories is one of valuation. Typically that issue is left to juries, with rather vague verbal standards for ceilings on the dollar amounts they award—words and phrases like "grossly excessive," "shocking to the judicial conscience," and "monstrous." It is the job of courts to use language like that to put limits on awards. Illustrations of how damages may be awarded for short periods of emotional trauma are cases involving the fear that airline passengers suffered when they perceived that planes were about to crash—in one case a federal appellate court affirmed an award of $15,000 for four to six seconds of a plane passenger's apprehension of death.[32]

Other categories of noneconomic damages are the deprivation of the capacity to enjoy life, the intangible item called consortium—which includes things like sex and companionship—and, in death cases, the related item of bereavement. These categories may blur into one another. For example, it is difficult to make the conceptual separation between emotional loss at witnessing the death of a family member and the sorrow felt as a result of that loss.

There has been criticism of the award of damages for intangible losses at all, from persons with different political perspectives. All opponents of these types of damages emphasize how unquantifiable they are. Businesspersons and healthcare givers find such damages a wild card in a legal universe that they consider unacceptably uncertain. Left wing critics oppose them as a "commodification" of human beings. Yet, every

American state allows these awards, subject to judicial review, and they have been part of the law of diverse cultures across the world for centuries.

Commentators have offered several rationales for the award of compensatory damages. One, borrowed from Aristotle, rests on the idea of "corrective justice," which—in an admittedly rough and often quite unrealistic way—says that someone who injures another should give up the gain he or she got from the injuring event. A related idea is that of restoring the injured person to the life she had before the event—entirely unrealistic in death cases, and arguable in many cases involving disabling injuries. A principal rationale is that of deterrence—making risk-takers behave more carefully. And in cases involving both emotional injury and physical contact, there is rabbinical commentary which states as a "general principle" that "it all depends on a person's dignity." Again the problem arises of quantifying things that have no sales value in permissible markets.

The other major category of damages is punitive damages, sometimes called exemplary damages. Just those labels suggest the many arguments that surround the propriety of giving such awards and the question of how courts and legislatures may limit them. Obviously, one purpose of punitive damages is to punish. Another is to provide deterrence, which already is an accepted rationale for compensatory damages. Related to punishment is retribution—a justification that emphasizes holding up a wrongdoer's conduct to the condemnation of society generally.

A major argument against the award of punitive damages, which are not allowed in a few states, is that such awards are an improper use of the kind of social punishment delivered by the criminal law, under which people can be convicted only with constitutional safeguards. In the many states that allow punitive damages in civil cases, courts have developed abstract verbal standards for making such awards. Some courts require plaintiffs to show "outrageous" conduct. One decision mentioned several words and phrases, including "malice, vindictiveness, ill-will, or wanton, willful or reckless disregard of plaintiff's rights." Another decision uses the terms "illegal, outrageous and grossly unreasonable." It is clear that simple negligence will not support a punitive award, but some courts will allow plaintiffs to show "gross negligence." Beginning in 1991, the Supreme Court ventured into the review of the amounts of punitive damages, a topic on which it has now decided several cases. One factor on which it has fixed is the "degree of reprehensibility of the defendant's conduct." It has also suggested that an appropriate limit on punitive damages is the ratio they bear to compensatory damages. In one case, it suggested that a good safeguard against excessiveness was to draw the line at "[s]ingle-digit multipliers." In another case that arose from maritime law, historically a specialized field of tort law, a decision by the Court said that the proper ratio was 1 to 1.

One should note that although punitive damages are a favorite target of critics of tort law, they have been awarded in only a very small percentage of personal injury cases. That fact, however, has not lowered the volume of argument from those who would forbid them entirely or would place dollar limits on them—the latter a topic discussed in Chapter 10.

Since the bottom line of tort law is dollars, it is not surprising that there should be such high levels of combat about damages issues, including whether certain kinds of damages should be awarded at all or whether they should be limited in amount. We shall elaborate in Chapter 10 on the disputes about when courts and legislatures are the proper bodies to make, or give, law in these areas.

Endnotes

1. Roscoe Pound, Interests of Personality, 28 *Harv. L. Rev.* 343, 356 (1915).

2. W. Schwartz & N. Komesar, *Doctors, Damages and Deterrence: An Economic View of Medical Malpractice*, 15 (Rand, R-2340-NIH/RC 1978).

3. *Martin v. Ryder Truck Rental, Inc.*, 353 A.2d 581, 587 (Del. 1976).

4. Jason M. Solomon, Equal Accountability through Tort Law, 103 *NW. L. Rev.* 1765, 1785 (2009).

5. Restatement (Second) Torts, §402A, cmt. k (1965).

6. *Brown v. Superior Court*, 751 P.2d 470, 482 (Cal. 1988).

7. *Allison v. Merck & Co.*, 878 P.2d 848, 854 (Nev. 1994).

8. Restatement (Second) of Torts § 402A, cmt. i (1965).

9. *Morris v. Adolph Coors Co.*, 884 S.W.2d 578, 584 (Tex. Ct. App. 1987).

10. *Hon v. Stroh Brewery Co.*, 835 F.2d 510, 514 (3d Cir. 1987).

11. *Brune v. Forman Corp.*, 758 S.W.2d 829 (Tex. Ct. App. 1988).

12. *Roysdon v. American Tobacco Co.*, 849 F.2d 230, 236 (6th Cir. 1988).

13. See, e.g., *America Tobacco Co. v. Grinnell*, 951 S.W.2d 420, 433 (Tex. 1997).

14. Texas Civ. Prac. & Remedies Code §82.004.

15. *Tompkin v. American Brands*, 219 F.2d 566, 572–73 (6th Cir. 2000).

16. *Rogers v. R.J. Reynolds Tobacco Co.*, 557 N.E. 1045, 1054 (Ind. Ct. App. 1990).

17. *Philip Morris USA v. Arnitz*, 933 So.2d 693, 697 (Fla. Dist. Ct. App. 2006).

18. *Hill v. R.J. Reynolds Tobacco Co.*, 44 F. Supp.2d 837, 843 (W.D. Ky. 1999).

19. *Heaton v. Ford Motor Co.*, 435 P.2d 806, 809 (Or. 1967).

20. *Linegar v. Armour of America*, 909 F.2d 1150, 1154 (8th Cir. 1990).

21. *Evans v. General Motors Corp.*, 359 F.2d 822, 825 (7th Cir. 1966).

22. *Larsen v. General Motors Corp.*, 391 F.2d 495, 502 (8th Cir. 1968).

23. *Alami v. Volkswagen of Am., Inc.*, 766 N.E. 574, 577 (N.Y. 2002).

24. *Gonzales v. Caterpillar Tractor Co.*, 571 S.W.2d 867, 872 (Tex. 1978).

25. Sexton by and through *Sexton v. Bell Helmets, Inc.*, 928 F.2d 331, 337 (4th Cir. 1991).

26. *Adams v. Fuqua Indus.*, 820 F.2d 271, 275 (8th Cir. 1987).

27. *Norton v. Snapper Power Equip. Div. of Fuqua Indus. Inc.*, 806 F.2d 1545 (11th Cir. 1987).
28. *Bell Helicopter Co. v. Bradshaw*, 594 S.W.2d 519, 530 (Tex. Ct. App. 1979).
29. *Green v. Smith & Nephew AHP., Inc.*, 629 N.W.2d 727, 754 (Wis. 2001).
30. *Hansen v Baxter Healthcare Corp.*, 764 N.E.2d 35 (Ill. 2002), affirming 723 N.E.2d 302 (Ill. Ct. App. 1992).
31. *Brockert v. Wyeth Pharms.*, 287 S.W.3d 760, 771 (Tex. Ct. App. 2009).
32. *Haley v. Pan American World Airways*, 746 F.2d 311, 317–18 (5th Cir. 1984).

Chapter 6

Information about Risk and Assumption of Risk

An important factor in many kinds of law involving injuries of various kinds is information about risk.

The typical faceoff in litigation is between a defendant who arguably had superior information and a plaintiff who claims disadvantage from not having enough information. However, at the threshold of the subject are cases in which the plaintiff knew about a risk and in which the defendant shows that the plaintiff agreed in some kind of written document to assume that risk. In some cases, for example cases involving participation in auto racing, courts will enforce those agreements. In other cases, they will refuse to enforce them, often citing the imbalance in bargaining power between the parties. The California Supreme Court employed a number of those arguments when it barred the use of an exculpatory clause in a hospital admission form, saying that the clause was "contrary to public policy." The court cited hospitals as falling in the category of businesses that "perform[] a service of great importance to the public." In addition to remarking on "superior bargaining power" on the part of the defendant, it spoke of the plaintiff being "under the control of the hospital."[1] We will discuss other aspects of express assumption of risk in Chapter 7, which focuses on medical care.

A subtle kind of defense is that which is called implied assumption of risk, which is a complete bar to recovery against plaintiffs. There are various legal formulations of this defense, but we may begin with the basic definition: A plaintiff's voluntary confrontation with a risk about which he or she knows. The main elements of this defense are that the plaintiff must know of the risk and must voluntarily encounter it. A case involving a lawnmower accident presents a rigorous application of this doctrine. Rejecting a suit based on the mower's lack of safety devices, the court declared that this was "apparent" when the plaintiff bought the product and that "in a free market," he "had the choice of buying a mower equipped with" the devices, "of buying the mower which he did, or of buying no mower at all."[2] A plaintiff's repeated exposure to a risk will also be a bar to recovery, as in a case in which a motorcyclist claimed that the headlamp on his cycle was too dim. The court thought it "inescapable" that "by his continuing use of the motor cycle even after he believed that the light was insufficient," the plaintiff "assumed any risk attendant to continued operation" of the vehicle.[3]

The degree of knowledge becomes an important factor with respect to assumption of risk. An important feature of the defense is the obviousness of a risk. A simple example is a case in which a court concluded that a centerfielder for the New York Yankees could not recover when he was hurt slipping on wet outfield grass, a condition the court called "obvious," commenting that "playing on an open wet field" was "part of the game of baseball."[4] We will note other uses of the "obviousness" defense as it links up to other defenses based on the plaintiff's conduct.

A case rejecting a suit by a nurse's aide injured by a combative Alzheimer's patient presents an argument that ties together the plaintiff's knowledge with a policy argument based on the ability to avoid risk. The court noted that the plaintiff, who worked with Alzheimer's patients, knew that violence was a "common trait" among them and said that she had "placed herself in a position where she assumed the duty to take care of" such patients and "to protect such patients from committing acts which might injure others." It reasoned that it was "the health care provider, not the patient, who is in the best position to protect against the risks to the provider rooted in the very reason for the treatment."[5]

Decisions involving various athletic activities, both professional and recreational, also employ the defense. It barred a champion jockey in a case in which he sued another jockey and a race track for crippling injuries that occurred when the other jockey's horse bumped him. That bump created a situation in which the plaintiff's mount clipped the heels of another horse and tripped, causing the plaintiff to fall. Noting that the plaintiff was claiming only negligence by the other rider and not intentional or reckless conduct, the court said that "a professional clearly understands the usual incidents of competition resulting from carelessness, particularly those which result from the customarily accepted method of playing the sport, and accepts them." The court described the plaintiff's conduct as "actual consent implied from the act of electing to participate in the activity."[6]

On the recreational side, both courts and legislatures have been unsympathetic to skiers, using variations on the terminology of assumption of risk, phrases which include the idea that defendants—principally operators of slopes—have "no duty" of care to the skier. Several legislatures, indeed, have effectively declared a public policy that protects operators of ski facilities. In a case in which an experienced skier chose a slope marked with an international symbol designating it "one of the most difficult slopes" at the facility, the court simply said that the plaintiff "took his chances." Although his conduct might have been "quite reasonable" in light of "his extensive skiing experience and ability," the court said his choice of that slope "absolved" the facility "of any obligation to exercise care for his protection."[7] The court in that case was interpreting the Pennsylvania Skier's Responsibility Act, in which the legislature essentially adopted "[t]he doctrine of voluntary assumption of risk," referring to a recognition of "the inherent risks in the sport of downhill skiing."[8] The Idaho skiers' legislation broadly declares that "[e]ach skier expressly assumes the risk" of injury associated with many conditions and fixtures, including "lift towers and components thereof."[9]

A legal cousin of assumption of risk, which sometimes overlaps with it, is the doctrine of contributory negligence, for which a standard definition is conduct by a plaintiff that "falls below the standard of care to which he should conform for his own protection."[10] The use of the term "should" in this definition suggests a moral element with subjective features, but the traditional view of the defense is that it has an objective measure, rather than the subjectivity usually associated with assumption of risk—that is, actual knowledge of a risk paired with voluntary conduct. An example of the objective test for contributory negligence is a case in which the plaintiff, working in a yarn mill, put his hand into an opening in a machine in which a moving part, a "beater roller," was "a large, rapidly rotating cylinder with thousands of steel spikes." The plaintiff said he had "no idea there were any parts moving inside the … opener when he inserted his left hand through the narrow clearance between" parts of the machine. However, the court emphasized that the "plaintiff's subjective awareness of danger is not determinative on the issue of his contributory negligence." The court said he "should have been aware of the danger" posed by "the spiked beater roller" and that the jury could find that the "plaintiff was contributorily negligent in placing his hand inside the … opener so soon after power to it had been cut off without first determining that no parts were moving inside it."[11]

Two cases involving psychiatric patients illustrate the room for argument about the application of the defense. In one, the patient sought to "fool" the hospital staff "into thinking that he was still in his room," "cover[ing] his tracks" with a series of maneuvers that included fluffing his bed pillows and putting them under blankets. He then used a bent toothbrush to pry open a part on a window. When he jumped through the window, he suffered paralyzing injuries. The court concluded that he was contributorily negligent, saying he had taken "measures like those of an ordinarily prudent person acting to conceal an illicit activity, and … evinced a piqued level of planning and cognizant dexterity." It noted that in deposition, the plaintiff "explained his motivations and the execution of his escape plan with a clarity that suggests the incident was the product of a lucid plan."[12]

A contrast appears in another case in which a psychiatric patient jumped out of a hospital window. The New Jersey Supreme Court framed the plaintiff's conduct within the duty of care of the hospital and individual healthcare defendants, who were sued for not preventing her leap from the window. Agreeing with an appellate court decision for the plaintiff, the Supreme Court referred to a standard that "recognizes that a mentally disturbed plaintiff is not capable of adhering to a reasonable person's standard of self-care, but at the same time holds that plaintiff responsible for the consequences of conduct that is unreasonable in light of the plaintiff's capacity." However, the court said that the "capacity-based standard" did not apply "because the plaintiff's inability to exercise reasonable self-care attributable to her mental disability was itself subsumed within the duty of care defendants owed to her."[13]

The defenses based on both parties' knowledge and the defendant's conduct overlap and in some cases merge with one another. The field of products injuries presents these questions in contexts that vary with the legal labels that courts give to the cases and with the kinds of products at issue. We have noted that a very basic set of theories for products suits lies in direct representations about the qualities or characteristics of products—representations made in advertising and other forms of product promotion, and in printed consumer contracts. The background of product portrayal will influence courts to some extent in cases involving product injuries. Once a basic case has been made in favor of plaintiffs—either on the ground that product sellers have been negligent or have sold products deemed to have an unreasonably dangerous defect—the question shifts to defenses related to what the plaintiff knew and did.

The courts have employed several different labels to describe these defenses. A fine illustration is a case that generated strong disagreements in the Michigan appellate courts about an experienced swimmer whose dive into 3-1/2 feet of water in an above-ground pool led to quadriplegia. The state appellate court, holding for the plaintiff in a suit against the pool manufacturer, said that "[n]othing in the appearance of the pool itself gives a warning of the very serious consequences to which a mundane dive can lead."[14] So controversial was the case that the Michigan Supreme Court wrestled with it for two full sets of opinions, with a majority of the court holding for the manufacturer both times. In the first decision, the majority employed no fewer than four theories to rationalize its ruling for the defendant. It said that "the dangers associated with diving into visibly shallow water in an above-ground pool are open and obvious to the reasonably prudent user," thereby incorporating the "obviousness" defense and the objective idea of contributory negligence. In the same sentence, the court said that the plaintiff "must ... be held to the knowledge and appreciation of the risk likely to be encountered in the head-first dive," thus articulating a subjective assumption of risk defense. It concluded that the manufacturer "owed no duty to warn the plaintiff."[15] This language added a fourth label, that is, no duty to warn, to the available defenses. We should add a fifth phrase, one used along with assumption of risk language in cases like the skiing case mentioned above—that is, that the defendant simply owes no duty of care to the plaintiff: A legal cousin of the idea of no duty to warn.

The tensions of fact and law in cases like the swimming pool case are evident in comments in a separate opinion by a supreme court judge favoring the plaintiff. This judge asked, "[e]xactly *what* was obvious in this case? Injury in general? Danger in general?" He mentioned testimony by the plaintiff about "a lack of specific recognition that his physical liberty lay in the balance," which he said was "a fact which *could* have been made obvious by the presence of an explicit visible warning."[16] Demonstrating the ability of lawyers to mold words and phrases to facts, a writer for the majority in the second hearing of the case—which held for the manufacturer—responded that "the obvious nature of the danger serves the exact function as a warning that the risk is present."[17]

This discussion has focused on the information available to the plaintiff, including its impact on the plaintiff's standard of conduct. We now turn to focus on how the information available to the defendant affects the defendant's duty. Here there is an overlap among at least three concepts: The idea of a product defect, the mantra of obviousness, and the assumption of risk type defenses. An example is a case in which a hockey puck penetrated a gap between sections of the helmet the plaintiff was wearing, which had been designed in sections to allow adjustment of the helmet. The trial court held that the defendant should get judgment "as a matter of law" on a count of negligent design of the helmet, given the defendant's argument that the plaintiff knew of the risks of such an injury because the gaps were obvious. But the Massachusetts Supreme Judicial Court reversed in favor of the plaintiff, saying that it did "not think that these gaps were so large or so obvious as to require the conclusion, as matter of law, that the plaintiff possessed the awareness necessary to support an assumption of the risk defense."[18]

There are interesting comparisons in other cases involving safety helmets. A case won by the defendant involved injury to the cervical spine, resulting in quadriplegia, that occurred to a high school football player who used his head in making a tackle. The court rejected his claim that there should have been a warning on the helmet, summarizing "testimony from plaintiff's and defendant's expert witnesses that the intended function of a safety helmet is to protect against head injury," and testimony by the plaintiff's expert that "he knew of no helmet designed with the intent of protecting the neck." The court invoked the "well settled" rule that "a duty to warn is not required where the product is not defectively designed or manufactured, and where the possibility of injury results from a common propensity of the product which is open and obvious." Again, the court meshes several concepts—duty to warn, design defect, and obviousness of danger.[19]

A contrasting result governed a case in which the plaintiff sued the maker of a motorcycle helmet for injuries that occurred when he lost control of his cycle and hit debris in the road while traveling at 30 to 45 miles an hour. The trial court ruled for the defendant against a suit based on a failure to warn theory "on the ground that it was open and obvious that the AGV helmet would not protect an operator traveling at 30 to 45 miles an hour." Although experts for both sides agreed that that "no helmet currently marketed could protect a wearer traveling at speeds of 45 miles an hour," the appellate court said that this did not "mean that this fact is patent to a purchaser," remarking that the defendant had given "no evidence tending to show that it is open or obvious that its helmet would not protect the wearer at speeds of 30 to 45 miles an hour."[20] Just to balance the scales, we can mention a case in which the plaintiff cyclist sustained injuries from a collision with a car. The defendant had embossed on the helmet stickers saying, "Warning—Some Reasonably Foreseeable Impacts May Exceed This Helmet's Capacity to Protect against Serious Injury," and "Warning! No Helmet Can Protect The Wearer Against All Foreseeable Impacts." The appellate court held for the defendant, effectively agreeing with the trial court's conclusion that the helmet maker was "under no duty to warn" of the "open and obvious" dangers in the case.[21]

A substantial number of cases deal with an issue that is often linked with whether there should be a warning, that is, whether a warning was adequate. These cases focus on information that initially is entirely within the control of manufacturers and service providers, including healthcare providers. The cases involving medical products often involve the "learned intermediary" defense, the basic idea of which is that in the case of prescription products, manufacturers of drugs or devices need communicate warnings only to physicians rather than directly to patients.

A wrenching case in which the plaintiff alleged that his father killed his mother and then committed suicide—events that the plaintiff attributed to his father's taking of Prozac— illustrates the limitations of the learned intermediary doctrine. A focal point of the case was the fact that at the time of the event, the maker of the drug had not yet implemented a black box warning that it published later. The defendant argued that the plaintiff could not show that a failure to warn about the risk of suicide caused the deaths of the plaintiff's parents because the father's doctor testified that he would have prescribed Prozac to the father, "even knowing there had been concerns raised regarding suicide and violence." However, the court reversed a judgment for the defendant on some of the plaintiff's claims because the doctor also testified that after the defendant had adopted the black box warnings, he "warn[ed] patients about the risk of antidepressant-associated suicidality." This, the court found, raised a "material issue of fact" about whether the defendant's failure to warn was a proximate cause of the deaths.[22] The court even denied a summary judgment to the drug maker on claims for punitive damages, concluding that a jury could have inferred from internal documents of the defendant "that it was aware of an alleged problem with Prozac, suicidality, and violence in 1990 before" the issuance of the black box warnings and before the events that gave rise to the case.[23]

In another case in which punitive damages were allowed, although reduced, the product was a silicone gel-filled breast implant, around which scar tissue had formed. A surgeon had used a closed capsulotomy to loosen the capsule but the plaintiff's problems continued, leading to an open capsulotomy, which was itself followed by operations to remove granulomas. A former vice-president of the maker of the implants testified that "he would never recommend a closed capsulotomy because the ... implant is too fragile and too likely to rupture." The defendant relied on a warning that it "cannot guarantee the structural integrity of its implant should the surgeon elect to treat capsule firmness by forceful external stress." However, saying that the defendant's "management knew that the product was likely to rupture when pressure was applied" and "also knew that physicians were routinely performing an operation in which such pressure was applied, and ... continue to perform this procedure today," the court said that "[t]he jury could reasonably conclude that the warning provided to physicians ... did not properly convey the risks of the closed capsulotomy."[24]

The question of adequacy of warning also extends to the frequency of injuring events and to the severity of the risk at issue. With respect to statistics on amount of occurrences, one view of the obligation of manufacturers appears in a case in which the package insert of DPT vaccine said that "[t]he incidence" of convulsions or seizures are "unknown but they seem to be exceedingly rare." However, there was evidence that studies on the frequency of these reactions varied from 1 in 800,000 immunizations to 1 in 1,750, and indeed a pediatrician who testified for the plaintiff testified that his review of internal documents of the manufacturer indicated that the seizure rate was "1 in 300 injections." Seizing on the latter figure, the court said that rate "cannot be considered 'exceedingly rare' as a matter law."[25]

Another court identifies the severity of the risk as a factor in a case involving a catheter placement unit used in open heart surgery. A bold-face warning for the product identified a hazard, known as retrograde shear, associated with the pulling out of the catheter before the needle. The plaintiff's surgeon did not employ the unit in a "use for which it was designed" and there was evidence that the manufacturer "knew or should have known that its product was being used in this manner during cardiac surgery." A magistrate judge, who held for the plaintiff, said that "[h]aving such knowledge, the manufacturer had a duty to warn of the dangers associated with this usage." Positing that "even if a warning is given and understood by an experienced consumer of the product, it may yet be found to be 'qualitatively insufficient' in failing to convey the degree of intensity or urgency of the risk involved." He said that a jury finding that the defendant's "warnings were inadequate implies either that the risk involved was of a different quality or character than the discrete risk warned against or that the warning was not sufficiently forceful in relation to the degree of danger involved."[26]

One exception to the learned intermediary doctrine has been applied when "direct warnings to the user of a prescription drug have been mandated by a safety regulation promulgated for the protection of the user." The Oklahoma Supreme Court articulated this rule in a case involving a fatal heart attack ascribed to nicotine patches. Although "[a] relatively thorough warning was given to physicians" about the patch, a consumer insert that said that an "overdose might cause you to faint" "did not mention the possibility of a fatal or cardiac related reaction." In an opinion favoring the plaintiff, the court, noting that the FDA had required warnings on patches be given directly to patients, said that "the manufacturer is not automatically shielded from liability by properly warning the prescribing physician" and that the question of whether a patient warning was adequate presented a factual issue.[27]

A decision that held for the maker of a corticosteroid inhaler captures the overlap of the issues of adequacy of warning with the role of the doctor as a learned intermediary. The court said that "[I]f a pharmaceutical manufacturer warns doctors that specific adverse side effects are associated with the use of a drug, then a causal relationship between use of the drug and development of potential side effects is implicit in the warning, as is the doctor's need to monitor the patient and to consider alternative therapies." The court noted that the prescribing physician "was aware of AstraZeneca's warnings, and that he took the risks that [the patient] would develop adverse side effects into account when prescribing" the inhaler.[28] A similar result governed a Viagra case in which the court held for the manufacturer. The patient was taking nitrates as treatment for his stable angina. The doctor who prescribed the drug told the patient that he should not take nitrates for at least 24 hours after he took Viagra. In finding that the learned intermediary doctrine applied, the court noted that the doctor told the patient to stop any sexual activity if chest pains occurred and that "if the pain did not subside, proceed immediately to a hospital." The court pointed out that the facts indicated that the doctor "at least was aware of the notice" in the original package insert that the use of Viagra in patients "concurrently using organic nitrates in any form is therefore contraindicated." It said that the evidence showed that the doctor, "a learned intermediary, was provided with a warning about the risk that Viagra posed to patients in [the patient's] circumstances, that he was aware of the risk, that he nevertheless chose to prescribe Viagra," and that the patient "relied on his physician to advise him about the effects of the medication."[29]

Another decision concluded that the defense applied when the maker of the antipsychotic drug Clozaril provided a patient pamphlet that the court characterized as giving *"some direct information"* about the drug. Noting that the doctor had "signed a document stating he was familiar with all Clozaril package labeling" and that the plaintiffs had not argued the warning given to the doctor "was inadequate," the court said that the drug maker had "no duty to directly warn" the plaintiffs "of the potential hazards of the use of Clozaril." It said that "the pamphlet does not constitute an effort to inform patients of all the dangers of Clozaril and does not purport to do so." Rather, the court said, the pamphlet was only stating "that it 'provides answers to many common questions about CLOZARIL,' but cautions the reader: 'If there are any other questions about CLOZARIL therapy, be sure to ask the doctor, nurse, or pharmacist.'"[30]

There are cases involving medicines in which plaintiffs are eligible to sue both manufacturers and doctors. One such case involved a technical legal issue concerning whether the plaintiff had properly joined together as defendants both a doctor and a drug maker. The plaintiff alleged that the doctor had "simply handed professional samples of a drug" to a patient without telling her "what type of medication he was providing" and "did not provide any literature about the drug's FDA-approved uses," simply saying that the patient should "'give it a try' and come back in one week." The patient killed herself the next morning. The manufacturer argued that the learned intermediary doctrine and the so-called "sophisticated user" doctrine barred the suit against it, claiming that the plaintiff "was fully informed of the risks ... by the treating physicians." With respect to the technical question before it—the procedural joinder of the doctor and the manufacturer—the court observed that the drug maker had admitted that common issues bound it and the doctor together, for example, the issue of whether the drug maker had informed the doctor of the suicide risks of the drug. Besides illustrating cases where both doctor and drug maker may be liable, the decision shows how technical questions, like whether parties are properly joined as defendants, can lead to substantively important results.[31]

A topic of considerable interest to physicians is direct-to-consumer advertising of prescription drugs. This author's own physician is a strong opponent of the practice, but as any television viewer can attest, it is universal. The New Jersey Supreme Court provided a nuanced treatment of this subject. The case involved the contraceptive implant Norplant, which had been the subject of a "massive advertising campaign ...

directed at women rather than at their doctors." The court's general conclusion was that "when mass marketing of prescription drugs seeks to influence a patient's choice of a drug, a pharmaceutical manufacturer that makes direct claims to consumers for the efficacy of its product should not be unqualifiedly relieved of a duty to provide proper warnings of the dangers or side effects of the product." It aligned this holding with a meditation on the way medicine had changed from the time when a physician "most likely made house calls if needed," and "[n]eighborhood pharmacists compounded prescribed medicines." Contrasting the era of direct-to-consumer advertising, it said that "[w]hen a patient is the target of direct marketing, one would think, at a minimum, that the law would require that the patient not be misinformed about the product."

It added that "when one considers that many ... 'life-style' drugs or elective treatments cause significant side effects without any curative effect, increased consumer protection becomes imperative, because these drugs are, by definition, not medically necessary." The court provided a balance to the duty of manufacturers with what was effectively a bow to the learned intermediary doctrine, saying that there was a "rebuttable presumption" that "a manufacturer satisfied its duty to warn" when it "complies with FDA advertising, labeling, and warning requirements." Yet, stressing that "[p]atient choice is an increasingly important part of our medical–legal jurisprudence," the court refused to entirely "insulate" manufacturers who "engaged in deceptive trade practices." It said that the question in the cases before it was whether there was "sufficient evidence for a reasonable jury to determine ... that the absence of information or presence of misinformation in Norplant advertising was in violation of FDA requirements and whether such violations, if any, were a substantial factor in bringing about the harm suffered."[32]

Other decided cases on the subject have shown shades of gray. In another Norplant case, in which the plaintiff received counseling from an advanced practice nurse who worked with an obstetrician/gynecologist, the court applied the learned intermediary doctrine, saying that "[t]he fact that a woman may have a voice in the choice of her contraceptive product, even if it is in fact the deciding voice, should not be enough to exempt this prescription drug from" the doctrine.[33] And in another case involving an insulin product that allegedly caused cancer, the court refused to apply the exception to the doctrine for direct to consumer advertising. It referred to FDA-approved language in the package insert for the product that "fully disclosed the carcinogenic potential" of the drug to physicians, noting that "[t]his Package Insert was included in the packaging of the ... samples provided" to the patient. It focused on the lack of evidence that the patient "even saw informational material" about the drug before visiting the doctor who suggested that he try the product and gave him two sample vials.[34]

Above, we discussed complete defenses based on the plaintiff's conduct-implied assumption of risk and contributory negligence. Most states have a body of law that, to one extent or another, balances the scales of fault between plaintiffs and defendants. These rules speak of comparative fault, most often comparative negligence, which typically asks the jury to assess percentages of negligence of each party. The state rules vary. One group of rules—"pure" comparative negligence—has the jury reduce the plaintiff's damages by the percentage of her negligence, however great that may be. Variations are rules that only allow the plaintiff to recover at all if her negligence was not greater than that of the defendant, or—in some states—only if her negligence was not as great at the defendant. This variation in rules is illustrative of the general point that in this federal system, there are many different rules that govern the same kinds of problems.

The arguments back and forth on the desirability of adopting comparative fault partake of considerations of both fairness and efficiency. A strong argument in favor of comparative rules is that they are appreciably fairer than complete-defense rules, under which the smallest amount of plaintiff negligence will completely bar a suit. An argument that cuts in favor of barring negligent plaintiffs entirely is that such a rule will provide the strongest incentive for people to take care against risks that may injure them. But, to round out the cycle, a rule of "pure" comparative negligence will provide the strongest incentive to potential injurers to avoid accidents.

A good example of how legal labels affect outcomes is the question of just what is being compared under "comparative fault." This question arises when the plaintiff's theory of liability is strict liability. How can one compare a plaintiff's negligence with the strict liability of a defendant, which theoretically is not based on fault? A practical answer that one court has given to this problem—that one can compare plaintiff's fault with strict products liability—is that "[f]ixed semantic consistency … is less important than the attainment of a just and equitable result."[35] This discussion of the comparative fault rules illustrates how lawyers can employ language to achieve results that may seem mysterious to nonlawyers, and particularly to people whose professional training inclines them to solutions with more quantitative precision. However, it is well to keep in mind the statement of a famous judge: Words often do better than logarithms.

We add one other set of weapons, using words, from the arsenal of potential defendants who wish to cut off any opportunity for injured persons to sue. These weapons, akin to the assumption of risk clauses discussed above, are the limitation of liability clause and the disclaimer, often employed in contracts for products that may have defects that cause injury or ruin the performance of a product. Courts generally are hostile to these kinds of clauses when they seek to bar or limit lawsuits for personal injury. In a case that arose from a severe electric shock from a power snake, a tool that the plaintiff used to clear a clogged pipe, the court declared that a disclaimer could not be used against a theory of strict products liability, saying that the plaintiff's "strict liability cause of action is independent of the contract, and therefore any contractual provisions, agreements or disclaimers are unenforceable."[36] Another court used similar language in a case involving a golf cart that overturned, saying that "strict tort liability is imposed by operation of law as a matter of public policy for the protection of the public" and that one held liable under that theory "cannot contract away his own responsibility for having placed a defective product into the mainstream of public use."[37]

A landmark case involving an allegedly defective car underlined a principal rationale for opposition to disclaimer clauses—a rationale that parallels the one employed in the case discussed earlier concerning a hospital's exculpatory clause. In the automobile case, where all the major auto manufacturers used disclaimers, the court said that because the auto owner's "capacity for bargaining is so grossly unequal, the inexorable conclusion which follows is that he is not permitted to bargain at all," that "he must take or leave the automobile on the warranty terms dictated by the maker" and could not "turn to a competitor for better security."[38]

A key idea summarizing this kind of holding in cases of personal injury is that it is "unconscionable" to enforce disclaimers or limitations of liability. Indeed, the Uniform Commercial Code declares that "[l]imitation of consequential damages for injury to the person in the case of consumer goods is prima facie unconscionable."

The Code also declares, however, that such limitations may be enforced "where the loss is commercial." This reflects a basic idea, mentioned in the case of the hospital exculpatory clause, that in a free market, "no public policy opposes private, voluntary transactions in which one party, for a consideration, agrees to shoulder a risk which the law would otherwise have placed upon the other party."[39] A straightforward application of this philosophy appears in a case involving "shaky pig syndrome" in infected piglets, born from sows allegedly infected by boars the plaintiffs bought from the defendant breeders. The court noted the plaintiffs' concession that "they agreed to the terms and that they were 'free to go elsewhere for breeding stock.'"[40]

Thus the question of what kinds of risks people assume, either by signing documents that absolve other parties or by their actions, depends on the contexts in which they agree to terms or in which they engage in risky conduct. It also includes the information both parties have about risk. These questions recur in the next chapter, which focuses on injuries in the process of healthcare.

Endnotes

1. *Tunkl v. Regents of University of Cal.*, 383 P2d 441, 446–47 (Cal. 1963).
2. *Myers v. Montgomery Ward Co.*, 252 A.2d 855, 864 (Md. 1969).
3. *Barnes v. Harley Davidson Motor Co.*, 357 S.E.2d 127, 130 (Ga. Ct. App. 1987).
4. *Maddox v. City of New York*, 108 A.D.2d 42, 45 (N.Y. App. Div. 1985), affirmed, 487 N.E.2d 553 (N.Y. 1985).
5. *Herrle v. Estate of Marshall*, 53 Cal. Rptr. 713, 715-16 (App. Ct. 1996).
6. *Turcotte v. Fell*, 502 N.E.2d 964, 968-70 (N.Y. 1986).
7. *Smith v. Seven Springs Farm*, 716 F.2d 1002, 1009 (3d Cir. 1983).
8. Pa. Stats. & Consolidated Stats. §7102(c).
9. Idaho Code Ann. §6–1106.
10. Restatement (Second) of Torts §463.
11. *Smith v. Fiber Controls Corp.*, 268 S.E.2d 504, 808–09 (N.C. 1980).
12. *Jankee v. Clark County*, 612 N.W.2d 297, 320 (Wis. 2000).
13. *Cowan v. Deering*, 545 A.2d 159, 163 (N.J. 1988).
14. *Glittenberg v. Wilcenski*, 435 N.W.2d 480, 482 (Mich. Ct. App. 1989).
15. *Glittenberg v. Doughboy Recreational Indus.*, 462 N.W.2d 348, 359 (Mich. 1992).
16. Id. at 363–65 (Archer, J., separate opinion).
17. 491 N.W.2d 208, 215 (Mich. 1992).
18. *Everett v. Bucky Warren, Inc.*, 380 N.E.2d 653, 659 (Mass. 1978).

19. *Lister v. Bill Kelley Athletic Inc.*, 485 N.E.2d 483, 486-87 (Ill. App. Ct. 1985).
20. *Sheckells v. AGV-USA Corp.*, 987 F.2d 1532, 1533-35 (11th Cir. 1993).
21. *Westry v. Bell Helmets, Inc.*, 487 N.W.2d 781 (Mich. Ct. App. 1992).
22. *Rimbert v. Eli Lilly & Co.*, 577 F. Supp.2d 1174, 1230–32 (D.N.M. 2008).
23. Id. at 1242–43.
24. *Toole v. McClintock*, 778 F. Supp. 1543, 1346-47 (M.D. Alab. 1991).
25. *Martinkovic by Martinkovic v. Wyeth Labs, Inc.*, 669 F. Supp. 212, 216 (N.D. Ill. 1987).
26. Knowlton, by and through *Tetrault v. Deseret Medical, Inc.*, 1989 WL 143158, at 3–6 (D. Mass. 1989), affirmed, 930 F.2d 116 (1st Cir. 1991).
27. *Edwards v. Basel Pharms.*, 933 P.2d 398, 303 (Okla. 1997).
28. *Ziliak v. AstraZeneca LP*, 324 F.2d 518, 521 (7th Cir. 2003).
29. *Brumley v. Pfizer, Inc.*, 149 F. Supp.2d 305, 313 (S.D. Tex. 2001).
30. *Presto v. Sandoz Pharms. Corp.*, 487 S.E.2d 70, 73–74 (Ga. Ct. App. 1997).
31. *Moote v. Eli Lilly & Co.*, 2006 WL 3761907, at 3 (S.D. Tex. 2006).
32. *Perez v. Wyeth Labs, Inc.*, 734 A.2d 1245, 1246, 1257, 1259–60 (N.J. 1999).
33. *Wyeth-Ayerst Labs, Co., v. Medrano*, 28 S.W.3d 87 (Tex. Ct. App. 2000).
34. *Mendes Montes de Oca v. Aventis Pharms.*, 579 F. Supp.2d 222, 230 (D. P.R. 2008).
35. *Daly v. General Motors Corp.*, 578 P.2d 1162, 1168 (Cal. 1978).
36. *Ruzzo v. LaRose Enters.*, 748 A.2d 261, 268 (R.I. 2000).
37. *Sipari v. Villa Olivia Country Club*, 380 N.E.2d 819, 829 (Ill. Ct. App. 1978).
38. *Hennington v. Bloomfield Motors*, 161 A.2d 69, 94 (N.J. 1960).
39. *Tunkl v. Regents of Univ. of Calif.*, 383 P.2d 441, 446 (Cal. 1963).
40. *Brunsman v. DeKalb Swine Breeders, Inc.*, 138 F.2d 358, 360 (8th Cir. 1998).

Chapter 7

Medical Malocurrences

Among the many areas of controversy in law and public policy, few exhibit the level of tension in the area of suits for injuries associated with healthcare. This chapter presents a precis of major issues in that area: First, the effort to define the standard of care; then, the problems arising from proof that a provider fell below the prescribed standard, and the associated question of when expert testimony is necessary in medical cases; and finally, the need to articulate the rules of informed consent.

7.1 The Standard of Care

The starting point for definition of the standard of care for healthcare providers is the general negligence standard, which in abstract terms has been defined positively as a standard of "reasonable care under the circumstances," and more negatively as a standard for protection of people "against unreasonable risk of harm." More economically oriented definitions speak in terms of comparing risk and utility of conduct or of comparing injury costs and prevention costs.

These generalized standards become more specific in application to medical injuries, as well as cases involving alleged malpractice in other professions. The Mississippi Supreme Court offered one standard in a case in which a surgical patient died of respiratory distress syndrome after his pulse rate was recorded at 140, allegedly without an effort by nurses to contact a physician. The court said that physicians were

> expected to possess or have reasonable access to such medical knowledge as is commonly possessed or reasonably available to minimally competent physicians in the same specialty or general field of practice throughout the United States, to have a realistic understanding of the limitations on his or her knowledge or competence, and, in general, to exercise minimally adequate medical judgment.

The court recognized that this standard was subject to "[m]ajor differences" in resources available in different communities—a geographical variation we discuss later. However, it also said that "objectively reasonable expectations regarding the physician's knowledge, skill, capacity for sound medical judgment and general competence are, consistent with his field of practice and the facts and circumstances in which the patient may be found, *the same everywhere*." Tartly applying these ideas to the facts of the case, the court said that "[a] pulse rate of 140 per minute provides a danger signal in Pascagoula, Mississippi, the same as it does in Cleveland, Ohio." It commented that "[b]acteria, physiology and the life process itself know little of geography and nothing of political boundaries."[1]

A subset of competence is judgment, referred to in the Mississippi court's opinion. Here, judicial opinions reflect some variations on the proper standard. In a case involving a child born with brain damage after a pregnancy alleged to have been too prolonged, the court evinced some discomfort with a standard that made allowances for an "honest error in judgment." Attempting to refine that standard, it set as a foundation the need for physicians to "use reasonable care to obtain the information needed to exercise his or her professional judgment." If that were done, the court said that when a doctor had to "make a decision on the basis of incomplete, unclear, or tentative data," the doctor would not be negligent "if the treatment chosen was an accepted treatment on the basis of the information available to the doctor at the time a choice had to be made."[2] A federal court employs a somewhat more lenient standard for physicians in a case in which a prisoner's suicide occurred after a doctor discontinued medication when the prisoner and her parents objected to the drugs. While allowing the case to go forward, the court applied a standard that required "deliberate[] indifference" on the part of the doctor.[3] Another variation appears in a case which involved a fatal overdose of aspirin given to a child by her mother, a recently released voluntary mental patient. The plaintiff alleged premature discharge of the mother from the hospital and failure to warn "necessary persons" of a propensity for violent acts. Applying the "professional judgment rule," the court said these allegations could support liability "only in the absence of good faith or a failure to exercise professional judgment."[4]

It has been argued that medical professionals should be able to avail themselves of the "business judgment rule," which two authors have summarized as one under which "courts generally refuse to substitute their judgment for the business acumen of corporate officials," with the result that "it is quite rare for a court to hold a corporate director for a negligent business decision." Seeking explanations for why courts have not applied this rule to medical negligence, they identify, among others, "differences in the role of risk-taking and failure, … lack of an accepted methodology with respect to business decision-making, differences in the threshold requirements to enter the business and health professions, differences in the ability to rely on market efficiency and differences in whether plaintiffs have voluntarily exposed themselves to risk."[5]

There is a range of opinion on the question of how geography relates to the standard of care. The "locality" rule, most sympathetic to doctors, made the standard that of "other doctors in the same community."[6] With increasing recognition of advancements in medical education and available technology, some courts adopted a "modified locality" standard, which "expand[ed] the area of comparison to similar localities."[7] Now more courts lean toward what might be called a nationalized standard of care, one which establishes a general foundation which all practitioners must meet, but also takes account of practical limitations in smaller communities. In one case, the court said that although "the appropriate community standard may require that ... doctors send such patients as may be taken to ... larger centers," "when this is not practicable, the small town doctor should not be penalized for not utilizing means or facilities not reasonably available to him."[8] Important to the qualifications in such statements is the question of what kind of witnesses can be used to prove the standard of care, a topic we treat below.

One standard that physicians have proffered as a defense is that they met the "industry standard" of care. Arguably, this idea is at the root of the rules requiring general competence on the part of physicians. However, there is support for a more expansive standard, for which a landmark opinion came in a case where the industry standard did not require that tugboats have working radio receivers on board. In this famous case, only one tugboat line maintained such sets, but as Judge Learned Hand put it in his opinion, "[a]n adequate receiving set suitable for a coastwise tug can now be got at small cost and is reasonably reliable if kept up; obviously it is a source of great protection to their tows." Although Judge Hand acknowledged that there were "cases where courts seem to make the general practice of the calling the standard of proper diligence," he said that "a whole calling may have unduly lagged in the adoption of new and available devices," that an industry "never may set its own tests, however persuasive be its usages," and that it was for courts in "in the end" to "say what is required." He declared that "there are precautions so imperative that even their universal disregard will not excuse their omission."[9]

A striking application of this idea appeared in a case in which an ophthalmologist did not give a pressure test to a 32-year-old woman who initially consulted him for myopia. Experts for the plaintiff as well as the defendant agreed that the industry standard did not routinely require such tests for patients under 40. However, given testimony that "the standards of the profession do require pressure tests if the patient's complaints and symptoms reveal to the physician that glaucoma should be suspected," the court applied the test of the tugboat case summarized above. Although it observed that "[t]he incidence of glaucoma in one out of 25,000 persons under the age of 40 may appear quite minimal," it remarked that the test was a "a simple pressure test, relatively inexpensive," and said that "there is no doubt that by giving the test the evidence of glaucoma can be detected," underlining the "grave and devastating effects" of glaucoma.[10]

Courts have applied the same idea in products liability cases. An example is a case in which the plaintiff's hand was caught in the rollers of a corn picker. The defendant argued that the machine met the "farm implement industry's custom and practice in the manufacturing of cornpickers"—specifically that such machines had "never had emergency stop devices." However, the court sliced a distinction between "state of the art," which it said was "a defense to a design defect claim," and industry "custom and practice," which it said was not.[11] Another court also ruled that industry custom was not a defense with respect to the design of the roof of a Ford Explorer, which rolled over without fault on the driver's part. It said, simply, that "[a] manufacturer cannot defend a product liability action with evidence it met its industry's customs or standards on safety," declaring that "in strict liability actions, 'the issue is not whether defendant exercised reasonable care'" but "whether the product fails to perform as the ordinary consumer would expect."[12] This group of cases teaches that courts may sometimes apply general language in one area of activity—for example, the standard for radio sets on tugs—to another, for example, eye examinations.

As a matter of abstract policy, there should be no difference in the application of medical malpractice rules because of the status of the patient. In practice, however, there are studies indicating "racial disparities in the quality of care across a wide range of diseases," including "asthma, heart attack, diabetes and prenatal care."[13] Beyond that, intuition suggests that the economic status of patients may dictate the quality of care. However, one will never find courts saying that there are different standards of care for rich and poor or for whites and persons of color.

Integrated into the question of the content of the standard of care is the question of how to establish it. There is a geographical element to this issue, typified by the question of whether a big city doctor should be able to testify on the standard of care in a small community. In a case involving the delivery of a child in Decatur, Indiana, although the court found legally "harmless" a jury instruction based on a modified locality rule because that rule applied at the time of the event, it effectively did not object to another instruction that allowed the testimony of a Pittsburgh doctor that the standard of care in Decatur required a cesarean section.[14]

A related question is whether in a case involving a medical specialty, only a specialist can give testimony. In another obstetrical case mentioned above, which focused on the question of whether the defendants had allowed a pregnancy to go too long, the plaintiff offered the testimony of a pediatric neurologist who had "never managed a pregnancy" and had not delivered a baby in the ten years before the trial. The court found the admission of this testimony to present an "extremely close" question, which it said that if it were the trial judge, who admitted the testimony, it would have barred the testimony. However, it allowed the evidence, noting that the defendants "were able to point out not only the inherent weakness" of the witness's opinion, "given the absence of clinical evidence, but also his minimal training and experience in the field of obstetrics." It noted that the defendants themselves had given an opinion from a pediatric neurologist.[15] This case is just one illustration of the many battles featuring competing experts that take place in medical malpractice litigation.

There are variations on the question of what kinds of witnesses may be used in medical cases. A Tennessee statute has required that medical witnesses be licensed to practice in that state, or at least in a bordering state. The state legislature modified this requirement further by giving trial judges the power to waive that requirement when they "determine[] that the appropriate witnesses otherwise would not be available." The state supreme court found the statute constitutional as having a "rational basis."[16] There are ways other than expert witnesses to prove the standard. One example is hospital bylaws, one of which was used in a case in which an emergency room physician did not notify the chief of the service about the refusal of a call in circumstances in which the bylaws required him to do so. In his application for the medical staff, the ER physician had affirmed that he had read the bylaws and "agreed to abide by them." The court found the bylaws to provide evidence of the standard of care.[17]

A complication for judging the standard of care is inherent in the welter of statistics on the opinions of doctors about what appropriate care is. Just one example is a study showing remarkable divergences of opinion about the appropriateness of coronary revascularization procedures and hysterectomies. The hysterectomy study, which involved responses from three expert panels conducted on 636 patients in seven managed care organizations, found ratings of inappropriate surgeries in 200, 153, and 331 among the panelists.[18] At least one of the first two panels rated 92 surgeries of the 331 called inappropriate by the third panel to be appropriate.

In litigation, the focus is much more on the testimony of individual witnesses rather than studies of this kind, since litigation by definition focuses on specific cases. Physicians, and indeed laypeople, may conclude that when research of this kind shows such levels of disagreement among experts—and when there is so much competition among expert witnesses in particular cases—it is difficult to find justice in the judicial process. As much of the rest of this book suggests, there are many differences of opinion about what we are willing to call justice.

7.2 Proving Violations of the Standard

Arguments about justice continue when the topic is how a medical injury occurred. This section focuses on the problem of injuries for which there is no direct explanation and for which plaintiffs must rely on circumstantial evidence of either negligence or causation. The legal doctrine at the heart of controversy in these cases is known by the Latin title *res ipsa loquitur*—the thing speaks for itself—which courts employ in the case of unexplained events. The general rule of res ipsa, which is applied with variations in different states, allows the jury to find negligence if "the event is of a kind which ordinarily does not occur in the absence of negligence" and the plaintiff has eliminated "other responsible causes, including the conduct of the plaintiff and third persons."[19] There is disagreement on other elements of the doctrine—for example, as to whether it is simply a rule of evidence or whether it creates a presumption of negligence. One variation, severely applied against doctors, requires the defendant to show that he or she was "free from negligence by evidence which cannot be rationally disbelieved."[20] Rules more sympathetic to doctors say it is not enough to show that a procedure had a bad outcome and that the rarity of a result is insufficient to make out a case. Generally, plaintiffs pleading a *res ipsa* case must present expert testimony, although there are some exceptions; the next sections discuss the role of expert testimony and the related doctrine of informed consent.

Various states have adopted several shadings of requirements for showing medical res ipsa. The most sympathetic of these rules for plaintiffs requires only the showing of an unusual event. Beyond that, variations include the occurrence of an unusual event plus the requirement of testimony by an expert that the kind of event at issue would not happen if due care had been exercised, and a requirement that in addition to an unusual event, the plaintiff must show evidence of specific acts of negligence. A case featuring two elements of *res ipsa* tests—each favoring a different party—is a case in which the plaintiff suffered a vaginal fecal fistula following a supracervical hysterectomy. The court found the testimony of an expert for the plaintiffs to be insufficient on probability of negligence, saying that it was unclear from the testimony whether the expert "meant fistula formation after hysterectomies is usually a result of negligence or whether there is an equal probability that they occur despite the exercise of due care." At the same time, however, the court pointed to testimony "about the inadvisability of operating on" the plaintiff when she had pelvic inflammatory disease "in an acute or an acute flare-up stage." This, the court found, was enough for a jury to conclude under the res ipsa doctrine that the plaintiff's expert "believed that this fistula, more probably than not, resulted from defendant's negligence." An example of the nuances in the evidentiary rules is the fact that the court affirmed a verdict for the defendant on straight negligence counts but reversed a dismissal of the plaintiff's case based on *res ipsa*.[21]

The topic becomes even more complex when the plaintiff seeks to use *res ipsa* against multiple defendants. The New Jersey Supreme Court imposed a heavy burden on defendants in a case in which the tip or cup of a pituitary rongeur broke off in the plaintiff's spine. The plaintiff sued the surgeon, the medical supply distributor for the instrument, the instrument's manufacturer, and the hospital, the latter on the grounds that it negligently furnished a defective rongeur. As the court viewed it, "It was apparent that at least one of the defendants was liable for plaintiff's injury, because no alternative theory of liability was within reasonable contemplation." It said that "the jury should have been instructed that the failure of any defendant to prove his nonculpability would trigger liability; and further, that since at least one of the defendants could not sustain his burden of proof, at least one would be liable."[22]

A judge who wrote a separate opinion in a case in which anesthesia wore off prematurely in a surgery captured a logical concern about some applications of res ipsa in the medical setting: "If one were to examine 100 operations in which this negligent technique had been employed, one would expect to find 2 operations in which such negligence caused premature termination, compared with 5 in which an overabundance of myelin caused premature termination." He said that to apply *res ipsa* "in every one of these hypothetical operations" "would invite the jury to infer a negligent cause without further guidance from the evidence before it." He found it "disturbing to note that in 5 out of every 7 cases of premature termination coupled with a specific negligent act, this inference would blame the doctor for an accident he did not cause."[23]

Other objections to the use of *res ipsa* in medical cases are that its results are like playing with dice, giving unlike results in similar cases; that, as one judge put it, it creates a "largely fictitious search for fault," and that the prospect of its use makes doctors too cautious. Fairness arguments appear on both sides, doctors contending that they may be stigmatized for injuries they did not cause, and patients' advocates saying that it is unfair to keep them from using circumstantial evidence to prove negligence, especially in cases where patients were under anesthesia. As the New Jersey court said in the rongeur case summarized previously, "[a] wholly fault-less plaintiff should not fail in his cause of action by reason of defendants who have it within their power to prove nonculpability but do not do so."

7.3 Expert Testimony

In most cases involving scientific and medical subjects, the courts require plaintiffs to provide expert testimony. Here, we focus on that requirement, with detailed discussion in Chapter 9 on the now-developing rules on the use of scientific evidence.

A good example of the application of the general rule requiring experts is a case involving spinal surgery, in which physicians advised the removal of bulging material from the "L5–S1 interspace." As it turned out, the plaintiff's surgery "removed material from between the first two sacral vertebrae (S1 and S2), and not between L5 and S1." After that operation, the plaintiff continued to suffer his preoperation symptoms, and tests indicated that his surgery "had been performed at the wrong site." He required a second operation for "removal of the bulging material at the L5–S1 interspace." As the court explained the surgeon's actions in the first operation, "[t]he procedure normally used in locating the operative site for a laminectomy was to make incisions exposing the spine, then to grasp vertebrae and use pistoning motions to find the sacrum, ordinarily the place where no further movement is possible; from that place, the surgeon would simply count vertebrae either up (through the lumbar area) or down (through the sacral area) until he reached the desired level." The surgeon, using that procedure, found "bulging and soft disk material between the lowest movable vertebra and the highest immobile vertebra," and decided "that he had located the L5–S1 interspace ... removed that material and concluded the operation." The result was that he did not remove the bulging disk material at L5–S1. The plaintiff had to undergo another operation for that purpose. The court rejected the plaintiff's attempt to make a case for malpractice without expert testimony. It acknowledged that there were cases where it was "clear and obvious" that lay jurors could understand that there had been negligence. However, it said it "doubt[ed] that a layperson would be equipped to judge, without expert assistance," whether the plaintiff could have avoided the pain he suffered and whether there would have had to be more surgery if the first operation "had been performed at L5–S1."[24]

To be sure, there are cases where courts have not required expert testimony—where the surgeon removes the wrong leg, or where a doctor fails to remove a wire embedded in a patient's foot, although the "foot had turned blue, and it was 'running' or oozing some sort of liquid substance."[25]

As is so in most areas of legal controversy, there are competing policy arguments on the requirement of experts. An important element of the problem lies in physicians' typical superiority in possession of relevant information. This has led plaintiffs' lawyers to emphasize the idea that there is a "conspiracy of silence" among doctors unwilling to testify against members of their profession, although this problem has been somewhat mitigated by the increasing availability of experts who may be from communities other than that of the defendant. On their part, defendants will argue that, particularly when there is a lack of expert testimony and the plaintiff uses circumstantial evidence, the results of litigation can be arbitrarily subject to the whims of lay jurors.

Generally, with respect to the availability of experts, we note that there now are companies that provide experts across the spectrum of litigation. A pamphlet from one of them offers a list of experts that goes through the alphabet from accounting, acoustics and aeronautics to zinc and zoology.

7.4 Medical Consent

When can a patient argue against a healthcare provider that she did not agree to a course of treatment? There are two traditional theories of tort law on which patients can rely. The most obvious is the intentional tort of battery, which is an intentional, unconsented touching of a person's body. The other is negligence, the failure to observe the proper standard of care in giving information. A third label, which came into use in judicial decisions only in the 1970s, is "informed consent."

The rationales for these doctrines include both philosophical premises and ideas of efficiency. A major philosophical argument appeared as far back as 1914 in an opinion by a great judge, Benjamin Cardozo, who declared that "[e]very human being of adult years and sound mind has a right to determine what shall be done with his own body." Employing the battery idea just discussed above under the label assault, he said that "a surgeon who performs an operation without his patient's consent commits an assault for which he is liable in damages."[26] A set of arguments with an economics focus has to do with the cost of giving relevant information to patients, which in the case of some courses of treatment theoretically might require a doctor to recite the contents of entire chapters in specialty treatises.

A separate problem, with elements of both philosophy and economics, arises when a patient simply says he does not want to know about the risks of a procedure and tells the doctor to do what she thinks is best. This kind of statement contains yet another issue, involving general exculpatory clauses, where the plaintiff says he will not sue for injuries even if they are caused by negligence. It may be argued that in a free market, adults should be able to bind themselves to such assumptions of medical risk. However, as a general matter courts are hostile to such clauses, reasoning that in terms of information and expertise, the relation between doctor and patient is not a free market.

There are competing general standards about what constitutes informed consent. One, the "professional" standard, requires disclosure "determined by what a reasonable medical practitioner would have disclosed to the plaintiff." By contrast, the "lay standard" "obligat[es] the doctor to disclose that information which a reasonable patient in plaintiff's position would have found material for making a decision to undergo or forgo treatment."[27]

With these abstract standards in mind, we can summarize some more specific elements of informed consent. One of the broadest statements, in a Rhode Island case, requires disclosure of "all the known material risks peculiar to the proposed procedure."[28] Although a "full disclosure" standard may be an ideal, we can identify some more specific elements of the doctrine, on which there is more or less agreement by the courts. The details to be disclosed include the nature of a procedure—to take one example on which there are opposing cases, the use of forceps in delivering a baby. They also include the severity of possible injury. Courts have described the element of the incidence of occurrence to a point where a risk of 1 percent of permanent incontinence and paralysis of the bowels after a laminectomy[29] or of 0.1 to 0.3 percent of recanalization of the fallopian tubes after a cauterization[30] are material.

The requirement of disclosure may extend to alternative courses of treatment. A striking application of the requirement is a decision in a case in which the defendant used a needle biopsy on a patient with lupus, without mentioning that this procedure might puncture the gall bladder. As the court summarized it, "[h]e did not discuss the alternative of an open biopsy, which would require an incision and would be conducted under general anesthesia, because he did not consider that procedure advisable." Concluding that the defendant should have disclosed the alternative of the open biopsy even though it was more hazardous, the court referred to the idea that "the patient must be provided with sufficient information to allow him to make an intelligent choice."[31]

Another court arrived at the same conclusion in a case in which a surgeon recommended immediate reduction surgery on an injured arm without disclosing the alternative of immobilizing the arm with an indefinite delay of surgery "to facilitate spontaneous regeneration of [a] damaged nerve." The court said that "[a]lthough a physician may, and indeed should, express his opinion regarding preferable methods of treatment, he may not neglect to set out in a fair manner the alternatives to the procedure he advocates." The court said presentation to the patient's parents of the alternative of immobilizing the arm was "undoubtedly information that reasonable parents would consider material in deciding whether to permit immediate surgery on their child's arm," and concluded that the defendant had not conveyed to the parents "the information they needed to make an informed choice."[32]

Physicians may even have to disclose the risks associated with not employing a procedure. This is the lesson of a case in which the plaintiff did not follow her doctor's recommendation that she have a pap smear, and the doctor did not "specifically" inform her of the possibility that she might have a cancer that a pap smear would detect. The doctor said that "[w]e don't say by now it can be Stage Two ... or go through all of the different lectures about cancer. I think it is a widely known and generally accepted manner of treatment and I think the patient has a high degree of responsibility. We are not enforcers, we are advisors." Emphasizing the right of patients "to make decisions about their own bodies," the court quoted a precedent from the original set of informed consent decisions on "the 'fiducial qualities' of the physician–patient relationship," saying that "patients who reject a procedure are as unskilled in the medical sciences as those who consent." Adding that the defendant "was not engaged in an arms-length transaction" with the plaintiff, the court concluded that "he was obligated to provide her with all the information material to her decision."[33]

The issue of whether information is material is subject to interpretation. There are two concepts linked together here—materiality and causation. A simple statement of that linkage is that the question is whether if the patient had been given the information it would have been likely to alter her decision to have a course of treatment. There are differing arguments on whether the test is a subjective one, focused on the individual patient, or an objective one. In the case summarized above that involved a sterilization operation, the court chose an "objective, prudent-person standard," quoting another decision on the idea of "what a prudent person in the patient's position would have decided if informed of all relevant factors." This test obviated the need for a patient's testimony about what she would have done, reflecting "distrust of the patient's hindsight testimony."[34]

A related issue lies in the question of how to inform patients with particular sensitivities that arguably would require disclosure. In the sterilization operation case, the court decided that the plaintiff should have been told about the possibility of recanalization because of a medical history that suggested that another pregnancy might have serious consequences, even fatal ones. The court thought a jury "could conclude that a reasonable person in what [the defendant] knew to be the plaintiff's position would be likely to attach significance to the risk."[35]

We briefly discussed efficiency in medical decision-making above. Basic notions of efficiency make various assumptions about the rationality of those who make choices about risk. There are, however, a number of qualifications. People's intelligence levels differ, as do their capacity to understand what a doctor may think are clear instructions. There are statistics indicating that large numbers of surgical patients could not identify the most basic aspects of their treatment within a day of signing consent forms.[36]

One group of authors has noted a group of factors that can compromise the rationality of patient decisions. These include the difficulty of defining the reference points of patients as influenced by a physician's framing of options, patients' loss aversion, and the difficulty of predicting future preferences.[37] Finally, we come back to the philosophical question of how much belief we have in free will.

Endnotes

1. *Hall v. Hilbun*, 466 S.2d 856, 870–72 (Miss. 1985).
2. *Oullette by Oullette v. Subak*, 391 N.W.2d 810, 815–16 (Minn. 1986).
3. *Rogers v. Evans*, 792 F.2d 1052, 1058–59 (11th Cir. 1986).
4. *Littleton v. Good Samaritan Hosp. & Health Ctr.*, 529 N.E.2d 449, 461 (Ohio 1988).
5. Hal R. Arkes and Cindy A. Schipani, *Medical Malpractice v. The Business Judgment Rule: Differences in Hindsight Bias*, 73 Ore. L. Rev. 587, 590, 622 (1994).
6. See, e.g., *Vergara v. Doan*, 593 S.E.2d 185, 186 (Ind. 1992) (summarizing the rule).
7. See id.
8. *Gambill v. Stroud*, 531 S.W.2d 945, 950 (Ark. 1976).
9. The T.J. Hooper, 60 F.2d 737, 740 (2d Cir. 1932).
10. *Helling v. Carey*, 519 P.2d 981, 982–83 (Wash. 1974).
11. *Hillrich v. Avco Corp.*, 514 N.W.2d 94, 98 (Iowa 1994).
12. *Buell-Wilson v. Ford Motor Co.*, 46 Cal. Rptr.3d 147, 164 (App. Ct. 2006).
13. Rachel Pearson, How Doctors Can Confront Racial Bias in Medicine, *Sci Am.*, Nov. 2015, at 14 (summarizing studies).
14. *Vergara v. Doan*, supra note 5, 593 N.E.2d at 188.
15. *Oullette by Oullette v. Subak*, supra note 2, 391 N.W.2d at 816.
16. *Sutphin v. Platt,* 720 S.W.2d 455, 458 (Tenn. 1986).
17. *Hastings v. Baton Rouge Gen'l Hosp.*, 498 S.2d 713 (La. 1986).
18. Paul G. Shekelle et al., The Reproducibility of a Method to Identify the Overuse and Underuse of Medical Procedures, 338 *N. Eng. J. Med.* 1888, 1891–92 (1998).
19. Restatement (Second) of Torts §328D (1965).
20. *Clark v. Gibbons*, 426 P.2d 525, 533 (Cal. 1967).
21. *Spidle v. Steward*, 402 N.E.2d 216, 219–20 (Ill. 1980).
22. *Anderson v. Somberg*, 338 A.2d 1, 4 (N.J. 1975).

23. *Clark v. Gibbons*, supra note 20, 426 P.2d at 536 n.2 (Tobriner, J., concurring).
24. *Sitts v. United States*, 811 F.2d 736, 741 (2d Cir. 1987).
25. *Runnells v. Rogers*, 396 S.W.2d 87, 90 (Tenn. 1980).
26. *Schloendorff v. Society of New York Hosp.*, 105 N.E. 92, 93 (N.Y. 1914).
27. Alan Meisel & Lisa Kabnick, Informal Consent to Medical Treatment: An Analysis of Recent Legislation, 41 *U. Pitt. L. Rev.* 407, 423 (1980).
28. *Wilkinson v. Vesey*, 295 A.2d 676, 688 (R.I. 1972).
29. *Canterbury v. Spence*, 464 F.2d 772, 794 (D.C. Cir. 1972).
30. *Hartke v. McKelway*, 707 F.2d 1544, 1549 (D.C. Cir. 1983).
31. *Logan v. Greenwich Hosp. Ass'n*, 465 A.2d 294, 301 (Conn. 1983) (summarizing trial court's instruction).
32. *Marino v. Ballestas*, 749 F.2d 162, 168 (3d Cir. 1984).
33. *Truman v. Thomas*, 611 P.2d 902, 906 (Cal. 1980).
34. *Hartke v. McKelway*, supra note 30, 707 F.2d at 1550–51.
35. Id. at 1549.
36. Barrie R. Cassileth et al., Informed Consent—Why Are Its Goals Imperfectly Realized? 302 *N. Eng. J. Med.* 896 (1980).
37. See Redelmeiier, Rozin and Kahneman, Understanding Patients' Decisions: Cognitive and Emotional Perspectives, 270 *JAMA* 72 (1993).

Chapter 8

The Duty/Proximate Cause Problem

An intriguing set of legal issues in tort law arises from events and situations familiar to providers of healthcare and professionals in the sciences and technological disciplines. These are occurrences with high levels of unpredictability which inject uncertainty into decision-making.

Courts use a variety of terms in their efforts to deal with these problems. Sometimes these different words do not differ in concept and in the outcomes they produce in court, but sometimes they reflect very different ways of looking at events. Thus, often words matter when they are words that courts use to describe their reasoning processes.

One group of these problems has to do with the types of harm that occur in injury cases. A category of this kind is what is called *economic loss*, which in this area of law courts often distinguish from injury to person or tangible property. One example of economic loss is the kind of pocketbook harm that happens when an event causes losses resulting from the idling of machinery. In frequently refusing recovery under tort law for economic loss—although sometimes they do allow it—courts attempt to draw lines to avoid liabilities they are afraid might prove to be without enforceable limits.

Generally courts will refuse claims for expectation-type loss by plaintiffs who were in a contractual relation with the defendant, reasoning that the plaintiffs could have protected themselves against such loss by provisions in the contract. The more difficult cases are those in which there is no prior contractual relation between the parties. A much-cited decision in such a case that denied recovery arose from a suit by an employee for wages he lost because his employer's plant was shut down due to a large fire that erupted in liquefied natural gas, negligently stored on the premises of the defendant, which were located near the plant of the plaintiff's employer. In refusing the suit, the court fashioned a parade of hypotheticals involving "remote" losses, giving as examples cases in which

> the power company with a contract to supply a factory with electricity would be deprived of the profit which it would have made if the operation of the factory had not been interrupted by reason of fire damage; a man who had a contract to paint a building may not be able to proceed with his work; a salesman who would have sold the products of the factory may be deprived of his commissions; the neighborhood restaurant which relies on the trade of the factory employees may suffer a substantial loss.

The court said that "to permit recovery of damages in such cases would open the door to a mass of litigation which might very well overwhelm the courts so that in the long run while injustice might result in special cases, the ends of justice are conserved" by a general rule opposing liability.[1]

Courts rejecting recovery in this type of case use different labels to justify their decisions—labels they stick on cases in several areas discussed in this chapter. One is the idea that the defendant's negligence was not the "proximate cause" of the plaintiff's loss. The other is that the defendant did not have a "duty" to the plaintiff to avoid that type of loss. Courts rationalize decisions for defendants in such cases by stressing the "limitless possibilities" for liability. They also say that tort law—as opposed to contract law—was not intended to apply to economic loss as contrasted with injuries to persons or to tangible property. And they point out that in many cases, the plaintiff could protect itself by acquiring insurance against the loss at issue.

A much-cited application of the "economic loss rule" is a decision of the Supreme Court in a case in which allegedly defective components on turbines in supertankers caused damage to the turbines that required repairs. The Court, in rejecting the suit, viewed "[d]amage to a product itself" as being "most naturally understood as a warranty claim." It said that "[s]uch damage means simply that the product has not met the customer's expectations, or, in other words, that the customer has received 'insufficient product value,'" commenting that "[t]he maintenance of product value and quality is precisely the purpose of express and implied warranties"— remedies given by contract law rather than tort law.[2]

Many other decisions, including decisions by state courts, have invoked the Court's opinion in that case to support their rejection of tort claims for economic loss. They have done so even in cases where there was physical injury to some property—that is, the exact goods that the plaintiff purchased, saying that tort recovery was limited to damage to "other property." For example, decisions have denied recovery when fires erupted in a front-end loader, in a recreational vehicle, and in several other vehicles, destroying those products.[3]

So strong has been judges' reliance on the "economic loss rule" that in a case where milking machines led to mastitis in the plaintiffs' cattle and a loss of milk production, the Michigan Supreme Court applied the rule. It viewed the case as one in which the plaintiffs' "commercial expectations were not met," which it viewed as "attempts to recover for lost prof- its and consequential damages, losses which are compensable under the" Uniform Commercial Code that fell "squarely within the economic loss doctrine."[4]

One of the most extreme applications of the rule appeared in a case in which a 40-foot section of pipe exploded in a unit of the plaintiff utility, Detroit Edison. In the federal appellate court's summary of this devastating occurrence,

> The blast injured seventeen people, damaged the pipe itself and immediately adjacent equipment, demolished the brick walls of a storage room and office more than forty feet away from the pipe, blew out windows, knocked out part of an aluminum wall, caused wall panel deformation, displaced floor plating panels, damaged hydraulic lines, wires and insulation, causing an oil fire to ignite, and blew asbestos-containing material throughout the entire plant, requiring substantial clean-up.

The utility, claiming a manufacturing defect in the pipe, sued for damages associated with the "cost of repairing or replacing the defective pipe and surrounding machinery, repairing other property damaged by the explosion, cleaning up and removing the asbestos." It also claimed for losses associated with "purchasing replacement power from other utilities" while the affected unit "was repaired and inspected" and while other units "were operating at reduced capacity to minimize the risk of another explosion." In denying the utility's claim the court emphasized that "[t]ort and contract law normally occupy distinct spheres," with contract law operating on "the premise that commercial actors, because of their ability to bargain for the terms of the sale, will be able to allocate the risks and costs of a product's potential nonperformance." It said that the consequences of "inherent hazards" in "the operation of a power plant," including the possibility of pipes exploding, "were not beyond Detroit Edison's contemplation and Detroit Edison should have internalized some of the cost of the risks attendant to doing business."⁵ Notably, the federal court relied on the state court's ruling in the milking machines case. It should be pointed out that the federal court's decision would not have barred personal injury suits brought by workers in the explosion, claims that would have been for personal injury.

The argument for plaintiffs in such cases is clear enough: The defendant was negligent, the plaintiffs' losses would not have occurred but for the defendant's negligence, and it would be unjust to keep the plaintiffs from recovering for what was, after all, a wrong. A decision that gave recovery focused on the escape of a dangerous chemical, ethylene oxide, from a tank car owned by a defendant. The plaintiff, an airline, had to evacuate its nearby premises and suffered a shutdown of is business operations with "resultant economic losses." Although the court said that the plaintiff airline would have a "difficult task in proving damages, particularly lost profits, to the degree of certainty required in other negligence cases," it ruled that the case should go to trial. It mentioned the "close proximity" of the airline to the freight yard where the chemical spill took place:

> the obvious nature of the plaintiff's operations and particular foreseeability of economic losses resulting from an accident and evacuation; the defendants' actual or constructive knowledge of the volatile properties of ethylene oxide; and the existence of an emergency response plan prepared by some of the defendants ... which apparently called for the nearby area to be evacuated to avoid the risk of harm in case of an explosion.⁶

Federal appellate courts have differed, to an extent, on suits for economic loss resulting from major oil spills. One of these events occurred in the Mississippi River Gulf Outlet, where a collision between vessels led to the spillage of twelve tons of pentachlorophenol, PCP, "assertedly the largest such spill in United States history." The diverse group of plaintiffs, whose businesses were affected by the closure of the outlet to navigation by the Coast Guard, included "shipping interests, marina and boat rental operators, wholesale and retail, seafood enterprises not actually engaged in fishing, seafood restaurants, tackle and bait shops, and recreational fishermen." The court affirmed a dismissal of those plaintiffs' claims, although it let stand a trial court finding that recovery could be granted to "commercial oystermen, shrimpers, crabbers and fishermen who had been making a commercial use of the embargoed waters." It rested the part of its decision denying recovery on "the principle that there could be no recovery for economic loss absent physical injury to a proprietary interest." Although it seems intuitively clear that injury from the spill to many of the plaintiffs whose suits were rejected would have been foreseeable, the court cited precedents on the idea that "restrictions on the concept of foreseeability ought to be imposed where recovery is sought for pure economic losses."[7]

The other case arose from the release of oil from platforms near Santa Barbara, California. The court at this case approved recovery for commercial fishermen, which in fact had been approved by the appellate court in the Gulf Outlet case when it denied the claims of many other plaintiffs. However, the court in the Santa Barbara case differed in spirit on the element of foreseeability. It said that "[t]o assert that the defendants were unable to foresee that negligent conduct resulting in a substantial oil spill could diminish aquatic life and thus injure the plaintiffs is to suppose a degree of general ignorance of the effects of oil pollution not in accord with good sense."[8]

The most disastrous 20th century spill that made its way into court occurred when the supertanker Exxon Valdez ran aground in Prince William Sound off Alaska. Among the plaintiffs who recovered for economic losses were commercial fishermen and, mostly by settlements, Native Alaskans who lived in the vicinity and whose livelihoods were compromised. An even more catastrophic event was the BP oil spill on the Gulf Coast in 2010, with damages that dwarfed even those of the Exxon Valdez. In Chapter 11 we discuss the complex compensation arrangements that developed around the impact of that spill, including the creation of a fund based on money provided by BP.

Quite different from the economic loss problem is a specific category of personal injury—that is, emotional harm. Practically all American courts have come to agree that there should be recovery for highly culpable infliction of emotional distress. Most courts have followed a verbal formula designed to reserve this kind of tort claim, usually labeled intentional infliction of emotional distress, for serious injuries. That formula requires that plaintiffs show that the defendant's conduct was intentional or reckless, that it was outrageous, and that the emotional distress was severe.

The term "outrageous" provides a good example of the flexibility that words afford for judicial interpretation. There have been many decisions on this kind of tort action that demonstrate that flexibility and there have been commentaries on whether the term refers to the subjective reaction of ordinary citizens—which would make the issue generally a jury question—or to the cooler response of judges, one of whose roles is thought to be keeping the law from overheated responses. A colorful example is the litigation by Paula Jones, then an Arkansas state employee, who sued Bill Clinton, then the governor of the state, for a hotel room episode that involved several separate events that could be labeled sexual harassment. Susan Webber Wright, the federal trial judge who decided the case in favor of Clinton, said that the incident fell "far short" of the requirements of the tort of intentional infliction of emotional distress. She described Clinton's conduct, although it involved some touchings, as "a mere sexual proposition, albeit an odious one, that was relatively brief in duration, did not involve any coercion or threats of reprisal, and was abandoned as soon as plaintiff made clear that the advance was not welcome." She also showed skepticism about the severity of Ms. Jones' emotional distress, expressing dubiety about the testimony of a "purported expert" for the plaintiff.[9] A human interest postscript to this decision is that the female judge who wrote the opinion had been Bill Clinton's student at the University of Arkansas School of Law. A comment on Judge Wright by a professor at that school, which may imply the idea of the judge as a cooler head, was that she "follows the law and pays attention to the facts." Also of interest is that it was President George H.W. Bush who appointed Wright to her judgeship.

Although the case law includes many decisions on both sides about whether particular kinds of conduct were outrageous, as we have said almost all courts recognize intentional infliction as a tort. The picture is rather different as to acceptance of a tort of negligent infliction of emotional distress, at least in cases where there has been no physical impact on the plaintiffs' body. There is certainly case law that allows recovery in that category. A good example is a case in which a husband sued for his distress after an erroneous report from a healthcare organization that his wife had syphilis.[10]

In another case, the plaintiff sought therapy with the defendant for difficulties in her relationship with another woman. As part of the therapy, the defendant held joint therapy sessions with the plaintiff and the other woman. She then "stopped counseling the plaintiff on an individual basis, and transferred her to group therapy because she had developed 'some emotional feelings' toward" the other woman. The defendant "did not reveal to the plaintiff her emotional involvement" with the other woman but "instead falsely stated that [the healthcare organization] could no longer provide individual counseling because it was the policy of the program to limit individual counseling to a period of six months." In concluding that the defendants, including the therapist's organization, had "breached their respective duties," the court focused on the idea that because a "therapist undertakes the treatment of a patient's mental problems and … the patient is encouraged to divulge his innermost thoughts, the patient is extremely vulnerable to mental harm if the therapist fails to adhere to the standards of care recognized by the profession."[11]

Courts have cited many different reasons for allowing actions for negligent infliction of emotional distress. They have pointed to the reality of the injury, especially when the distress is severe and to the idea that modern medicine recognizes that it is often impossible to separate physical from mental injury. With reference to the difficulty of proving such cases, they have expressed confidence that trials can sort out the trivial cases from the serious ones.

Yet the many courts that have refused to impose liability in such cases have referred exactly to the difficulty of doing that kind of sorting. They have mentioned the twin specters of a liability they view as both unpredictable and unlimited—arguments that recur with respect to the general question of whether a defendant has a duty to a plaintiff. And besides expressing skepticism about proof of mental injuries, they have suggested, in effect, that people must "tough out" emotional harms, which are part of everyday life.

A specific type of these problems is the case in which the plaintiff sues for fear of disease. Plaintiffs who failed on such a claim, in a case famous in the legal literature, were the "Snowmen of Grand Central," workers in the tunnels below the terminal who became covered with asbestos dust. This case went all the way to the Supreme Court, which rejected the argument that the asbestos dust constituted a "physical impact." In denying recovery, the Court referred to the threat of "unlimited" liability, expressed concern about the "'potential for a flood' of completely unimportant, or 'trivial,' claims," and also mentioned that the plaintiffs had not shown symptoms of disease.[12] In a later case, where the plaintiff railroad employees had established asbestosis, the Court made a linguistic distinction in holding for those claimants. The Court contrasted the prior case, and another one, as involving "claims of negligent infliction of emotional distress," and the case before it, in which it said that the plaintiffs "complain of a negligently inflicted physical injury (asbestosis) and attendant pain and suffering." The crucial distinction for the Court was the plaintiffs were not suing for "discrete damages for their *increased risk* of future cancer," but that rather, they "sought damages for their *current* injury, which, they allege, encompasses a *present fear* that the toxic exposure causative of asbestosis may later result in cancer."[13]

A subcategory of negligent infliction of emotional distress is the law on bystander witnesses. These are people who suffer distress from their proximity to an event that causes physical injury to another person. The courts have tried to formulate standards that limit liability in these situations because of their concern—if that sounds familiar—that otherwise there would be an unacceptable number of suits. One element of these standards is the requirement of a close relation between the parties; usually this means that the plaintiff and the third person are close relatives, although courts have made a few exceptions. Another is that the plaintiff must have been a direct witness to the accident. Finally, the plaintiff's distress must be severe. Presenting a fairly restrictive view of one of these elements is a case in which a mother was informed that her son had been hit by a car. Rushing to the scene, she saw the boy lying in the street and thought that he was dead. Although understandably she claimed "great emotional disturbance, shock, and injury to her nervous system" from seeing this scene, the court rejected her suit because she was not an on-the-scene witness to the accident. Although it acknowledged that drawing a direct-witness line was "arbitrary," it said that drawing such lines was "unavoidable if we are to limit liability and establish meaningful rules for application by litigants and lower courts."[14] In many cases of the sort discussed in this chapter, the plaintiffs argue that injury was foreseeable, but this case teaches that foreseeability is not invariably the measure of duty.

An example of how thinly courts may slice such decisions is a case in which an eight-year-old girl heard the noise of a vehicle that fatally struck her six-year-old brother and "turned to observe his body as it rolled off the highway." In reversing a judgment for the defendant, the court employed a "direct involvement" criterion, under which a person could recover by showing that she "actually witnessed or came on the scene soon after the death or severe injury of a loved one" in a family relationship.[15]

Competing policy arguments have flown around these cases. Plaintiffs emphasize individual justice, citing the simple fact that a negligent defendant caused an injury and the idea that the plaintiff witness' distress was foreseeable given her relationship to the direct victim. Defendants contend that fairness and common sense require that there be only a "single recovery" rule—that the direct victim of the accident is the only person who should get a tort judgment and that compensation to the witness is principally compensation to an injury to family relations. In response, plaintiffs argue that their suits go beyond their injuries to family relations to their emotional interests as individuals. And defendants will come back with the argument that we all have to put up with vicissitudes of life, which are, are one court put it, "unavoidable aspect[s] of the 'human condition.'"[16] Plaintiffs may contend that a liberal rule will increase deterrence to accident-causing behavior. However, it can be argued that it seems questionable whether people will act more carefully because of emotional injuries to bystanders than they would with reference to the possibility that they will cause direct physical injury to the relatives of the witnesses.

The way these arguments fly back and forth is an indicator of how judges employ varied rationales, which themselves may have emotional roots, to justify opposing conclusions about concrete legal issues.

A large and intellectually challenging group of cases includes events that intuitively would have been unpredictable before they happened, including events where the manner in which those events occurred is unusual. Those occurrences include consequences that are strung-out in time and place, and injuries to people outside the ambit of those who ordinarily would not be expected to be injured by a defendant's culpable conduct. Many decisions in these cases seek to set boundaries that will keep litigation from overloading the judicial system.

The courts have used many different terms to label the results that they reach in these cases. As indicated above, they may use the terminology of "duty" and "no proximate cause." They may use the variant of no "legal cause." Another verbal test employed by courts is to ask whether the defendant's act was the "natural and probable cause" of the plaintiff's harm. In cases where some event or events occurred in the time between the defendant's conduct and the plaintiff's injury, they will use terms like "intervening cause" or "supervening cause." Using geography and time, they will say that an injury was "too remote" from the defendant's negligence to impose liability. Sometimes in holding for defendants, they will fall back on the unforeseeability of an event. They also have said that even if the defendant's conduct was negligent in the abstract, the plaintiff's injury was not "within the risk" of that conduct. A similar, rather subtle basis for defendant-oriented decisions is the idea that the defendant's conduct—though below the standard of care in that activity—was not negligent as to the plaintiff. Now I turn to a discussion of particular cases involving unpredictable or unusual events and of commentaries on the policy arguments that move courts in different directions on these issues.

An interesting contrast on time and space appears in two decisions, separated by more than a century and an ocean. The first was an English case in which the sparks from the defendant railway's locomotive started a fire in grass cuttings that the railway's workers had heaped up near the rails for two weeks in very hot weather. The fire burned over 200 yards through a hedge, over a stubble field, across a lane, and destroyed the plaintiff's cottage. The appeals court affirmed a judgment for the plaintiffs. The writer of the first opinion acknowledged that "no reasonable man could be expected to foresee consequences of these many accidents, which together led to the destruction of the plaintiff's house." However, he observed "that there was negligence on the part of the defendants and that that negligence caused the accident," and said that given the defendants' knowledge of the dry condition of the grass cuttings, "they were bound to provide against the possible consequences of such an accident."[17]

The comparison case, featuring multiple arguments against liability, arose from a collision of ships on the Mississippi River. At the time of the collision the barge on which the plaintiff was working was approximately six miles downstream from the collision site. The current at the time of the collision was one knot. Some oil from one of the colliding ships moved down the river and, six hours later, washed onto the deck of a barge where the plaintiff was working and congealed there "into a soft, tar-like substance." Two days later, as he started to clean the deck, the plaintiff slipped and fell. The court rejected his claim, saying that the defendant "should not be held responsible for *all* injuries which occur as a result of the oil spill, no matter how far removed in distance and time." It declared that to impose liability "would be to stretch the concept of legal cause too far." The defendant's negligence, the court said, was "at best, a fortuitous event for which defendant's conduct was not a legal cause." It declared that the plaintiff's injury was "too remote from the collision, both in time and space, for plaintiff to recover." The court also employed an unforseeability argument, saying that "it simply was not foreseeable that oil which spilled into the Mississippi as a result of a collision would splash aboard a barge miles away and cause someone to slip some two days after the collision."[18]

Another set of dividing lines appears in cases involving chains of events that many people would think improbable. Again we contrast cases, both famous in legal literature, from both sides of the Atlantic. In the English case, workers on a ship carelessly knocked a plank into the hold of the vessel, where petrol vapor had collected. A spark set off when the plank hit the hold ignited the vapor, causing a fire that destroyed the ship. The English Court of Appeal held for the plaintiff, the owner of the ship, unpersuaded by the defendant's unforeseeability argument. It said that there were various harms that could be foreseen from the defendant's negligence—that the plank falling into the hold of the ship "might easily cause some damage either to workmen, or cargo, or the ship." As one judge generalized it,

> if the act would or might probably cause damage, the fact that the damage it in fact causes is not the exact kind of damage one would expect is immaterial, as long as the damage is in fact directly traceable to the negligent act and not by the operation of independent causes, having no connection with the negligent act, except that they could not avoid its results.[19]

The American case, with an even more complex chain of events, is a classic to which every law student is exposed. The role of disputed facts in litigation is evident when I mention that there are many versions of the facts, including testimony by one of the plaintiff's daughters, who was standing with her mother on the defendant's rail platform waiting for a train for which they had bought tickets. A man, who was carrying a package and whose identity will be forever unknown, ran to catch another train as it began to move. The railway's guards tried to help him into the car. The plaintiff claimed that they were negligent in their efforts to help him, which jarred the package loose. Containing explosives, of which the guards had no knowledge, the package fell to the rails and exploded. At least in the version of the facts that the court accepted, "[t]he shock of the explosion threw down some scales at the other end of the platform many feet away," and the scales struck the plaintiff.

A four-to-three majority turned down the plaintiff's suit against the railroad for her injuries. Judge Benjamin Cardozo, one of the greats of American judicial history, used foreseeability as the basis for his conclusion that the railroad did not have a duty to the plaintiff: "the orbit of the danger as disclosed to the eye of reasonable vigilance would be the orbit of the duty." He also employed another concept of the several we mentioned at the beginning of this discussion. First, he declared that even if the negligence of the defendant's employees was a wrong to the man with the package—which he said might "very well be doubted"—"it was a wrong to a property interest only, the safety of his package." And, he asserted, it certainly "was not a wrong in its relation to the plaintiff, standing far away. Relatively to her it was not negligence at all."[20]

Judge William Andrews, himself a distinguished jurist, disagreed in a dissenting opinion. For him, the keynote legal concept was not duty but "proximate cause." Noting that "[t]hese two words have never been given an inclusive definition," he said that its meaning would "depend in each case upon many considerations."

The meaning he gave "is that, because of convenience, of public policy, of a rough sense of justice, the law arbitrarily declines to trace a series of events beyond a certain point." Then he posed a number of questions—a favorite occupation of lawyers:

> The court must ask itself whether there was a natural and continuous sequence between cause and effect. Was the one a substantial factor in producing the other? Was there a direct connection between them, without too many intervening causes? Is the effect of cause on result not too attenuated? Is the cause likely, in the usual judgment of mankind, to produce the result? Or, by the exercise of prudent foresight, could the result be foreseen? Is the result too remote from the cause, and here we consider remoteness in time and space.

Judge Andrews acknowledged that "we draw an uncertain and wavering line," but said that "draw it we must as best we can." For him, it was "all a question of fair judgment, always keeping in mind the fact that we endeavor to make a rule in each case that will be practical and in keeping with the general understanding of mankind." He concluded that he could not "say as a matter of law"—as Judge Cardozo had—"that the plaintiff's injuries were not the proximate result of the negligence."[21] This case has been cited many times, but it is of some interest that Judge Andrews' dissent has been quoted very often.

Important lessons that this case provides for nonlawyers are not only how powerful the opposing arguments can be about the facts of a litigated case, but how different the legal concepts that lawyers and judges bring to bear on the same fact situation can be.

A decision in a case involving a child's mischief and the alleged negligence of a bank, and, for good measure, the carelessness of a driver, illustrates the variety of legal concepts that may be employed in a relatively simple case. In this case, the court refers to both the labels of duty and of proximate cause and also the defenses of unforeseeability and "intervening cause." The initiating cause of a traffic accident was a three-year-old boy who became fascinated with an alarm button that faced outward from the desk of a bank employee. On several occasions over a period of months he pressed the button, with the result that police officers rushed to the scene. The plaintiff in this case was an officer who made an emergency response to an alarm that the boy set off. One defendant was a motorist whose negligent driving caused the plaintiff to swerve, with the result that he hit a telephone pole. The other two defendants whose liability was discussed in the case were the boy's mother and the bank, with the mother being sued for not keeping a close enough watch on the boy and the bank for not guarding against his antics with the alarm button, with one possible precaution being relocation of the button.

The court rejected the defendants' argument that this series of events was "freakish." In holding that the facts raised "a duty at law" on the part of the bank, the court said that "the consequences of placing the burden of guarding against the risk of harm on the defendant in this case does not appear to involve extraordinary cost or problems." It commented that a bank "charged every day with the safekeeping of the property of its customers can be expected to handle the consequences involved in securing a safe location for a silent emergency alarm button." It also referred to an "undue emphasis on foreseeability as a 'make or break' factor insofar as the court's duty determination is concerned."

As to the mother, the court referred to the idea that "a parent has a special power of control over the conduct of the child which the parent is under a duty to exercise reasonably for the protection of others," particularly when "the parent has notice of a specific type of harmful conduct, and an opportunity to interfere with it." It said that given the plaintiff's allegations, the mother "had both the knowledge of the need to control" the child, "and the opportunity to do so." In the circumstances, the court said, the plaintiff's complaint had "sufficiently allege[d] a duty owed by" the mother under the elements of "a traditional duty analysis; that is, consideration of public policy and social requirements, foreseeability, the likelihood of injury, the magnitude of placing the burden of guarding against the injury on the defendant, and the consequences of placing that burden on the defendant."[22]

The court also found that the defense of no "proximate cause" did not save the defendants from a jury trial, saying that "reasonable men may differ as to whether either defendant's failure to warn the police department about the false alarm or to ascertain whether the button had been pushed constituted a breach of the duty owed plaintiff since the extent of either defendant's knowledge and observation of the boy's activities is not certain." It rejected both defendants' contention that "their alleged negligence was only a condition to, and not a cause of, plaintiff's injury" and their "intervening cause" argument. It observed that the precise "nature of the risk created by the defendants' alleged negligence was the danger that the responding emergency vehicle would be involved in a collision," a situation in which the other motorist's "car caused the plaintiff to swerve to avoid that very risk." It said that "the so-called condition may be viewed as having done quite as much to bring about the harm to the plaintiff as did the intervening cause," the other motorist's car.[23] Thus, what may have seemed to onlookers to be a simple auto accident drew forth an opinion that required a court to discuss at least five legal concepts.

Another group of categories where persons or events intervene between the defendant's activities and the plaintiff's injuries includes cases where the intervening events are crimes. In a case involving one such crime, the defendant was *Soldier of Fortune* magazine, which ran a personal service advertisement that included the words "GUN FOR HIRE. 37-year-old professional mercenary desires jobs. … All jobs considered." A man who wanted to kill his business partner responded to the ad and hired the man who placed it, who then murdered the partner in his own driveway and wounded the partner's son. The court decided that the magazine could not avail itself of the guarantee of freedom of the press by the First Amendment.[24] It also rejected the magazine's argument that the publication of the advertisement was not the proximate cause of the murder, a defense based on the ideas that the "events that intervened between its publication of [the murderer's] ad and the carrying out of the murder plot were entirely unforeseeable" and that the publication of the ad was "too remote in the chain of events leading to" the murder. The court recognized that there was state law saying that an "intervening criminal act" would supersede the negligence of a defendant like the magazine. However, it quoted a precedent on the idea that if "the criminal act was a reasonably foreseeable consequence of the defendant's conduct, the casual connection between that conduct and the injury is not broken."

Declaring that the language of the ad "should have alerted a reasonably prudent publisher to the clearly identifiable unreasonable risk" that the person who placed it "was soliciting violent and illegal jobs," the court said "a reasonable jury could conclude that the criminal act that harmed [the plaintiffs] was reasonably foreseeable and, accordingly, that the chain of causation was not broken."[25]

A very different result, bolstered by an unforeseeability argument, appeared in a case in which a man bent on killing Jews entered a Jewish Community Center (JCC) in the Los Angeles area and shot a child, whose family sued the center for failure "to provide adequate security measures." The court's summary of the facts might have seemed to slant toward the plaintiffs' case. It noted that the attack took place during a time that Jewish organizations called the "summer of hate." It also noted that "[t]he Anti-Defamation League sent notices to Jewish groups throughout the nation advising them to increase security," that its west coast office had "notified Jewish organizations that there was a 'strong potential' of violence against their members," and that two centers including the one with the camp attended by the plaintiffs' son had "received anonymous telephone calls threatening their members with physical violence." Moreover, it mentioned that the center, which "had a large sign identifying it as a Jewish facility," "had no locks on the entry door, no security guards, and no emergency evacuation plan, notwithstanding that the JCC had implemented those precautions at other locations."

Despite those facts, the court denied recovery, saying that "[i]mposing a duty … would not prevent future harm," and essentially folding the duty issue into the fact-based question of whether the defendant had been negligent. The court pointed out that it was not alleged that the shooter had made any of the anonymous calls, and saying that his assault "took the North Valley Center completely by surprise." It said that "[a] general concern about security, absent a sufficiently specific threat, does not require an organization to prepare for the worst imaginable scenario." It opined that "[t]he characteristics of a camp ... are not conducive to the use of security guards or similar measures." It concluded that the circumstances of the plaintiff's injury "were unique, shocking and ... unforeseeable," commenting that "[d]espite the efforts of an organization to protect individuals on its premises, a crazed bigot who has declared 'war' on a particular group in society may find a way to breach security measures."[26]

One of the most discussed decisions imposing liability for a third person's crime was the California case in which a voluntary outpatient at a university hospital, Prosenjit Poddar, told his therapist at a university hospital that he was going to kill a woman who he did not name, but who was "readily identifiable" as the plaintiffs' daughter, Tatiana Tarasoff. The therapist, with the concurrence of a doctor who first examined the patient, and the assistant to the director of the department of psychiatry at the hospital, decided that Poddar "should be committed for observation in a mental hospital." However, police officers asked to assist in securing his confinement, being satisfied that he was "rational," "released him on his promise to stay away from" Tatiana. The director of the department of psychiatry "directed that all copies of the letter and notes" that the therapist had taken should "be destroyed, and 'ordered no action to place ... Poddar in a 72-hour treatment and evaluation facility.'" Poddar "persuaded Tatiana's brother to share an apartment with him near Tatiana's residence," and shortly after she returned to California after being overseas, he "went to her residence and killed her."

The plaintiff sued the therapists and policemen, and the regents of the University of California as their employer. In its much-discussed opinion, the court "recognize[d] the public interest in supporting effective treatment of mental illness and in protecting the rights of patients to privacy ... and the consequent public importance of safeguarding the confidential character of psychotherapeutic communication." However, it said that "[a]gainst this interest ... we must weigh the public interest in safety from violent assault." In part focusing on the fact that Tatiana was an identifiable target for Poddar, it referred to a summary of case law supporting "the conclusion that by entering into a doctor–patient relationship the therapist becomes sufficiently involved to assume some responsibility for the safety, not only of the patient himself, but also of any third person whom the doctor knows to be threatened by the patient." It declared that "[i]n this risk-infested society we can hardly tolerate the further exposure to danger that would result from a concealed knowledge of the therapist that his patient was lethal."

The court thus allowed the plaintiff's claims to go forward against the medical defendants "for breach of a duty to exercise reasonable care to protect Tatiana," although it held in favor of the police defendants as not having "any such special relationship to either Tatiana or to Poddar sufficient to impose" on them "a duty to warn respecting Poddar's violent intentions." It generally concluded that "the public policy favoring protection of the confidential character of patient–psychotherapist communications must yield to the extent to which disclosure is essential to avert danger to others." The court epitomized its view in the memorable statement that "[t]he protective privilege ends where the public peril begins."[27]

Summing up the Duty/Proximate Cause Problem

The duty/proximate cause problem arises in many guises: Different kinds of plaintiffs, odd ways in which accidents happen, remoteness of injuring events in time and space, different kinds of harm (emotional harm, economic loss), intervening events and acts—for example, third party crimes. The problem for courts is finding an intellectually efficient solution that makes room for giving justice when negligent conduct is the cause in fact of a plaintiff's injury but requires checks against limitless liability.

Courts have used varied words and phrases in the effort to define the boundaries of liability. Besides duty and proximate cause, these include illegal cause, foreseeability, injury not "within the risk" of the defendant's negligence, natural and probable consequence, remoteness, intervening cause, cause "independent" of the defendant's negligence, a requirement that the defendant's conduct be a "substantial factor" in causing the injury, the idea that the defendant's conduct was a "condition" for but not a "cause" of the injury, and the description of an event as a "fortuity."

They have identified numerous policy rationales for imposing liability or rejecting claims. Among these are the incremental incentives to avoid accidents, determining the most efficient ways to insure against the costs of injuries, including predictability of injuring events and the availability and affordability of insurance, and intuitive fairness.

Courts and commentators have articulated many standards for limiting liability. I have identified as many as fifteen different views. These include liability for all "direct consequences" of the defendant's conduct, a formula that focuses on the relation between the parties and the defendant's recognition of the risk in its context, a concept of duty defined by risk and specifically by foreseeability of risk, a proximate-cause limitation on risk based on considerations of public policy, and intuitions of "fair judgment." They also include the ideas that liability will be imposed only for a result "within the risk" of a negligent act or only for harms of which the "negligent aspect" of the defendant's conduct is a cause in fact.

Many factors influence courts and commentators. Some academic disputes pit against one another the idea that the problem is basically one of public policy, including economic balancing, and the idea that the question is basically one of individualized justice between the parties alone, without reference to considerations of policy. For those whose focus is economics, the question is how to figure out the optimally efficient result in a case, which requires estimating the quantum of increased risk generated by the defendant's conduct. A related empirical question is how predictable an injury is—a factor crucial to calculating insurance premiums. Another factor, related to both economics and process, is the administrative expense of resolving disputes by litigation.

General comments on the topic include the idea that duty includes a cluster of economic, moral, and administrative elements, and the view that the principal question is the weighing and balancing of accident costs and accident avoidance costs. A very specific factor is the individual sensitivities of injured persons, for example in cases involving plaintiffs with hemophilia or with psyches that are more vulnerable than those in the general population.

Courts also will consider broad alternatives to imposing liability on those who cause injury. These include leaving the question to contractual relations between the parties or to how people work out private relationships, relegating potential victims to protect themselves through first-party insurance, and the hard-headed view that people should be philosophically resigned to the occurrence of all kinds of misfortune. Another consideration for courts judging tort cases, which are civil cases, is the strength of the public policy involved; occasionally this factor might be manifested in decisions to leave judgments, or elements of judgments, to the criminal law.

A major practical issue in litigation is which questions are the province of judges alone, and which may be submitted to juries. The conventional answer is that judges deal in "questions of law," including matters involving legal policy, and juries resolve "questions of fact." But many margins between "law" and "fact" are blurry, and sometimes judges will decide that issues with some policy content should be left to jurors as representatives of the community.

Finally, there are considerations of justice, abstractly defined by different metrics. As lawyers are apt to do, I pose these questions: Is an injuring event simply one too quirky to require compensation? Before the fact, would ordinary persons, without knowing whether they would be injurers or victims in particular cases, believe that compensation should be awarded? What will be the long-range impact on people similarly situated, including the impact on their conduct—either as potential injurers or victims? How much ability do potential injurers have to absorb, or spread, the costs of injuries, either with or without insurance? What will be the effects of decisions imposing liability on the distribution of wealth between individual parties or groups of parties? What are the chances that a socially valuable business enterprise will be ruined by a tort judgment? How much volition did either party exercise or have the opportunity to exercise with respect to minimizing the risk of injury?

It is worth emphasis, with respect to these questions of justice, that intuitions about social mores and culture will influence decisions.

One indicator of how much dispute there is on terminology is that an important commentary on the topic on which this chapter focuses, using illustrations, runs to more than 50 pages. It may be noted that the writers of that commentary say that "[a]lthough the term 'proximate cause' has been in widespread use in judicial opinions, treatises, casebooks, and scholarship," the authors do not use the term "because it is an especially poor one to describe the idea to which it is connected."[28]

This summary has included reference to different concepts that courts and commentators employ in resolving these questions, to the words and phrases they use to label those concepts, and to the many elements of justice to which they refer. Readers who are not trained in the law may find all of this awfully complicated and may wish for simpler language and fewer slicings of concepts. I would suggest only that in this area of difficult legal questions, the law simply reflects the complexities, and the difficulties, of living itself.

Endnotes

1. *Stevenson v. East Ohio Gas Co.*, 73 N.E.2d 200, 203–04 (Ohio Ct. App. 1946).
2. *East River S.S. Corp. v. Transamerica Delaval, Inc.*, 476 U.S. 858, 872 (1986).
3. For examples, see Marshall Shapo, *The Law of Products Liability* §27.05[G][2], text with notes 155.a.1–8 (7th ed. Elgar 2017).
4. *Neiberger v. Universal Coops, Inc.*, 486 N.W.2d 612, 621 (Mich. 1992).
5. *Detroit Edison Co. v. NABCO, Inc.*, 35 F.3d 236, 239–42 (6th Cir. 1994).
6. *People Express Airlines v. Consolidated Rail Corp.*, 495 A.2d 110, 118 (N.J. 1985).
7. *State of La. v. M/V Testbank*, 752 F.2d 1019, 1027 (5th Cir. 1985).
8. *Union Oil Co., v. Oppen*, 501 F.2d 558, 569 (9th Cir. 1974).
9. *Jones v. Clinton*, 990 F. Supp. 657, 677–78 (E.D. Ark. 1998).
10. *Molien v. Kaiser Foundation Hosps.*, 616 P.2d 813 (Cal. 1980).
11. *Rowe v. Bennett*, 514 A.2d 803, 804, 806–07 (Me. 1986).
12. *Metro-North Commuter R. Co., v. Buckley*, 521 U.S. 424, 430, 437 (1997).
13. *Norfolk v. Western Ry. Co. v. Ayers*, 538 U.S. 135, 148, 152 (2003).
14. *Thing v. La Chusa*, 771 P.2d 814, 828 (Cal. 1989).
15. *Groves v. Taylor*, 729 N.W. 569, 573 (Ind. 2000).
16. Thing, supra note 14, 771 P.2d at 829.
17. *Smith v. Landon & S.W. Rail Co.*, [1871-73] All E.R. Rep. 167, 169–170 (Kelly, C.B.).
18. *Brown v. Channel Fueling Service*, 574 F. Supp. 666, 668 (E.D. La. 1983).
19. Re Polemis, Worthy & Co., [1921] All E.R. Rep. 40, 42 (Scrutton, L.J.).
20. *Palsgraf v. Long Island R. Co.*, 162 N.E.99, 99–100 (N.Y. 1928).
21. Id. at 104–05 (Andrews, J., dissenting).
22. *Duncan v. Rzonca*, 478 N.E.2d 603, 610-14 (Ill. Ct. App. 1985).
23. Id. at 615–16.
24. *Braun v. Soldier of Fortune Magazine*, 968 F.2d 1110, 1116–21 (11th Cir. 1992).
25. Id. at 1121–22.

26. Kadish ex rel. *Kadish v. Jewish Community Ctrs. of Los Angeles*, 5 Cal. Rptr.3d 394, 402–06 (App. Ct. 2003), dismissed and remanded, 96 P.3d 1055 (Cal. 2004).
27. *Tarasoff v. Regents of Univ. of California*, 551 P.2d 334, 341–49 (Cal. 1976).
28. Restatement (Third) of Torts §29 (2010).

Chapter 9

Scientific Evidence

A major ongoing story in litigation of many kinds lies in the rules on admission of scientific evidence. The foundation for that story is the 1993 Supreme Court decision in *Daubert v. Merrell Dow Pharmaceuticals, Inc.*[1] That case involved claims by two children that Bendectin, the anti-nausea drug taken by their mothers, had caused birth defects. The Court rejected a prior rule that, in cases of expert testimony "deduced from a well-recognized scientific principle or discovery," "the thing from which deduction is to be made must be sufficiently established to have gained general acceptance in the particular field in which it belongs." Rather, without providing "a definitive checklist or test," the Court identified factors that would "bear on the inquiry." Among these factors were whether the "theory or technique" at issue "can be (and has been) tested," and whether it had "been subjected to peer review and publication," although the Court said that "[t]he fact of publication (or lack thereof) in a peer-reviewed journal ... will be a relevant although not dispositive, consideration." It also referred to "the known or potential rate of error." Finally, it said that the "general acceptance" test of the prior decision "can yet have a bearing on the inquiry." Emphasizing that expert testimony must be "not only relevant, but reliable," the Court used the language of a Federal Rule of Evidence to articulate a "helpfulness" standard—that an expert's evidence should "assist the trier of fact to understand the evidence or to determine a fact in issue."[2]

The Court tailored this principle in two subsequent decisions. The plaintiff in one of these cases claimed that his exposure to the chemical PCB promoted his small cell lung cancer. The Court agreed with a trial court holding that animal studies used by the plaintiff's experts did not support this conclusion. It noted that those studies involved infant mice, which developed cancer after direct injections of "massive doses" of PCBs into their peritoneums or stomachs. The Court concluded that "the studies were so dissimilar to the facts presented in [the] litigation" that the trial court did not abuse its discretion in rejecting the reliance on them by the plaintiff's experts. In his opinion for the Court, Chief Justice Rehnquist said that the trial judge did not have to "admit opinion evidence which is connected to existing data only by the *ipse dixit* of the expert"—in colloquial English, the expert could not say, "accept my opinion because I told you so."[3] This aligned the Court with the sardonic remark of a court of appeals judge in the Bendectin case. This judge, noting that "[n]one of the plaintiffs' experts has published his work on Bendectin in a scientific journal or solicited formal review by his colleagues," said that "[i]t's as if there were a tacit understanding that what's going on here is not science at all, but litigation."[4]

The Court's other decision that tailored its holding in the Bendectin case concluded that the elements of that case—which have been termed as enforcing the "gatekeeping" function of courts for expert evidence—included "technical" or "other specialized" knowledge in addition to "'scientific' knowledge."[5]

A summary of the trio of Supreme Court decisions led by *Daubert* has now been codified in a federal rule of evidence. The impact of *Daubert* has been considerable in the federal courts, which are required to follow it, and in the state courts that have adopted the *Daubert* rules. Some state courts retain the "general acceptance" test of the prior decision.

The practical impact of these rules is that in a large range of cases involving scientific evidence, courts now require "*Daubert* hearings" that test expert testimony before trials are held. One of the most important inquiries in these hearings, following the language of the *Daubert* case, concerns the "reliability" of an expert's opinions. Courts have presented long lists of factors that may be considered in making this judgment. In a case involving the design of a forklift, the court mentioned nine "[i]ndicia of reliability," ranging from whether an expert had "referenced standards published by independent standards organizations" to "the centrality of scientific testing and the court's scrutiny of the soundness of that testing" and including "whether an expert has supported his conclusions through discussion of the relevant literature, broadly defined."[6] Another court identified no fewer than seventeen factors, one with eight subcategories, that could be "germane" to its "gatekeeping" function on *Daubert* issues.[7]

Yet another set of criteria are those of Koch's Postulates, originally developed in 1890 to test the hypothesis that particular bacteria caused a specific disease. In a case involving a suicide attributed to a drug used to treat depression, the court finds an expert's testimony insufficient when he "adequately addressed only one of the postulates"—that is, temporal relationship, but not the other six—"strength of association, consistency with other research, alternative explanations, ... biological plausibility, specificity of association and dose-response relationship."[8]

The decisions of many courts apply various factors outlined in the *Daubert* case. Here we discuss these and other criteria used with reference to scientific evidence. One of these is the criterion of peer review. An example is a case involving a heart medication which the plaintiff claimed caused him to lose his eyesight. The court's opinion captures several themes common to cases excluding expert opinion on scientific causation. Noting that none of the opinions of the plaintiff's experts had been "tested or subjected to peer review," the court says that "[w]ithout testing, epidemiological study, or controlled experimentation," those opinions "constitute no more than scientific speculation and cannot be admitted as reliable scientific knowledge." Harking to the theme of opinions "developed exclusively for purposes of litigation," the court finds testimony to be inadequate when it was "based primarily on anecdotal case studies, adverse drug reaction reports, and Defendants' own warnings—information that the scientific community regards as not reasonably reliable for an opinion on causation."[9]

It should be noted, though, that some decisions refer to the *Daubert* court's recognition that "while peer review may be helpful, it is not absolutely necessary for an opinion to be admissible." Saying this, a court allowed testimony not subjected to peer review to go to the jury in a case involving the design of a football helmet.[10] In a case on auto design that arose from a vehicle rollover, the court noted that a test conducted by a plaintiff's witness had "not been published in a peer-reviewed journal," but it said that "this fact alone should not render his expert testimony inadmissible." Rehearsing an idea sometimes used in decisions that are relatively liberal about admitting expert testimony, the court said that "the reliability of a test should be brought into question through vigorous cross-examination and the presentation of contrary evidence."[11]

A series of cases involving breast implants teaches a number of lessons on expert testimony. In a case in which the plaintiff claimed that implants coated with polyurethane foam (PUF) caused breast cancer, the court split its holdings on an expert's testimony. It found reliable his "assessment that the available epidemiological studies do not reach even tentative conclusions about whether *PUF-coated implants* (as opposed to implants generally) are carcinogenic." However, it would not credit his testimony about a study in which "the sample size of subjects with PUF implants was vanishingly small" and "the overall response rate ... was only 'borderline acceptable.'" It commented that that study was "unreliable, because it ignores the rigorous standards and methodology [the witness] himself applies to ... other studies."[12]

An example of testimony on breast implants that passed judicial muster is a case with a foundation in the qualifications of an witness who was the chief of the division of rheumatology, immunology, and allergy at a medical school, and based his testimony "on his research and treatment of more than 700 women with silicone gel breast implants." He opined that "there is a unique constellation of symptoms seen in approximately five percent of women with silicone breast implants, and that these symptoms, taken together, constitute an atypical autoimmune disease." He also testified, after a review of the plaintiff's medical records, that "her symptoms were consistent with this atypical autoimmune disease and were caused by her ruptured silicone gel breast implant." Another witness, a rheumatologist who made a physical examination of the plaintiff, opined that many medical problems of the plaintiff "were related to her exposure to silicone gel," and that "her future was 'guarded.'" The court summarized the qualifications of both witnesses as their possession of "the knowledge, skill, and experience to qualify as experts in their fields, having conducted research, published in peer reviewed journals on silicone-related topics, and treated hundreds of women with silicone gel breast implants in their clinical practices."[13]

In another breast implant case, the court referred to the lag in publication of scientific research when it admitted evidence from an immunologist and a rheumatologist who testified for the plaintiff in addition to her treating neurologist. The court's opinion reflects the difficulty in aligning law and science in what it called "scientifically controversial" areas such as litigation on breast implants. The court said that the plaintiffs "did not need to wait until the scientific community developed a consensus that breast implants caused her diseases," given that they might be subject to statutes of limitation in bringing a lawsuit. Strikingly, in language to which many scientifically trained observers might object, the court said that the plaintiffs' "complaint was not tried in the court of scientific opinion, but before a jury of her peers who considered the evidence and concluded that Dow Corning silicone gel breast implants caused her injuries" and that they provided "substantial evidence" on the issue of causation.[14]

A federal appellate court set a liberal standard in a breast implant case where there was "no solid body of epidemiological data to review." It summarized the testimony of several experts, including a toxicologist described as "a recognized expert on the immunological effects of silicone in the human body" who "testified that his opinion was based on his experience as a toxicologist, his review of medical records," studies by the defendant, and his "general scientific knowledge of silicone's ability to cause immune disorders as established by animal studies and biophysical data." It concluded that this evidence, and testimony by a witness who participated "in a preliminary epidemiological study involving over 200 women," and a rheumatologist who referred to "medical records, his clinical experience, preliminary results of an epidemiological study and medical literature," were "based on scientific techniques that satisfied the requirements established in *Daubert*."[15]

In another case the witness guarded against one of the hurdles in *Daubert* by establishing "an error rate of five to seven percent" in his evaluations of a group of 50 patients and established a further shield for his opinion by "eliminat[ing] other potential causes through differential diagnoses." The defendant attacked the testimony of the plaintiff's witness on the ground that he admitted that he "as yet does not understand the mechanism that he believes produces the silicone-related neurological harm." However, the Oregon appellate court said that "[a]lthough a differential diagnosis under these facts assumes that silicone is a possible cause, that assumption [was] logically supported by the unique symptoms and neurological patterns displayed by the women that were examined."[16] Although the witness' causation hypothesis "had not been tested by others," "had not been subjected to peer review and had not been published," the Oregon Supreme Court said that its state's rules did "not preclude the admission of novel scientific evidence" and that "neither peer review nor publication is a *sine qua non* for the admissibility of scientific evidence."[17]

A contrasting result on breast implants appears in a federal appellate case in which the court rejects the plaintiff's objection to epidemiological evidence offered by the defendant. It refers to the "body of epidemiology" that "largely finds no association between silicone breast implants and immune system diseases." Although saying it is "not holding that epidemiological studies are always necessary in a toxic tort case," the court opines that "where there is a large body of contrary epidemiological evidence, it is necessary to at least address it with evidence that is based on medically reliable and scientifically valid methodology." It rejects the testimony of two experts for the plaintiff, who it says "relied solely on differential diagnosis and case studies to support their belief that silicone gel breast implants can cause systemic disease." It declares that "[t]heir reliance on differential diagnosis without supporting epidemiological evidence is misplaced and demonstrates the unreliable nature of the testimony."[18]

In a case involving a diet pill containing phenylpropanolamine (PPA) the court found sufficient strength in the opinion of an expert for the plaintiff. The court referred, among other things, to the basis of the witness' opinion in "five studies he published on the topic, the published articles of other medical researchers, case reports, his experience treating patients who had ingested PPA-containing compounds, his clinical experience with PPA in other studies, and his experience directing endocrine and obesity clinics." Tracking the criteria of *Daubert*, it said that all of the papers on which the witness relied "have clearly explained, solid scientific methodologies upon which they have tested their theories, and all have been peer-reviewed and published in reputable medical journals." It also noted that the error rates of those papers were "published and their impact on the studies explained."[19] The court distinguished a Bendectin case it had previously decided as one in which an expert "had based his testimony on 'personal belief or opinion,'" and "not 'on the basis of the collective view of his scientific discipline'" and in which he did not explain "coherently the 'grounds for his differences' with his scientific peers."[20]

Another case that specifically tracked *Daubert* factors dealt with a bottom-fire pneumatic nailer, the alleged defect of which was the way it rapid-fired nails "when the operator depresses and holds the trigger and bounces the bottom contact point off the surface of the work." As the court summarized it, the defendant "produces a second type of pneumatic nailer, a sequential-fire tool," which required an operator to release and squeeze the trigger each time he fired a nail. The court was unpersuaded by the defendant's argument that the strength of the testimony of a plaintiff's witness was compromised because he had given testimony in about 40 cases involving nailers. Referring to an article written by the witness, the court did not find it an obstacle that the article was not peer-reviewed. It noted that "the article was published prior to the present litigation and [came] to the identical conclusion as proffered in this case: bottom-fire pneumatic nailers are unreasonably dangerous." Among other things, the court observed that "some propositions are too new to be published," an idea it partly quoted from *Daubert*, and instanced a report by a state agency that the "increased popularity" of nailers of the type at issue in the 1990s "appears to have triggered an increase in injuries due to their use." Saying that "[t]he general acceptance factor dovetails with ... peer review," the court referred to the state agency report and testimony by a user to the effect that "[b]ottom-fire pneumatic nailers are known for problems associated with double-fires throughout the industry." It also mentioned "general acceptance" of the sequential-fire design that the witness had proposed, instancing the report by the state agency.[21]

One test favorable to defendants, although not one requiring broad agreement on methodology, insists that a party who offers expert evidence must show general acceptance by a "recognized minority" of experts—a formula applied in a case in which the plaintiffs claimed that a fertility drug caused birth defects.[22]

The courts exhibit hostility to anecdotal evidence. An example is a case in which the plaintiff alleged that a drug for the prevention of postpartum lactation caused a stroke. The court, noting that the plaintiffs' "anecdotal case reports" were "not controlled studies and do not eliminate confounding variables," said that "the reported effect or injury could be due to some other cause than" the drug at issue. It quoted a prior decision on reports that "are not reliable scientific evidence of causation, because they simply describe reported phenomena without comparison to the rate at which the phenomena occur in the general population or in a defined control group."[23]

Another case featured an attack on an expert's reliance on "reports, temporal methodology," and the "atypical symptoms" of a patient who attributed scleroderma to breast implants. The court said that the plaintiff's "heavy reliance on case reports" proved "her undoing." It referred to a "uniform body of evidence" presented by the defendant "including epidemiological studies failing to establish a causal link between silicone breast implants and connective tissue disease" and to the conclusion by a National Academy of Sciences report that there was "insufficient evidence" of "a causal relationship."[24]

A statement by a very well-regarded appellate judge cautions that "an insightful, even an inspired hunch" will not quality as evidence. Affirming a judgment against a man who claimed that a nicotine patch caused a heart attack, this judge rejected the causation testimony of "a distinguished cardiologist and department head at the University of Chicago." He said that the witness' "deposition offers neither a theoretical reason to believe that wearing a nicotine patch for three days, or removing it after three days, could precipitate a heart attack, or any experimental, statistical, or other scientific data from which such a causal relation might be inferred or which might be used to test a hypothesis founded on theory." Although he said that the witness' stature merited "careful attention," he declared that "the courtroom is not the place for scientific guesswork, even of the inspired sort. Law lags science; it does not lead it."[25]

Courts often insist on details that show causal connections. Denying a claim that Accutane caused cataracts, the court emphasized the *ipse dixit* idea that "an expert cannot establish that a fact is generally accepted merely by saying so." It said that the plaintiff's witness had "failed to identify any authoritative source which recognizes as generally accepted the proposition that all photosensitive chemicals produce cataracts when they become photobound to lens protein." It pointed out that the witness had "not attempted to determine the amount of Accutane that he claims reached [the plaintiff's] lenses" and had not said "how much of a photosensitive drug must be present in the lens to produce a cataract." It concluded that "[w]ithout such information, it would not be possible to reliably opine that therapeutic doses of Accutane cause cataracts simply because it is generally accepted that unspecified doses of other photosensitive drugs produce cataracts when they become photobound."[26] A similar holding governed a Viagra case involving a heart attack. The court found irrelevant a study, cited by the plaintiff's expert, that "show[ed] the deleterious effects of a drug related to Viagra known as milrinone" "where there was no showing that the effect of milrinone was the same as that of Viagra."[27]

One sector of the judicial struggles over proof involves epidemiology. We have noted a breast implant case in which the court emphasized the strength of epidemiological evidence. However, not every claim of scientific causation requires epidemiological proof. An example is a case involving no more unusual a product than Tylenol, in which the manufacturer argued that the plaintiff had not proved that "combining alcohol with therapeutic doses of acetaminophen causes liver disease." The evidence included various details mentioned by treating doctors who concluded that acetaminophen toxicity probably caused liver and kidney failure in the plaintiff. Other experts for the plaintiff "relied upon a similar methodology: history, examination, lab and pathology data, and study of the peer-reviewed literature." Remarking that "[u]nder the *Daubert* standard, epidemiological studies are not necessarily required to prove causation, as long as the methodology employed by the expert in reaching his or her conclusion is sound," the court said it would not "declare such methodologies invalid and unreliable in light of the medical community's daily use of the same methodologies in diagnosing patients."[28] Among the other cases not requiring epidemiological proof are decisions involving asbestos and an artificial elbow.

Although epidemiology is often a basis for defense arguments by manufacturers of medical products, it has sometimes been a friend for plaintiffs in suits against drug makers. One such case involved birth defects ascribed to Depo-Provera. The court credited testimony by an epidemiologist, who emphasized that "epidemiologists evaluate the totality of the data," saying that the witness' statement that he "conducted [an] extensive search of the entire medical literature in terms of the epidemiology of the link between progestins and birth defects, reviewed every paper that is relevant to this in the medical literature, and applied absolutely conventional epidemiological methods and criteria to draw conclusions of causation."[29]

There has been warfare on epidemiological evidence in a number of judicial opinions about the relative risk number that is appropriate to apply in asbestos cases, specifically with respect to the risk of colon cancer. An example is a case in which the plaintiff's witness, an epidemiologist and biostatistician, relied on a study in which the relative risk for a group of asbestos insulators was found to be 1.55. The New Jersey Supreme Court refused to accept the defendants' argument for a 2.0 figure, a standard that several cases have adopted. It said that "a relative risk of 2.0 is not so much a password to a finding of causation as one piece of evidence, among others, for the court to consider in determining whether the expert has employed a sound methodology in reaching his or her conclusion." It left it to the trial judge to assess "both his qualifications and his methodology."[30]

In another case where causation of colon cancer was also an issue, the trial court had discredited testimony about studies which concluded that standardized mortality ratios (SMR)—essentially the relative risk—ranging from 1.14 to 1.47 were "statistically significant when taken together." The trial judge asserted that an SMR of less than 1.50 is "statistically insignificant." However, the federal appellate court sent the case back to the trial court, noting that the trial judge had "cited no authority for the bold assertion that SMRs of less than 1.50 are statistically insignificant and cannot be relied upon by a jury to support a finding of causation." The appellate court said that "[a]lthough perhaps a floor can be set as a matter of law, we are reluctant to adopt such an approach" and that it much preferred that the trial judge "*instruct* the jury on statistical significance and then let the jury decide whether many studies over the 1.0 mark have any significance in combination."[31]

One kind of epidemiological evidence that tends to be convincing is "fingerprint" evidence, data on diseases that recur in connection with exposure to particular products or activities. A common example is mesothelioma, which almost always afflicts people who have been exposed to asbestos. Fingerprint evidence also has been persuasive with reference to injuries in repetitive physical work. A good example is the occurrence of spinal fractures and disc degeneration in workers operating coal hauling machines, who linked their injuries to the design of the machines. An appellate court affirmed a judgment for the workers, rendered by a trial court that referred to "a body of literature dealing with repetitive trauma back injuries," and found reliable the testimony of the plaintiff's experts. The trial court had noted that the experts' theories could be tested, and that their methodology "derived from other accepted methodologies."[32]

Sometimes courts track the *Daubert* criteria one by one, as in a case in which the court rejected the plaintiffs' claim that latex paints caused asthma. First, although the court noted that the claim "could be tested," it noted that it had not been. The court employed some detail in its analysis of the factor of peer review publication. It said that although "[t]he literature does conclude that certain irritants can create respiratory problems, resulting in asthma," the plaintiffs had

> cite[d] no authority for the propositions that irritating chemicals in latex paints become bioavailable in relevant amounts, that actual exposure levels from any particular uses of latex paint are high enough to cause any reaction, that prolonged, unspecified low level exposure to irritants can cause asthma, or that latex paints generally (or these paints in particular) cause asthma.

The court said that the factor of the potential rate of error was "inapplicable … because Plaintiffs' theories are vague and untested" and that "[t]hus no rate of error in identification of victims can be ascertained." Finally, with respect to general acceptance, the court said that although the plaintiff's hypotheses were "not outlandish or pseudo-science," they were not "generally accepted theories."[33]

Scientific studies are usually fair game for argument in litigation, but occasionally courts will give special credit to a particular study. An example is a case that focused on whether Premarin increased the risk of breast cancer. In concluding that the testimony of a witness for the plaintiff should be excluded, in part because she "selected study data that best supported her opinion, while downplaying contrary findings or conclusions," the court favorably spotlighted a study by the Women's Health Initiative (WHI) on the health effects of hormone replacement products. The court referred to citations to that study by "[s]everal major authorities" on "the proposition that Premarin does not increase the risk of breast cancer," saying it believed "these authorities represent the generally accepted scientific view of the issue." It concluded that an analysis by the plaintiff's expert of observational studies could not "cannot overcome the reliable and generally accepted findings of the WHI clinical study" and therefore excluded that witness' opinion.[34]

A very expensive practical lesson in scientific evidence played out in public over a period of several years. It involved the diabetes medicine rosiglitazone, which achieved headline status under the brand name Avandia. This saga captured several of the themes discussed in this chapter—notably, conflicts among experts about proof of causation and the associated uncertainties.[35] A principal early marker in the story was an article by Steven Nissen and Cathy Wolski that summarized a meta-analysis of 42 clinical trials of the drug. Although acknowledging "important limitations" in their study, they summarized their results as showing a statistically significant "43 percent excess incidence of heart attack in Avandia-treated patients." The uncertainty factor was evident in a statement by House committee chair Henry Waxman at a 2007 hearing where Nissen testified. Waxman, observing that "millions of Americans" had taken the drug, expressed his concern that there had been "no post-market studies ... to say conclusively whether Avandia increases or decreases the risk of heart attacks." It was further evident in a statement by Dr. Brian Stromm, chair of biostatistics and epidemiology at Penn. He said that the Nissen meta-analysis was "a very weak study" that "might ultimately" prove "to be correct" but that "it may not be." He proposed a "large outcomes-related randomized clinical trial." Later that year, the FDA's advisory committee voted 22 to 1 to recommend that Avandia stay on the market but with a new warning that referred to the Nissen data.

With tort litigation swelling in the background, by 2010 two FDA doctors condemned GSK, Avandia's manufacturer, for a new trial that they said was "unethical and exploitative." And the Senate Finance Committee issued a 342-page report saying that "GSK representatives attempted to intimidate independent physicians," tried "to minimize or misrepresent findings that Avandia may increase cardiovascular risk," and sought "to downplay findings that a competing drug might reduce cardiovascular risk." Two bipartisan members of the committee sent out a press release about the FDA being "too cozy with drug makers." Although the focus of this book is not on the public relations image of persons and businesses who engage in risky activities, these events may carry some lessons for potential defendants.

Another illustration of scientific uncertainty was a statement by the usually conservative *Medical Letter*, also in 2010, observing that there still was "no prospective double-blind trial comparing the cardiovascular safety" of Avandia and the competing drug Actos. Following this came a report that GSK had covered up a study indicating that Avandia was "riskier to the heart" than Actos. On the heels of that report was a vote by a divided FDA panel, with representatives from two committees, about the safety of Avandia. The votes ranged from twelve members who recommended that the drug be taken off the market, ten voting that "sales should be restricted," seven opining that it required "enhanced warning," and three who supported continued marketing with the then existing warnings. The chair of the combined committee published an essay with a complex interpretation of the vote. Included in his remarks were references to two new meta-analyses showing a 30 to 80 percent higher risk of acute heart attacks from Avandia, but also "several new data sets" with conclusions that Actos was either no riskier or, "in some circumstances, protected against" heart attacks. As we noted in Chapter 4, he also commented that "very little" had been said in the panel hearing "about the balance of risks and benefits" of Avandia, noting that "there was virtually no discussion of any unique benefits" of the drug. In September of the same year, the FDA clamped down with a limitation on eligibility for new users of the drug—to those who were "unable to take Actos"— although it permitted use for current users "who are benefitting from the drug." Evidencing the stringency of this action were requirements that doctors "attest to and document their patient's eligibility" and that patients acknowledge that they understood statements they were given about the risks of the drug.

What I have called the roller-coaster aspect of the story continued three years later with a journal article that mentioned an "extensive" study providing "reassurance" that Avandia and two other drugs "appear to be relatively safe" "from a cardiovascular perspective." The FDA followed in the next month with a "safety announcement," referencing the study just mentioned, which it described as based on "comprehensive, outside, expert re-evaluation of the data." This statement said that "recent data" indicated that the generic form of Avandia did not "show an increased risk of heart attack compared to" two "standard type 2 diabetes medicines." With this report on the research table, the FDA decided to remove the restrictions it had published in 2010.

Various elements of the story reflect dark and light shades of a controversy about product safety that exhibits a high degree of uncertainty. Just after the FDA's 2010 announcement of prescribing restrictions, an essay by three top agency officials said "there was no reliable evidence to refute" "cardiovascular safety concerns" about Avandia. Underlining the uncertainty was these authors' remark about "strongly held differing positions on how the agency should respond to emerging safety data, both inside the FDA and in the biomedical community." They acknowledged "the benefits in glycemic control" of Avandia and that evidence of its cardiovascular risk was "concerning, but it is not definitive." At the same time, they cited "serious questions" about the design of a GSK study, and said that a crucial question facing the FDA was how it could "prevent such uncertainty about a major risk happening again." Even in its 2013 removal of prescribing restrictions, the agency said there "still remain[ed]" "some scientific uncertainty about the cardiovascular safety of rosiglitazone medicines," including Avandia. Evidence of assumptions about supplier behavior appeared in the agency's statement that "sponsors will assume that healthcare professionals" likely to provide Avandia-type medicines "are provided training based on the current state of knowledge" about their cardiovascular risk.

In Chapter 4, we explored the tensions inherent in regulatory controversies about medical products, using the case of Avandia as an especially sharp illustration of the difficulties regulators face in those thickets of argument. Avandia also continues to figure prominently in product liability suits under the tort law introduced in Chapter 5. Among other things, litigation on Avandia is representative of procedural frameworks the law has developed for dealing with caseloads that may run to thousands of cases. By statute, such cases—typically spread over the country, are assigned to panels on "multidistrict litigation," established to deal with "actions involving one or more common questions of law or fact" in multiple lawsuits in different districts.[36] It may not be surprising that there frequently are disputes about whether such "common questions" exist.

GSK, faced with thousands of Avandia suits, had settled 50,000 of them by 2016, with one mass settlement of 10,000 cases resulting in a payout of $460 million. Dwarfing that figure, and emblematic of the reach of criminal law, GSK agreed to a $3 billion settlement with the Department of Justice concerning its failure to report clinical data on Avandia.[37]

The role of experts often plays a pivotal part in legal controversies involving scientific evidence. The case law on qualifications of experts has many nuances, which depend on such factors as the training, education, and professional experience of those offered to testify. We apply here our illustrations earlier in the chapter about the qualifications of scientific experts.

A foundation in academic training may not be enough when a proposed witness has not had experience with particular subject matter. An example is a case involving alleged design defects in a snow thrower. The court refused to admit the testimony of a witness it described as "an eminently qualified mechanical engineer and professor of mechanical engineering whose courses include Machine Design and Mechanical System Failure Analysis." The court's skepticism about his qualifications was evidence in its labeling of him as a "classic hired gun" who had prepared "close to 200 'product liability'" reports on a large variety of products ranging from ladders and step stools to staplers, chaise lounges, and debris chippers. Its precise concern with his testimony was that he had "no professional experience with respect to the design, manufacture, operation, or safety of outdoor power equipment, including snow throwers," had not "conduct[ed] a review of the literature on snow throwers," and had "never been involved with any industry or governmental body charged with the responsibility of developing or overseeing safety standards for snow throwers or any similar device."[38] On the point of "hired guns," another court said, in a case involving a birth control pill, that "[p]erhaps the time has come for a vigorous discussion and examination of the problem" of expert witnesses "becom[ing] partisans."[39]

Another decision, one of the many that dealt with breast implants, was specific in its targeting of the lack of particular expertise of a witness who directed the biomedical engineering program at a state university. He had "published several papers about medical devices and biomaterials," and held "several patents on medical devices," and indeed had "worked in the quality control department of a pharmaceutical company" for two years. However, the court found this background "insufficient to qualify" him on the question of "when and whether it is 'unreasonable' not to conduct biodegradation tests on a biomaterial before using it in an implantable medical device" when was no evidence that he had "any experience developing an implantable medical device for general use or that he has any foundational knowledge about what standard practices exist in the industry in this regard."[40]

A comparison, favoring admissibility of testimony of a witness with a rather specific background of experience, appears in a case involving the alleged uncrashworthiness of a vehicle that rolled over. The automaker argued that the plaintiff's expert, who proposed requirements on the strength of vehicle roofs and headroom, was "not qualified to give expert testimony ... because he lacked experience designing car roofs or supporting structures." However, the court admitted his testimony, noting his "twenty-two years of experience in automotive engineering," including fourteen years at Ford, where he "spent nine years in the vehicle components engineering division and five years in vehicle engineering where he was involved in the development of the Ranger Supercab pick-up truck roof design." Although the witness had "never conducted or observed rollover tests or static tests for roof crush while at Ford," in the eight years after he left Ford "to become a 'consulting engineer,'" he had "performed numerous design analyses on the roof and roof support structures of various vehicles." Noting that he had "based his testimony upon general engineering principles and concepts," the court said that "[a]lthough another witness might certainly have provided greater expertise in the area of roof design and support structures," it thought his "education and experience as an automotive engineer were sufficient to permit his testimony."[41]

General experience sometimes has won the day with courts at various levels of discussion. An illustration is a case involving a battery explosion. The defendant attacked a witness' use of microprobe analysis because he "testified that he knew of no published literature advocating his methodology for testing a bulk sample of an alloy for its constituents," focusing "entirely on use of a microprobe with respect to bulk alloy rather than finished product." The court rejected this argument, noting that "with respect to a finished product," the witness had pointed out that "microprobe use is 'standard methodology' in metallurgy, has been the subject of hundreds, if not thousands, of publications, has been addressed in textbooks, and has several chapters dedicated to it in a metallurgical reference book that [he] referred to as 'the bible of material science.'"[42]

The court becomes somewhat playful in a case in which a hemi-walker failed. Admitting the testimony of three witnesses for the plaintiff, the court says that the defendant's requirements for specificity in expert testimony are too narrow. It says that under the defendant's interpretation of that rule,

> Sir Isaac Newton should not have been permitted to offer his theory of gravity after watching an apple fall from a tree until he first demonstrated a special expertise in the field of horticulture, and Benjamin Franklin should have been precluded from discussing his experiments with electricity unless he supported his theories with a documented aptitude for championship-caliber kite flying.

Invoking the "helpfulness" standard of the Federal Rule of Evidence used in *Daubert,* and describing the case as "[u]ltimately" "present[ing] the question of why a mechanical device failed," the court declared that "it cannot be seriously suggested that two mechanical engineers and a metallurgist with nearly 150 years of experience among them cannot 'assist the trier of fact to understand the evidence or to determine a fact in issue.'"[43]

In a case in which the plaintiff claimed that a corn chip caused an acute tear in his esophagus, the court admits a combination of opinions from an engineer and a doctor. A retired professor of chemical engineering testified that "sharp triangular chip tips can readily pierce the esophagus when driven into the walls of the esophagus by peristaltic action." The doctor, an otolaryngologist, citing case reports in medical literature that "substantiate[d]" that danger from "tortilla type chips," testified that "within a reasonable degree of medical certainty" the plaintiff's ingestion of the defendant's chips "caused him to suffer a laceration of the esophagus."[44]

Yet, however long a list of work experiences an expert presents, he may fail the *Daubert* test if his testimony relies on "common knowledge" of physical phenomena. In one case, the plaintiff's work pants caught on fire as he walked by a heater made by the defendant, which he claimed was the cause of the event. The court ticked off several *Daubert*-related factors, including the witness' failure to conduct testing, which it said kept it from "even begin[ning] to review whether his theory has been tested, subjected to peer review, has a known or potential rate of error, or has been generally accepted in the engineering field." Broadly, it faulted the witness for offering no more than "a general conclusion based upon general principles of engineering and combustion."[45]

Similar reasoning underlay an appellate court's refusal to allow a polymer scientist to testify on the cause of the bursting of a tire. In this case the court effectively does a judo turnaround on the court's remarks about Newton and Franklin in the hemi-walker case described previously. Noting that the plaintiff's witness had "never worked in or studied the tire industry in any capacity, nor had he ever testified as a tire expert," the court was not impressed with his claim that "[a] tire is simply an application of the fundamental issues of polymer science." The trial court had said that although it would allow the witness to testify about "polymer fibers and their adhesive properties," it would not accept his opinion about "(1) the cause of the tire's failure, and (2) the proper design or manufacture of tires generally." Agreeing with the trial court, the appellate court noted the witness' assertion that "[a] tire is simply an application of the fundamental issues of polymer science." However, it said that while "[t]hat is true in some sense, just as it is true that asbestos, heart valves, and cupcakes can all be broken down into their basic atomic particles," that did "not mean an atomic physicist is qualified to testify regarding any asbestosis, medical malpractice, or confectionary issue." Emphasizing that "[i]t's the science's application to tires that concerns us here," it pointed out that the witness had "absolutely no experience applying polymer science to tires."[46]

In academic specialties, the degree of specialization can be dispositive on the admission of an expert's testimony. An illustration is a case involving a fungicide, alleged to have caused birth defects in several children in other countries. The plaintiffs offered a witness with an impressive resume: "consultant with the EPA and the World Health Organization," presentation of "papers and speeches on topics relating to human exposure to environmental contaminants," regular publication of "articles in peer reviewed scientific journals discussing human exposure to pesticides in residential settings," and research on "human exposure to chemical hazards in community and occupational settings." Despite this background, however, the court would not admit his opinion because he was not qualified as an expert on dermal absorption. It specified that a model he used was "the least favored method of measuring dermal absorption," in fact one that EPA guidelines recommended should "be used only when no comparable human studies exist." The court made a generalization of a sort that has governed some other decisions involving particular specialties. It said that while it recognized "that at times an expert may be qualified by criteria outside of his formal training or designated specialty, we must scrutinize an expert's qualifications with 'due regard for the specialization of modern science.'"[47]

Although specialization counts in academically oriented professions, practical experience may weigh heavily in favor of proposed experts. An example of testimony that was admitted is a case in which a milking system made by the defendant allegedly caused mastitis and sores on the teat ends of the plaintiffs' cows. The plaintiff proffered as an expert a man who for most of a quarter century worked for the Michigan Milk Producers Association, supervising its laboratory and quality control program. He had "conducted numerous seminars on milking machinery and mastitis," and had "published at least one paper in the area." Moreover, as a milking-management consultant, he had "worked with farmers in fourteen states and two provinces of Canada," and over his career, he had "inspected milking operations on some 15,000 farms." The trial court refused to admit his testimony because he was not a licensed veterinarian, but the appellate court disagreed, referring to his "extensive" studies and experience. Although he was "frank in his admission that he was not an expert on animal diseases in general," the appeals court pointed out that "[h]e was not ... called upon for such testimony" nor to diagnose mastitis, there being no dispute that there was mastitis in the plaintiffs' herd. Rather, the court said, he was "simply called upon to give an opinion as to the relationship between a particular milking machine defect and the most common of dairy herd diseases." Here the court delivered a counter-specialization lecture. Although it said that "[t]he proliferation of academic degrees and increasing specialization of labor is evident for all to see," it said it believed there was "a world of wisdom apart from college campuses and urban high-rises" and that there was "much to be gained from the practical student of the common arts." It found that wisdom in the plaintiffs' witness, who it said was "not simply a well-qualified expert, but perhaps *the* expert in this particular junction of science and industry."[48]

A Texas court admitted the testimony of a varied group of specialists in a shooting accident case in which the plaintiffs claimed that defects in the defendant's ammunition were responsible for a hang fire. The plaintiffs' witnesses included a firearms training officer who had "trained approximately 7000 cadets how to safely use firearms," the chief engineer of "the world's largest and oldest independent testing laboratory for guns and ammunition," and a registered gunsmith who "had served as gunsmith to the United States Olympic shooting team, the United States shooting team at the Pan American Games, and the elite United States Marine Corps rifle and pistol teams." The latter witness "testified that several ammunition reloading treatises define the term 'hang fire' as something unrelated to mechanical firearm defects." He said that "several ammunition reloading treatises define the term 'hang fire' as something unrelated to mechanical firearm defects," thus bolstering the claim that the problem was with the defendant's ammunition. In finding the testimony of these experts admissible under the rule of evidence adopted in *Daubert*, the court referred to "testimony of their technical and specialized knowledge, based on skill, training, and experience"—"not only ... years of experience in manufacturing firearms, testing firearms, and training others to use firearms, but on experience and actually observing ammunition-related hang fires lasting in the" relevant range of time.[49]

To be sure, there are boundaries to practical knowledge set by subject matter. An example is a case involving the alleged failure of a collapsible steering column in a car. The court refused to admit testimony from a police officer with experience as an accident investigator, saying that "he could not properly be termed a qualified expert in accident reconstruction," given his testimony "that he had only minimal training in preliminary aspects of this field." Also noting that "he had only minimal training in the area of physics and movement of bodies," the court found that he was "not qualified to offer an opinion of the movement" of the plaintiff's body "inside the vehicle at the time of the accident."[50]

With that qualification, many decisions exhibit courts' willingness to give leeway to experts. An example is a case in which a spare tire flew out of its retention system and hit the back of a bench seat. In an opinion applying the *Daubert* rules, the court admitted the opinions of the plaintiffs' accident reconstruction expert although it acknowledged his calculations "reli[ed] heavily on educated guesswork and theory." It said that "such guesswork falls within the ambit of expert knowledge and scientific methodology and can, if well-articulated, assist the jury in understanding the physics that governed the spare tire's motion." The court recognized that such an expert "might predetermine his 'conclusions' based on the inputs he specifies," but, in language of a sort that appears in many decisions, it said that "cross examination is the more appropriate vehicle for exposing that possibility or any of the perceived weaknesses" in the witness's assumptions.[51]

Another decision that provides leeway to an expert favored the defendant, in a case where the plaintiff alleged that a swimming pool was defectively designed. At issue was the testimony of a witness "acknowledged" to be an expert on swimming pool standards, who said that "[t]here are probably within sixty and a hundred injuries in residential swimming pools on an annual basis," and that there had been "about four to six cervical spine injuries of the type sustained by" the plaintiff "over a seventeen-year period in pools with diving boards that met" the standards of the trade association for swimming pools. As the court summarized it, he said "he had obtained his information by interviewing some people who had been injured, but had not reviewed public court dockets." He said he had "made an analysis of data that [were] available and I went through and picked out the cervical spine injuries from diving boards, yes, as well as interviews with diving board manufacturers and fabricators of vinyl liner swimming pools in the mass market." He "acknowledged that he did not know how to verify" his information and "agreed that manufacturers might have a vested interest in underreporting the number of injuries." However, interpreting a state rule of evidence as requiring "that a court make an inquiry into and a finding on whether experts in the given field rely on certain information," the court said that "[i]f such reliance be found, then it is presumed to be reasonable."[52]

At some point, courts will find the devil in the omitted details. A detail weighed against the maker of a hair bleach, whose expert was a dermatologist who was vice president for medical affairs of the research division of the defendant's parent corporation. The court excluded his testimony about an "experiment or test" he carried out on a woman whose hair had previously been bleached, using the defendant's product and competitive products. It said that the description of his test "lacked detail and exactitude," pointing out that jurors "were not told the precise condition of the particular woman's hair, or the instructions, if any, given to the hairdresser, or how the particular product exemplar was selected." Saying that "[t]here were manifest possibilities of conscious or unconscious skewing of the test by the one supervising it, ... a person associated with the defendant," the court noted that "[t]here was but one test, an unimpressive number."[53]

Litigation on products alleged to cause injury is expensive, and a significant expense lies in employing experts. A case involving diet drugs illustrates this, along with the potential conflicts among expert opinions that may arise in a single case. The court reviewed the testimony of no fewer than six experts, using a *Daubert*-based scrutiny to reject most of their opinions. It concluded that a pathologist had "not adequately explained how or why he can reliably extrapolate the results of the rat study to human beings." Speaking of two witnesses with specialties in cardiology, it said that "[n]either is an expert in treating obesity or in evaluating diet drug efficacy," and noted that one had "never prescribed a diet drug." It did allow some testimony from a molecular biologist who did research in "the molecular and hormonal bases of obesity." It said that the fact that this witness was not an MD did not, "on its own, ... preclude him from testifying about whether or not these drugs were demonstrated to be as effective as diet and exercise in reducing fat." It noted that "in fact, the National Institutes of Health Evidence Report on the treatment of obesity was compiled by a panel of 24 experts, 11 of whom were not medical doctors and many of whom had PhDs." However, it rejected some of even that witness's opinions on two subjects. It said that he "clearly lacks the qualifications and methodology to opine about whether [the drug] met FDA efficacy criteria," having "no expertise in FDA regulations," and that he was "unqualified to opine about" the manufacturer's "marketing efforts and disclosure obligations."[54]

Scientists and physicians reviewing the cases described here may find concern about many nuances, even seeming contradictions, in judicial opinions on the subject of expert testimony. If there is a general explanation for how judges reason when they must decide whether an expert is qualified in such cases, it would lie in a diagram of concentric circles from which courts select the most relevant circles between relatively general bodies of knowledge and the most intense kind of specialization. Elements of those circles include practical experience, academic training, and professional specialties and subspecialties. The job of judges is to exercise judgment—in this case, to draw lines that sensibly assess the potential contributions of experts in the intermediate circles.

Hovering over the subject is the label of "junk science," which has been attached to expert opinions that critics condemn as literally unscientific. At the heart of the problem are emerging bodies of knowledge, in areas where there is uncertainty about whether novel hypotheses may turn out to have a sufficient basis in "truth" that they should at least be admissible in evidence. Courts are properly wary of anecdotes and of testimony from experts out of their depth. But courts have recognized that sometimes the law must make decisions in particular controversies that cannot wait for a process of continued falsification of theories. A most striking example of how long it may take brilliant scientists to develop a theory that works out in practice is the story of the development of the nuclear bomb.[55]

Endnotes

1. 509 U.S. 579 (1993).
2. Id. at 591–94.
3. *Joiner v. Gen'l Elec. Co.*, 522 U.S. 136, 144–46 (1997).
4. *Daubert v. Merrell Dow Pharms.*, 43 F.3d 1311, 1318 (9th Cir. 1995).
5. *Kumho Tire Co. v. Carmichael*, 526 U.S. 137, 141 (1999).
6. *Milanowicz v. Raymond Corp.*, 148 F. Supp.2d 525, 533–36 (D. N.J. 2001).
7. *Williams v. Daimler Chrysler Corp.*, 2008 WL 4449558, at 3–4 (N.D. Miss. 2008).
8. *Miller v. Pfizer*, 196 F. Supp.2d 1062, 1084 (D. Kan. 2002).
9. *Nelson v. Am. Home Prods., Corp.*, 92 F. Supp.2d 954, 972–73 (W.D. Mo. 2000).
10. *Miller v. Bike Athletic Co.*, 667 N.E.2d 735, 741 (Ohio 1998).
11. *Ford Motor Co. v. Ammerman*, 705 N.E.2d 539, 554 (Ind. Ct. App. 1992).
12. In re Silicone Gel Breast Implants Prod. Liab. Litig., 318 F. Supp.2d 879, 896–98 (C.D. Cal. 2004).
13. *Vassallo v. Baxter Healthcare Corp.*, 696 N.E.2d 909, 913–17 (Mass. 1998).
14. *Dow Chem. Co. v. Mahlum*, 970 F.2d 98, 108–09 (Nev. 1998).
15. *Hopkins v. Dow Corning Corp.*, 33 F.3d 1116, 1124–25 (9th Cir. 1994).
16. *Jennings v. Baxter Healthcare Corp.*, 954 P.2d 829, 834 (Or. Ct. App. 1998).
17. 14 P.3d 598, 600 (Or. 2000).
18. *Norris v. Baxter Healthcare Corp.*, 397 F.2d 878, 882–85 (10th Cir. 2005).
19. *Glaser v. Thompson Medical Co.*, 32 F.2d 969, 972–95 (6th Cir. 1994).

20. Id. at 975, referring to *Turpin v. Merrell Dow Pharms., Inc.,* 959 F.2d 1349 (6th Cir. 1992).
21. *Lauzon v. Senco Prods., Inc.,* 270 F.3d 681, 690–91 (8th Cir. 2001).
22. Lust by and through *Lust v. Merrill Dow Pharms.,* 89 F.2d 594, 597 (9th Cir. 1996).
23. *Hollander v. Sanchez Pharms. Corp.,* 95 F. Supp.2d 1230, 1236–37 (W.D. Okl. 2000).
24. *Meister v. Medical Eng'g Corp.,* 267 F.3d 1123, 1129–32 (D.C. Cir. 2001).
25. *Rosen v. CIBA-Geigy Corp.,* 78 F.2d 316, 319 (7th Cir. 1996).
26. *Grimes v. Hoffman-LaRoche, Inc.,* 907 F.Supp. 33, 38–39 (D. N.H. 1995).
27. *Selig v. Pfizer,* 735 N.Y.S.2d 549, 550 (2002).
28. *Benedi v. McNeil-P.P.C, Inc.,* 66 F.3d 1378, 1384 (4th Cir. 1995).
29. *Ambrosini v. LaBarraque,* 101 F.3d 129, 136 (D.C. Cir. 1996).
30. *Landrigan v. Celotex Corp.,* 605 A.2d 1079, 1087–89 (N.J. 1992).
31. In re Joint & Southern Dist. Asbestos Litig., 52 F.3d 1124, 1134 (2d Cir. 1995).
32. *Bartley v. Euclid, Inc.,* 158 F.3d 261, 267–68, 289 (5th Cir. 1998).
33. *Cartwright v. Home Depot U.S.A.,* 936 F. Supp. 900, 905–06 (M.D. Fla. 1996).
34. In re Prempro Prods. Liab. Litig., 738 F. Supp.2d 887, 891–93 (E.D. Ark. 2010).
35. This summary is largely based on Chapter 4 of Marshall S. Shapo, *The Experimental Society* (Transaction Publishers 2016), at 70–79.
36. 28 U.S.C. §1407.
37. Information from https://www.drugwatch.com/avandia/lawsuit.php, last modified May 16, 2016.
38. *Shreve v. Sears, Roebuck & Co.,* 166 F. Supp.2d 378, 393–94 (D. Md. 2001).
39. *Rubenstein by Rubenstein v. Marsh,* 1987 WL 30608, at 7–8 (E.D. N.Y. 1987).
40. In re Silicone Gel Breast Implants Prods. Liab. Litig., 318 F. Supp.2d 879, 902 (C.D. Cal. 2004).
41. *Compton v. Subaru of Am.,* 82 F.3d 1513, 1519–20 (10th Cir. 1996).
42. *Johnson Controls Battery Group v. Runnel,* 2003 WL 21191063, at 5 (Tex. Ct. App. 2003).

43. *Gibson v. Invacare, Inc.*, 2011 WL 2262933, at 4 (S.D. Miss. 2011).
44. *Grady v. Frito-Lay*, 789 A.2d 738 (Pa. Super. Ct. 2001).
45. *Bland v. H.R. Beck*, 2007 WL 748461, at 4 (E.D. Mo. 2007).
46. *Smith v. Goodyear Tire & Rubber Co.*, 495 F.2d 224, 227 (5th Cir. 2007).
47. *Bowen v. E.I. DuPont de Nemours & Co.*, 906 A.2d 787, 794–96 (Del. 2006).
48. *Mulholland v. DEC Internat'l Corp.*, 443 N.W.2d 340, 346 (Mich. 1989).
49. *Olin Corp. v. Smith*, 990 S.W.2d 789, 797 (Tex. Ct. App. 1999).
50. *Higginbotham v. Volkswagenwerk Aktiengesellschaft*, 551 F. Supp. 977, 982 (M.D. Pa. 1982).
51. *Thorndike v. DaimlerChrysler Corp.*, 266 F. Supp.2d 172, 179–80 (D. Maine 2003).
52. *Ryan v. KDI Sylvan Pools*, 579 A.2d 1241, 1244–47 (N.J. 1990).
53. *Sacks v. Roux Labs*, 521 N.E.2d 1050, 1051–52 (Mass. App. Ct. 1988).
54. In re Diet Drug, Prods. Liab. Litig., 2001 WL 454586, at 20–23 (E.D. Pa. 2001).
55. See Richard Rhodes, *The Making of the Atomic Bomb* (anniversary edition 2012), e.g., at 428–40 (on Fermi's experiment that led to chain reaction).

Chapter 10

Tort Reform

Healthcare professionals and product sellers bewail liability rules, but for them the end is not vocalizing but efforts to change the legal system. An overall label for these efforts is "tort reform"—or, as claimants' lawyers are fond of calling it, "tort deform." In the many pages that have been written on the topic, it is hard to find a crisp definition. I use the term here principally to refer to legislation—historically, mostly enacted by state legislatures—that restricts or even abolishes categories of lawsuits for injuries, including the placement of dollar limitations on amounts of damages.

It seems to be accepted that, putting aside asbestos claims, the number of injury suits filed in the country is a relatively small percentage of all litigation.[1] Statistics from the period beginning around 1995 indicated variations among the states with reference to increases and decreases in suits filed, with plaintiffs succeeding a little less than half the time.[2] In the decade from 1995 to 2005, the number of various kinds of tort suits declined, and between 2000 and 2007, verdicts for more than $100 million fell from 27 to 2.[3] Surely new categories of plaintiffs have entered the courts—since the early 1960s, claimants for products injuries; for healthcare-related injuries, an upsurge of litigation since the 1970s; and suits for injuries ascribed to toxicity of environmental chemicals. The problem of "mass torts" has been of particular concern to industry groups. The biggest segment of these cases has involved products that allegedly cause injury to large groups of people. Just to take one example, some 100,000 cases on vaginal mesh products were filed with a federal multi-district litigation panel. Asbestos has added very substantial increments to caseloads, with 750,000 suits filed by 2005 and many more predicted to come. Cigarette lawsuits have significantly added to the total number of lawsuits, and some litigation has bridged the two categories: asbestos workers who smoked.

10.1 Rhetoric and Results

The rhetoric of tort reform has included many references to "crises," particularly "insurance crises" and "liability crises."[4] Some of these were rooted in rises in medical malpractice premiums in the 1970s.[5] Others were the product of urban myths or semi-myths. One made-up story was about a man who sued for injuries occurring when he tried to use his lawn-mower to trim a hedge. A semi-myth was the much-publicized verdict against McDonald's for burns occurring from a spill of hot coffee. The plaintiffs' allegations in that suit, which was eventually settled, included the assertions that McDonald's coffee was hotter than the industry norm, and that it knew about the risk of serious burns and never warned consumers about them.[6]

The professional contestants are many. There are thousands of plaintiffs' attorneys, who try lawsuits. Their principal organization is the American Association for Justice, which does legislative lobbying in Washington and in the states. Abetting these efforts are such organizations as the Pound Civil Justice Institute, the Center for Justice and Democracy, and the Public

Citizen Interest Group. A principal advocate for defendants in a variety of risky businesses is the American Tort Reform Association (ATRA), the activities of which include representation in both courts and legislatures. On the healthcare side, the American Medical Association provides major lobbying efforts. Other groups on the defense side include the Product Liability Coordinating Committee, the Coalition for Uniform Product Liability Laws, The Institute for Legal Reform of the U.S. Chamber of Commerce, and, not limited to tort reform, the Business Roundtable.

Defendants' groups have mounted major public relations campaigns that employ advertising of various kinds to emphasize the costs to the public of tort suits—for example, in driving up the price of products and in forcing doctors into expensive "defensive medicine." A campaign by the Insurance Information Institute in 1986 generated an article headed "We All Pay the Price: An Industry Effort to reform Civil Justice." The titles of print advertisements at the time included "The Lawsuit Crisis is Bad for Babies," "The Lawsuit Crisis is Penalizing High School Sports," and "Even the Clergy Can't Escape the Lawsuit Crisis." The next year, Aetna mounted an eight-ad campaign that included an ad headed "Sue City, USA," which focused on a "lawsuit crisis" in which "helpless" municipal "victims" were "[p]arks, playgrounds and other recreational facilities."[7] An ATRA campaign's attack on litigiousness in general had a bumper sticker, "Go Ahead. Hit Me. (I Need the Money.)"

Catch phrases have abounded. One president of the United States inveighed against plaintiffs' lawyers in "tasseled loafers."[8] His son, later a president himself, declared in a State of the Union address that "[n]o one has ever been healed by a frivolous lawsuit."[9]

Part of the attack on tort suits was the identification by ATRA of "judicial hellholes," states with localities that allegedly featured pro-plaintiff decisions and large awards. A reflection of the intensity of controversy about injury litigation was an essay that said that these campaigns were "bolstered with false or misleading horror stories and fabricated or misleading numerical data (made more effective through eye-catching charts and graphs)."[10] There is research indicating that anti-lawsuit campaigns have minimized the amounts of jury verdicts in injury cases,[11] and have had general "framing" effects on public perception of injury suits.[12]

Lobbying effects by business groups have produced significant effects in state legislatures, which have passed statutes minimizing litigation and damage awards in the areas of medical malpractice and products liability. They have been less successful in Congress. In 1976, a bill to limit tort suits for auto injuries failed by just four votes in the Senate. In 1996, both Houses of Congress passed a rather limited bill that restricted products liability suits, but President Clinton vetoed the bill and the House could not override his veto.

10.2 Types of Laws

There are many different kinds of "tort reforms," most of them adopted by legislation, but some by judicial decision. We discuss them here in three categories, some of which blur into each other, so the classification system is somewhat arbitrary at its margins.

First, there are a number of laws that change the substantive content of legal doctrines. These include statutes that dispense with strict liability rules in products cases; the idea is that the liability should be based on fault—intentional misconduct or at least negligence. There are rules, which vary from state to state, that allow defendants to show that their behavior, or their product, lived up to the state of the art. Some laws fully immunize the makers of certain kinds of products—for example weapons manufacturers.

Other changes in the law may advantage plaintiffs. These are statutes that divide liability between negligent parties.

Their effects are often to override rules that set up a complete bar to recovery to a plaintiff who is contributorily negligent, even to a small degree. However, some comparative fault statutes—and judicial decisions—require that the plaintiff at least not have as great a percentage of fault as the defendant, or that the defendant have had a greater amount of fault.

Several kinds of tort reform statutes target the amount of damages. Some of the ones that are most adopted put dollar ceilings on the amount of "noneconomic" damages—principally, pain and suffering, and also capacity to enjoy life, fear without identifiable physical injuries, bereavement, and consortium, which has been epitomized as "sex, society, and services." Many of these statutes pertain only to medical malpractice cases.

We have reviewed in Chapter 5 arguments that fly back and forth on the propriety of giving dollar awards for noneconomic loss. Although those losses are nearly a universal item of damages in American tort suits, legislators who limit them emphasize what they view as the arbitrariness of such awards. The statutory ceilings, $250,000 in some states, are themselves arbitrary, but they respond to the sense that some dollar ceiling is needed to deal with harms that are not quantifiable in the same way as, for example, medical bills or lost wages.

Paralleling ceilings on noneconomic loss are dollar caps on punitive damages, which also have been enacted by many state legislatures. The kinds of caps vary considerably—$250,000, $500,000, no more than compensatory damages, and no more than two, three, or five times compensatory damages. As we noted in Chapter 5, the United States Supreme Court has articulated a number of standards for the limitation of punitive damages. Those include both verbal standards, such as the term "reprehensible," and other numerical ones that focus on the ratio of punitive to compensatory damages.

Another specific reform related to damages is the elimination of the rule of "joint and several liability," the effect of which is that when there are multiple defendants, each one may be held liable for the entire amount of a damage award. An example would have two defendants, Company A and Company B, both of which negligently pollute, with Company A's contribution to a plaintiff's injury being 10 percent and Company B's being 90 percent. Since both were negligent, they are "joint tortfeasors," and if Company B is bankrupt, Company A—although only 10 percent contributory—will have to pay the whole amount of the damages under joint and several liability. Some reforms to that rule would require that each defendant pay only the percentage of the award represented by his contribution to the injury.

Another damages-related rule that has been targeted by tort reformers is the so-called collateral source rule, the effect of which is that a plaintiff does not have to deduct from a personal injury award the payments she has received from a third party—often a medical insurer—already represented by the jury award. Many insurers have clauses in their contracts that allow them to get reimbursement from awards given for payments the insurers have made for items of damages covered by those awards. Where such clauses do not apply, some states have enacted laws that allow defendants to tell the jury about payments the plaintiff has received from collateral sources—the idea being to prevent double recoveries for the same item of damages. Another damages–related reform eliminates what is called the "ad damnum" clause, the naming of a very large total award figure by plaintiffs' attorneys. Reform legislation does not permit the use of these clauses on the theory that they tend to inflate jury awards.

We now come to changes affecting tort law that tie into the legal process itself. One such set of changes in the legal landscape are those wrought by the Supreme Court's *Daubert* rules on scientific proof, discussed in Chapter 9. This change has cut both ways in litigation. Plaintiffs' lawyers were inclined to applaud a rule that did not require them to show general acceptance of methodologies their experts offered. However, in the end the *Daubert* rules had strong elements of triumph for defendants, because parties, mostly plaintiffs, must face hearings, not previously required, in which they have to establish the qualifications of their witnesses.

A substantial set of rules that advantage defendants have to do with what is known as federal preemption: The existence of a body of statutory law that covers a particular area will be taken to prohibit—"pre-empt"—civil suits within that area. Some statutes have specific preemption clauses. An example is a section of the Food Drug and Cosmetic Act that prohibits states from "directly or indirectly establish[ing] ... any requirement for a food which is the subject of a standard of identity established" under the act "that is not identical" to the standard in the statute. In an illustrative case, a court applied this rule to preempt a suit against sellers of milk and milk products brought on the grounds that the sellers did not give warning labels about lactose intolerance, pointing out that there was "no dispute that milk is subject to a standard of identity."[13]

Other cases slice the onion more finely, providing room for interpretation of preemption-type language. An example is a case involving the Federal Insecticide, Fungicide and Rodenticide Act (FIFRA), which says that a state "shall not impose or continue in effect any requirement for labeling or packaging in addition to or different from those required" in the act. In this case the Supreme Court refused to apply preemption to a number of theories of liability advanced by plaintiffs suing for damage caused by a herbicide to peanut crops. One of those theories was breach of express warranty. Although the Court recognized that the defendant had an express warranty on the label of the product, it observed that a claim for express warranty "asks only that a manufacturer make good on the contractual commitment that it voluntarily undertook by placing the warranty on its product." Pointing out that court-created rules did not require manufacturers to make express warranties or "say anything in particular" in warranties they did make, the court said that the preemption rule in the statute did "not impose a requirement for 'labeling or packaging.'"[14] However, in the same decision the Court presented a different perspective on claims for fraud and negligent failure to warn. Although it did not flatly bar those claims on preemption grounds, it emphasized that plaintiffs using those theories must make claims that were "equivalent to, and fully consistent with" the misbranding provisions of the FIFRA statute.[15]

There are at least two lessons for non-lawyers in this decision. One is that the terms in which lawyers sheathe theories of liability may affect results in cases. The other, also having to do with the interpretation of words, concerns the way that courts put a gloss on language that may differ from how lay people might interpret those words. When the FIFRA statute says that "a state shall not impose" certain kinds of requirements, laypeople might think this is a limitation only on what state legislatures can do. But in cases involving preemption issues with respect to many products, courts take for granted that such language extends to judicial decisions in civil cases that have the effect of imposing such requirements. I also note that many of the most closely contested cases in this area involve a quintessential part of the law on preemption: These are cases in which the argument is not about whether a statute has expressly preempted civil suits in the area it covers, but about whether such cases are *impliedly* preempted.

There have been many judicial battles about preemption in cases involving prescription drugs and devices, and the choice of passenger restraints in automobiles, some of which have resulted in five-to-four decisions in the Supreme Court. This book does not permit extended discussion of those cases, but I mention here a case of judicial combat about a severe injury from a prescription drug, to illustrate the very different perspectives that may inform keen judicial minds on the same issue. Justice Stevens, speaking for the majority in supporting the plaintiff's claim that the labeling on the drug was defective, referred to the "limited resources" the FDA possessed "to

monitor the 11,000 drugs on the market" and to manufacturers' "superior access to information" about their products. He
said that "[s]tate tort suits uncover unknown drug hazards and
provide incentives for manufacturers to disclose safety risks
promptly" and that "[t]hey also serve a distinct compensatory
function that may motivate injured persons to come forward
with information."[16] Justice Alito's dissenting opinion revealed
a very different point of view. He said that the "real issue" was
"whether a state court jury can countermand the FDA's considered judgment" about a warning label.[17]

Sharply pointed arguments about the practical workings of
the legal process focus on attorneys' fees. A specific target of
reformers is the contingency fee used by plaintiffs' lawyers,
which gives them a percentage of total awards, often beginning at one-third. The argument of reformers is that this kind
of fee generates unhealthy incentives to bring unmeritorious
litigation which will force settlements that should not have to
be paid. Plaintiffs' lawyers emphasize that these fees open the
courthouse door to valid lawsuits that would not be brought if
injured persons had to pay at an hourly rate. There are various
kinds of laws that limit contingency fees—for example slid-
ing scales that put dollar limits on fees above certain amounts,
and rules that impose absolute percentage limits on the
amount of fees a lawyer can charge.

Another set of reforms pertains to the way jury trials are
conducted. Among the principal recommended changes are
proposals to allow juries to take notes, which in many states is
not permitted on grounds that this fosters distraction and may
negatively affect the deliberations of jurors. A good example of
how empirical assumptions affect the choice of process rules
is a response argument that "[n]ote taking might allow jurors
a sense of competence and mastery over the material" and
"serve as a resource during deliberations."

Another proposal would allow jurors to ask questions of
witnesses; an opposing argument is that, given the assumptions of the adversary process that control over the process

should reside principally in the minds and hands of lawyers, the ability to ask questions would cast jurors as advocates rather than neutral decision makers. Still another proposal would allow jurors to discuss a case while a trial is going on. Many states limit such conversations to the time when jurors have begun their deliberations. The concern at the heart of these limitations is that early discussions among jurors will lead to premature judgment of cases.[18]

A different set of reforms lies in a requirement that in some circumstances, parties must submit to alternative dispute resolution with a neutral third party, whose decision may be either binding or advisory. Arguments against such requirements emphasize that they result in "second class justice" by contrast with the product of full adversary trials, that they do not employ the safeguards of the rules of evidence, and that they favor parties with the most economic power.

Other proposals for changes in the legal process include a requirement for "speedy trials." This requirement already is embodied for criminal trials in the Constitution and appears in some state legislation for civil trials; an example is a Massachusetts law specifying advancement of trials for parties over 65 who request it.

The class action is a process element that has inspired the passage of laws that control litigation where there are many claimants, and sometimes many defendants. A federal rule of procedure contains requirements that pose obstacles to lawyers who want to meld multiple plaintiffs into one litigation, requirements that include a showing that there be "questions of law or fact common to the class," that their claims or defenses be "typical of the claims or defenses of the class," and that the persons designated as representative parties for the class "will fairly and adequately protect the interests of the class." An example of a case where the plaintiffs could not satisfy the requirements of the rule is litigation based on allegations that the antidepressant Paxil had caused suicides in children. In denying certification to the class, the court referred to "numerous critical factual and legal differences among the putative class members that preclude typicality." It said that "[e]ach class member took varying doses of Paxil, for varying indications, at various times, at different developmental stages and for different durations" and, that "[e]ach has different medical, psychosocial, and pharmaceutical histories." It also fixed on variances among the prescribing doctors: that "[e]ach had different specialties, varying levels of knowledge about Paxil and other SSRIs, different clinical experience with Paxil and similar medications for pediatric patients, and varying levels of contact with the patient." These differences, the court said, would allow the manufacturer to "potentially raise unique defenses to each plaintiff's claim."[19]

A contrasting result appears in a case against a cigarette maker in which the plaintiffs did not have symptoms of lung cancer but sought "medical monitoring," which would regularly screen them for signs of disease. The court found that the plaintiffs had shown "common questions" shared by each of them: "(1) Philip Morris' alleged breach of warranty; (2) causation; (3) exposure, subcellular harm, and increased risk of cancer; (4) the efficacy of LDCT testing; (5) the standard of care; and (6) the cost of the proposed monitoring program."[20] It also noted common questions of law, saying that given that all the claims were governed by the law of one state, "the plaintiffs may commonly prove issues related to the statute of limitations." The court rejected the defendant's argument that the plaintiffs could not prove causation on a class-wide basis on the grounds that "(1) Plaintiffs must prove that the alternative design *would have* prevented their injury, which they cannot do; and (2) proof of alternative design requires proof that the plaintiffs *would have* smoked the less carcinogenic cigarettes, which necessarily involves individual inquiries." It quoted precedents on the idea that "liability will … attach where the design defect enhances the injuries a person sustains in an otherwise foreseeable" way, and that "[p]roduct liability may be premised on 'existence of some enhanced injury, i.e., an injury "over and above" that which would have been sustained in the absence of the alleged defect."[21] These are just examples of the complexity of the law that applies where there are multiple parties on one side or the other.

A set of reforms that bridges the categories of substance and process would establish boundaries for damage amounts. One of these approaches would have judges compare the results of prior cases involving the same kind of injury. In an asbestos case that involved "enormous suffering" from mesothelioma, the court effectively reduced a $12 million award to $3.5 million. Although taking "as a given that reasonable people of [the plaintiff's] age would not have traded one-quarter of his suffering for a hundred million dollars, much less twelve," the court used as standards the results of other mesothelioma cases in the same district decided by the same administrative judge.[22] Other proposals would have charts given to juries that summarize "similar awards in cases of similarly situated plaintiffs" or would use "relatively hard schedules that provide a range of awards" in defined categories.[23] Plaintiffs' lawyers oppose such proposals, emphasizing the individuality of each claimant.

Another group of reforms at the boundary of process and substance aims at statutes of limitations and statutes of repose, which prescribe time periods in which actions may be brought. A principal group of controversies on statutes of limitations arises with respect to the "discovery rule," which allows plaintiffs to put off the time for bringing suit until they could reasonably have discovered their illness or discovered that the defendant's product or activity caused that disease. Much of the litigation centers on the question of whether the plaintiff was properly diligent in making the discovery. Two New Jersey cases with different results give a sense of the legal parameters. In one of these cases, the plaintiff sued a glue manufacturer for a heart attack, bringing his complaint two years and eight months after the event. Concluding the statute of limitations barred his suit, the state supreme court mentioned the plaintiff's "regular incidence of lightheadedness and dizziness while using the glue, and the disappearance of the symptoms shortly after" his exposure stopped. It said that his realization of "the connection between the glue and the symptoms (although at trial he denied such knowledge)," "furnishe[d] a substantial credible basis for an inference of knowledge by plaintiff at least shortly after the heart attack that the exposure to the fumes of the glue in [a] warm trench was in some way related to that attack."[24]

Almost a decade later, the court distinguished the glue case in a case in which the plaintiff sued on injuries attributed to exposure to toxic chemicals at a toxic waste disposal site. The court noted that for several years before that exposure the plaintiff had suffered from migraines after an auto accident and that "[t]he onset of severe migraine headaches began gradually after" he started work at the disposal site and "gradually subsided not merely when he left that job but after he was treated with Caforgot and aspirin." Importantly, his doctor "did not attribute the severity of the headaches to chemical exposure but rather to the stress component of his work situation." The court opined that "[t]he causal connection that was drawn was between his symptoms and high stress, not chemical exposure." In the context of the doctor's opinion, the court said that "in contrast to the almost unmistakable relationship" between the plaintiff's exposure to glue in the glue case, "any connection between the condition" of the plaintiff in the toxic disposal case "and his employment circumstances was at best obscure, dim, vague, speculative."[25] One finds distinctions like this in many cases involving products like chemicals, asbestos, and drugs—and usually the courts focus on particular facts.

A legislative tort reform that blends hazardous products and medicine grew out of efforts by plaintiffs' lawyers to mass-produce litigation over asbestos and silica. In some cases, these efforts included payments to doctors for mass screenings of potential plaintiffs who they did not examine. In one group of silica cases, a federal judge in Texas said that the diagnoses by these doctors "were driven neither by health nor justice; they were manufactured for money."[26] Counterattacks to these practices came from both courts and legislatures. In an asbestos case, the Texas Supreme Court required "scientifically reliable expert testimony that the plaintiff's exposure to the defendant's product more than doubled his risk of contracting the disease."[27]

An example of laws passed by state legislatures is the Ohio statute that sets as a "minimum requirement" for asbestos cases "[e]vidence verifying that a competent medical authority has taken a detailed occupational and exposure history of the exposed person from the exposed person," "based on a medical examination and pulmonary function testing of the exposed person." It also requires a finding that "[t]he exposed person has a permanent respiratory impairment rating of at least class 2 as defined by and evaluated pursuant to the AMA guides to the evaluation of permanent impairment" and has "asbestosis or diffuse pleural thickening, based at a minimum on radiological or pathological evidence of asbestosis or radiological evidence of diffuse pleural thickening."[28]

Yet another set of reforms, principally devised to reduce payouts in malpractice litigation, would mandate an administrative system for resolving all medical malpractice claims, employing a multi-member board that makes decisions on claims.[29] Other proposals have been for "health courts," tribunals that would replace juries, with caps on attorney's fees and rate schedules on damages.[30]

Much has been written on the effects of various tort reform statutes. I summarize here a few of these studies. There is an indication that one effect of these laws is to reduce the number of injury case that claimants' lawyers will accept, using more rigorous screening processes. Commentators have said that a result is that the cases lawyers will decide to take "are likely to be stronger and have a better chance of success."[31] There is evidence that between 1985 and 2002, there was a decline in civil jury verdicts of more than 50 percent.[32]

The evidence on death rates in states with such statutes as caps on noneconomic loss and punitive damages show that for men, at least, they actually decrease but that they increase when there are caps on total damages and reform-statute changes to the collateral source rule. Another conclusion is that "[n]oneconomic damage caps and punitive damage reforms benefit women less than men" but that "total damage caps and collateral source reforms harm men more than women."[33] Much cited data indicates that "for female plaintiffs, average non-economic damages accounted for 78 percent of average total compensatory damages, while for male plaintiffs the average was 48 percent."[34]

One statistic that puts into perspective the costs of malpractice litigation is that at least in 2005, malpractice insurance premiums were "only about 1 percent of total U.S. healthcare costs."[35] An empirical question on which there is some uncertainty is whether the effects of tort reform laws, or the lack of them, affect physicians' decisions to stay in practice, or to retire. The data indicates that "the presence or absence of caps on awards bears either no relationship or a best a very modest association with the per-capita number of patient-treating physicians in a state."[36]

More generally with respect to damage awards, it is necessary to distinguish between the statistics of mean and median awards. Illustrative is data from 1996 to 2001 that indicates that "mean awards outstrip medians because of the presence of a small number of very large awards." One observer has suggested that the "[g]rowth in mean plaintiff verdicts, coupled with large nominal awards, fuels the perception that juries are engaging in redistributive behavior (or are simply 'out of control')." She suggests that "an unexplained increase in average real dollar awards remains in the type of cases that typically involve individual plaintiffs facing off against corporations or higher status individuals."[37] As a general matter, one commentator declared that "[t]ort reformers have been extremely successful in scaling back punitive and non-economic damages in the majority of states."[38] And Oklahoma data from 2003 to 2007 indicated that during that period when there was a 17.5 percent decrease in tort filings, there was a 4 percent increase in all civil cases in 2007.[39] An interesting description of a kind of judo in lawsuits between doctors and patients is the assertion that "[h]ospitals and doctors sue patients far more often than their patients sue them."[40]

A battle over tort law that has raged for more than a generation centers on the question of whether courts or legislatures are the better lawmaking body. The argument surfaces most vigorously when courts make judgments the result of which is to affect substantial numbers of cases, for example in a given area of activity. An argument for limiting the power of courts is that "[l]egislatures are uniquely well-equipped to reach fully informed decisions about the need for broad public policy changes in the law."[41] A counterargument, focusing on products liability, is that the adoption of strict liability by courts in specific cases involving products injuries—in an era where manufacturers have much greater power over information— provided "a shift from a balanced playing field, negligence, to one that favored injured consumers."[42] Politics stands closely in the wings, and sometimes appears directly on stage, in state systems where judges are elected. Increasing amounts of money now fund judicial elections, and one focus of contributors is to swing the balance, in one way or another, between judges who lean toward plaintiffs or defendants in injury cases.

A battleground where courts and legislatures come into direct conflict involves the question of whether tort reform statutes are constitutional. The courts have divided on these questions, and their reasoning has sometimes been on rather technical legal grounds. The Illinois Supreme Court held unconstitutional a limitation on noneconomic damages on the ground that it violated the separation of powers clause of the state constitution. As the plaintiffs summarized this idea, to uphold the law as enacted would allow the legislature to "supplant the judiciary's authority in determining whether a remittitur [that is, an order that requires a plaintiff to accept a reduction of damages]—is appropriate under the facts of the case." The technical basis of the court's holding lay in the fact that the statute did not allow the damages cap to be severed from the rest of the law, and the court said that if that were changed, "the legislature remains free to reenact any provisions it deems appropriate." The court did stress, however, that none of the statutes the defendants cited in support of their position required "a court to reduce a jury's award of noneconomic damages to a predetermined limit, irrespective of the facts of the case," the statute having specified a $500,000 limit on noneconomic damages in suits against medical providers. The court was unmoved by the fact that many other states had passed such statutes: "That 'everybody is doing it' is hardly a litmus test for the constitutionality of the statute."[43] Thus, the question of the constitutionality of the statute required the court to opine on the relationship of its specific provisions with the state constitution while considering the existence of similar statutes in other states.

An interesting contrast appears in a case where a plaintiff sued doctors at an Oregon state university hospital for negligence, winning a jury award of more than $12 million including $6 million in noneconomic damages, and a statute limited damages against the state and its employees to $3,000,000. The court "recognize[d]" that the damages subject to the cap were "not sufficient … to compensate plaintiff for the full extent of the injuries that her son suffered." However, it concluded that the caps statute did not violate the provision of the Oregon constitution that "every man shall have remedy by due course of law for injury done him in his person, property, or reputation," and the constitutional right to a jury trial. Declaring that its decisions on remedy clause cases did "not deny the legislature authority to adjust, within constitutional limits, the duties and remedies that one person owes another," the court said that "legal limits on a jury's assessment of civil damages have been and remain an accepted feature of our law." It said that two kinds of limits on amounts of damages that a jury could award were not "an interference with the jury's fact-finding function."[44]

The discussion here has focused on tort reform statutes, which generally advantage defendants, but we should also mention judicial decisions that change the law in a way that benefits plaintiffs. An example is an Illinois case that adopted comparative negligence, overturning the rule that any contributory negligence by a plaintiff, however small, would bar him entirely from collecting any damages. Rejecting the defendant's argument that this was a choice that could be made only by the legislature, the court said a "stalemate" existed on the issue, given that the legislature had not adopted comparative negligence, with "a mutual state of inaction in which the court awaits action by the legislature and the legislature awaits guidance by the court." It said that when such a situation existed, with resultant injustice to claimants, it was the court's "imperative duty ... to repair that injustice and reform the law to be responsive to the demands of society."[45] A dissenting judge said he was "bothered by the fact that this court has snatched the problem from the 236 elected representatives" of the state's "11 million people and decreed that it, not the elected representatives, shall determine whether this State will follow comparative negligence" and which variety it should choose.[46] An interesting linguistic feature of the majority opinion was its use of the term "reform the law"—usually, as we have said, a term used to describe statutes that limit lawsuits or the amount of damages.

Proposals for tort reform dive into controversial areas of injury law, and the fact that those proposals generally advocate legislative enactments necessarily means that they deal with issues of public policy. Here, I briefly summarize the major arguments that both sides muster about such proposals. These arguments reflect tensions about the definition of justice as it is achieved both by courts and by legislatures.

Those who support the element of the pro-plaintiff tort law that existed before the advent of tort reform statutes argue that such developments as strict liability for products and expanded liability for medical malpractice have yielded significant benefits for injury reduction in both areas. One author cites evidence that strict liability, and the imposition of liability on automakers for lack of crashworthiness, cut the fatality rate for cars. He also suggests that "the stronger the malpractice litigation system the safer the health care system," specifically instancing a substantial drop in deaths from anesthesia.[47] There is evidence that, at the margin, tort law minimizes auto accidents.[48]

More generally, tort law has expanded with the occurrences of injuries associated with advances in modern technology. In fact, in areas of disease-causing toxic products that reach far back into the early 20th century, it has provided at least some compensation to people who have suffered from debilitating, often fatal, illnesses. The most powerful example is asbestos. Another product area, concerning which law continues to be made, is tobacco. Still another, with variations in the results of litigation, is lead poisoning resulting from paints used in households.

From the standpoint of its proponents, tort law has the great virtue of providing individualized justice to particular persons who suffer injuries that could have been avoided. Another benefit of tort law is that it is decentralized within the country, permitting states to experiment with different kinds of liability rules. From the defense perspective, this element of tort law can keep what turn out to be undesirable expansions of liability from dominating the entire nation.

Some of the arguments made by tort reformers show the other side of a coin that shines brightly for defenders of relatively broad tort liability. One argument is that society loses from individualized injury litigation—that recurrent injury problems are best dealt with by compensation systems that avoid the need for trials of specific injury-causing events and that eliminate judgments about the pain and suffering of particular persons. Part of this opposition to compensation awards from individual lawsuits is that tort law is a poor insurance vehicle. Reformers also criticize other elements of a decentralized tort law that permits state-by-state experimentation with liability rules. Business groups in particular lament that in that environment, uncertainty reigns—both as to question of what the rules are on liability and as to the amount of damages that may be awarded. Yet it is interesting that some business people indicate that they would rather face uniform rules that might increase their overall exposure to liability than a system in which they cannot figure out their chances of being sued and for how much. This set of arguments may resolve itself into questions about how each side estimates its chances of being a big winner or a big loser under rules that are uniform throughout the country.

Complicating the predictability of tort reform measures are data which point in different directions about the effects of reform statutes on medical care. One study, for example, exhibited bidirectional tendencies. It found in data from the Centers for Disease Control evidence that dollar caps on damages "simultaneously increase and decrease" the intensity of treatment "with an overall net decrease." At the same time, they found that caps "increase the probability" that doctors would do bypass operations, especially when the alternative was an angioplasty; bypasses were performed more often when doctors had "the strongest financial incentives" to do them, with the possible result that tort reform "may encourage riskier but more remunerative procedures." Their overall conclusion on mortality data—that "patient outcomes did not change greatly, and may have slightly improved, even though treatments changed"—was that the "combination of results is most consistent with a decrease in defensive medicine following tort reform."[49]

Paralleling those results was another author's conclusion that "evidence of the effect of tort reform in the medical malpractice field is mixed." This researcher found that "caps on noneconomic damages have reduced costs, thereby decreasing pressure on hospitals to improve care" and that "[c]onsistent evidence of effects on physician behavior and physician supply has not emerged." With respect to another kind of tort reform, that author found "little evidence ... that reform of punitive damages affected the ratio between punitive and compensatory damages." He remarked that this was "consistent with punitive damages not having been out of control and in need of reform." For this discussion, perhaps most striking was that author's general conclusion that "the most common theme of the empirical findings" on tort reform, "other than the effect of draconian caps, is the absence of robust evidence of effects."[50]

Doctors, scientists, and product developers must make their own personal judgments about the meaning of this welter of data, as ambiguous as it often is. I can only append a word of advice on punitive damages in particular, which I believe is a solid standard of conduct generally for those who engage in risky activity. As I put it in a treatise: "Behave sensibly. Act decently."[51]

Endnotes

1. Center for Justice & Democracy, Fact Sheet: Tort Litigation in the United States (Nov. 12, 2011) printed from the Internet, April 21, 2017.
2. Patrick Hubbard, The Nature and Impact of the "Tort Reform" Movement, 35 *Hofstra L. Rev.* 439, 443–44 (2006).
3. Jonathan Glater, To the Trenches: The Tort War Is Raging On, *N.Y. Times*, June 22, 2008, Business 1 & jump at 8.
4. See Sandra F. Gavin, Stealth Tort Reform, 42 *Valp. L. Rev.* 431, 444–47 (2008).
5. See Glen O. Robinson, *The Medical Malpractice Crisis of the 1970; A Retrospective*, 49 L. & C.P. 5 (1986).
6. See Nevada Justice Ass'n, The "McDonald's Coffee Case" and Other Fictions, *The Recorder*, Sept. 30, 1994.
7. Stephen Martin and Joanne Daniels, "The Impact It Has Had Is Between People's Ears": Tort Reform, Mass Culture, and Politics, 50 *DePaul L. Rev.* 453, 467–70 (2000).

8. George H.W. Bush, Acceptance Speech, 1992 Republican National Convention.

9. George W. Bush, State of the Union Message 2003.

10. See Elizabeth Thornburg, Judicial Hellholes, Lawsuit Climates and Bad Social Sciences, Lessons from West Virginia, 110 *W.Va. Rev.* 1097, 1098–1100 (2008).

11. See Gavin, supra note 4, at 452–53 (summarizing studies).

12. Timothy D. Lytton, Framing Clergy Sexual Abuse as An Institutional Practice: How Tort Litigation Influences Media Coverage, 36 *Wm. Mitchell L. Rev.* 169 (2009).

13. *Mills v. Giant of Maryland*, 441 F. Supp.2d 104, 108 (D.D.C. 2006).

14. *Bates v. Dow Argosciences LLC*, 544 U.S. 431, 444 (2005).

15. Id. at 447.

16. *Wyeth v. Levine*, 555 U.S. 555, 578–79 (2009).

17. Id. at 605 (Alito, J., dissenting).

18. Valerie Hans, Empowering the Active Jury: A Genuine Tort Reform, 13 *Roger Williams L. Rev.* 38, 54, 60–66 (2008).

19. *Blain v. Smithkline Beecham Corp.*, 240 F.R.D. 179, 188–89 (E.D. Pa. 2007).

20. *Donovan v. Philip Morris, Inc.*, 268 F.R.D. 1, 29 (D. Mass. 2013).

21. Id. at 14.

22. *Consorti v. Armstrong World Indus. Inc.*, 72 F.3d 1003, 1009 (2d Cir. 1995).

23. Joseph Sanders, Reforming General Damages: A Good Tort Reform, 13 *Rogers Williams L. Rev.* 115, 146-48 (2008).

24. *Burd v. New Jersey Tel. Co.*, 386 A.2d 1310, 1315 (N.J. 1978).

25. *Vispisiano v. Ashland Chem. Co.*, 527 A.2d 66, 74 (N.J. 1987).

26. In re Silica Prods. Litig., 398 F. Supp.2d 563, 635 (S.D. Tex. 2005).

27. *Bostic v. Georgia-Pacific Corp.*, 439 S.W.2d 332, 350 (Tex. 2014).

28. Ohio Rev. Code §2307.92.

29. Originally, A Proposed Alternative to the Civil Justice System for Resolving Medical Liability Disputes (AMA Specialty Society Medical Liability Project 1988). Some details are summarized in Chapter 11.

30. Critically summarized in Emily Chow, Health Court: An Extreme Makeover of Medical Malpractice with Potentially Fatal Complications, 7 Yale *J. Health Policy Law & Ethics* No. 2 (2007).

31. Martin & Daniels, supra note 7, 50 *DePaul L. Rev.* at 485.

32. Larry Lyon et al., Straight from the Horse's Mouth: Judicial Observations of Jury Behavior and the Need for Tort Reform, 59 *Baylor L. Rev.* 419 (2007).

33. Joanne Shepherd, Tort Reforms, Winners and Losers: The Competing Effects of Care and Activity Levels, 55 *UCLA L. Rev.* 905, 958-60 (2008).
34. Deborah R. Hensler, Jurors in the Material World: Putting Tort Verdict in their Social Context, 13 *Roger Williams L. Rev.* 8, 18 (citing Lucinda Finley in 53 Emory L.J. 1263).
35. Richard Posner, Tort Reform, *Jurist*, Jan. 17, 2005.
36. Neil Vidmar, Medical Malpractice Tort Reform, IV, in Andrew F. Popper, (ed.), *Materials on Tort Reform*, 24 at 25 (West 2010).
37. Hensler, supra note 34, at 22–23.
38. Michael Rustad, The Endless Campaign: How the Tort Reformers Successfully and Incessantly Market Their Group Thought to the Rest of U.S., in Popper, supra note 36, at 37.
39. Patricia W. Hatamayar, The Effect of "Tort Reform" on Tort Case Filings, 43 *Valparaiso Univ. L. Rev.* 559, 561 (2009).
40. Thomas Geoghegan, quoted by Adam Liptak, in "If There's Too Much Litigation, Blame Class Divisions, and Class Actions," reviewing book *See You in Court*, N.Y.Times, Nov. 24, 2007, at A25.
41. Mark Behrens, Who Should Decide Tort Law? A Fundamental Issue in the Public Debate over Civil Justice Reforms in Popper, supra note 36, at 47.
42. Frank Vandall, Tort Reform, A Power Plan, in Popper, supra, at 50.
43. Lebron v. Gottlieb Mem'l Hosp., 930 N.E.2d 895, 900, 913–14 (Ill. 2010).
44. *Horton v. Oregon Health & Sciences Univ.*, 376 P.2d 998, 1030, 1041 (Ore. 2016).
45. *Alvis v. Ribar*, 421 N.E.2d 886, 896 (Ill. 1981).
46. Id. at 902 (Ryan, J., dissenting).
47. Carl T. Bogus, Genuine Tort Reform, 13 *Roger Williams L. Rev.* 1, 6 (2008).
48. See Don Dewees et al., Exploring the Domain of Accident Law 22–26 (Oxford Univ. Press 22–26 (1996) (summarizing literature).
49. Ronen Avraham & Max Schanzenbach, The Impact of Tort Reform on Intensity of Treatment: Evidence from Heart Patients, 39 *J. Health Econ.* 273, 284 (2015).
50. Theodore Eisenberg, The Empirical Effects of Tort Reform, in *Research Handbook on the Economics of Tort*, 513 (Edward Elgar 2013).
51. Marshall S. Shapo, *The Law of Products Liability* §29.10[E] (Elgar 7th ed. 2017).

Chapter 11

Statutory Compensation Systems

There are many ways that society has provided for compensation of victims of injuries. Many of these, discussed previously, are through individual suits against injurers. Many others are through compensation plans enacted by legislatures.

11.1 Workers' Compensation

The most far-reaching of the statutory schemes is workers' compensation, which annually pays more money to injury victims than do judgments in tort suits. The historical background of these laws included a legal world in which deaths and injuries from workplace accidents went entirely uncompensated because workers' tort suits were barred by the doctrines of assumption of risk and contributory negligence. The basic rationales for workers' compensation laws include a combination of social justice and the economics-based belief that industry should internalize the costs of workers injured on the job. The British statesman Lloyd George summed up this idea in a memorable sentence: "The cost of the product should bear the blood of the working man."

American states began to pass workers' compensation laws in the first decade of the 20th century. Now they are part of the law in every state and there are also federal "comp" statutes, including one for federal employees injured or killed at work. These laws were passed as part of a legislative bargain—a "quid pro quo" that produced an exclusive remedy under which workers gave up their opportunity to bring tort suits in exchange for compensation payments that would be granted without litigation if an accident fulfilled the requirements of the statute and without a worker having to prove that the employer was at fault.

The language typical of "comp" statutes includes words like "accidental injury" and injuries "in the course of" or "arising out of" employment. One case in which the claimant succeeded involved her work in the laundry room of a nursing home, which obligated her to load into washing machines bags of laundry that weighed 25 to 50 pounds. The court upheld her claim for carpal tunnel syndrome, rejecting the argument that she should have to show that her injury was "sudden and completely disabling" rather than "gradual." It said that "[r]equiring complete collapse" in such a case "would not be beneficial to the employee or the employer because it might force employees needing the protection of the Act to push their bodies to a precise moment of collapse." It remarked that "a more severe standard would penalize" "an employee who faithfully performs job duties despite bodily discomfort and damage."[1]

Another decision granted compensation to a woman whose asthma was aggravated by working in a single room with 50 other employees, at least half of whom smoked and in which the ventilation system did not work properly, and who suffered two "sudden and traumatic asthmatic attacks" that required emergency room treatment. The court concluded that the plaintiff had shown an "accidental injury," rejecting the

arguments that "the asthma condition [was] solely an allergic or other type of sensitivity reaction to an everyday environmental condition and did not occur in an unexpected or
unusual circumstance" and that the "accidental injury" category in the statute required a "catastrophic or extraordinary"
event. It said that "[w]hile exposure to cigarette smoke in our
society and in workplaces may have been and still is relatively
endemic," the facts of the claimant's exposure "demonstrate[d]
an exacerbative and excessive quality." It also said that the
plaintiff's "predisposition with an asthma condition" did not
bar her recovery, citing precedent on the idea that it was "well
settled that where causally related injuries from a claimant's
employment precipitate, aggravate or accelerate a preexisting
infirmity or disease, the resulting disability is compensable." It
also was unpersuaded by the familiar argument that to allow
recovery would "open floodgates and make every allergic
reaction, common cold or ordinary ailment compensable." It
emphasized that in order to recover, claimants would have
to "make showings of unusual environmental conditions or
events assignable to something extraordinary that caused an
accidental injury."[2]

With respect to statutory language that requires that injuries
arise "in the course of" employment, one of the most remarkable results occurred in a case in which the plaintiff, a truck
driver, was injured when a train hit his vehicle as he followed
another truck across a crossing on which the signal arms
malfunctioned. According to at least one version of the facts,
the collision occurred when the claimant was having sexual
intercourse with his co-driver, who died in the accident. A
narrow majority of the Oklahoma Supreme Court upheld the
driver's claim for compensation on the ground that he was in
the "course of employment." The writer of the majority opinion distinguished that phrase from the phrase "arising out
of"—which he defined as a "risk incident to employment." His
premise was that "[a]n injury is compensable if it *arises out of*
the claimant's employment–*i.e.,* was caused by a risk to which

the employee was subjected by his work." He viewed the claimant's "assigned task—that of transporting goods to the West Coast"—as "requir[ing] his presence on the highways." Given that premise, he said that there was "[a] causal connection between the act in which [the claimant] was engaged, when injured" and that "his job description [was] clear," and concluded that "[b]ecause the perils of this servant's travel for his master are co-extensive with the risks of employment," his "injuries undeniably *arose out of* his work."[3]

Two cases from the Virginia Supreme Court involving back problems had contrasting results. In one the claimant was a customer service representative whose supervisor put her to work moving and unpacking boxes in connection with a move of the company's office. Wearing high-heeled shoes as she usually did, she suffered a severe lumbar sprain that put her in the hospital for five weeks, which an examining doctor posited was an "exacerbation" of a previous injury "from which she was still having minor residuals." The court upheld her claim, saying that the accident occurred while she "was exposed to a particular danger" and that medical reports by two specialists confirmed that her disability "was caused by the accident resulting from that danger." Paralleling the decision in the case involving the smoke-filled room, the court said that it was "immaterial whether her work incapacity was related solely" to her prior injury, quoting a precedent as saying that [w]hen an injury sustained in an industrial accident accelerates or aggravates a pre-existing condition, ... disability resulting therefrom is compensable under the Workers' Compensation Act."[4]

In the other decision, handed down the same day, the court affirmed a judgment against the claimant, who "felt acute pain in his lower back" as he bent over to tie his shoe as he was unloading packages from his truck. The court, concluding that the injury did not "arise out of" his employment, said that "the act of bending over to tie the shoe was unrelated to any hazard common to the workplace"—that "nothing in the work environment contributed to the injury." Observing that "[e]very person who wears laced shoes must occasionally perform the act of retying the laces," it said that "[t]he situation of a loose shoelace confronting the claimant was wholly independent of the master–servant relationship."[5]

A Michigan decision in 1960 at what was then the frontier of workers' compensation began to signal that that branch of the law would catch up with the realities of emotional life. The claimant in that case was a General Motors assembly line worker, recalled to work after a five-month layoff, who was assigned to a job he could not keep up with. After a couple of stressful weeks, he suffered a breakdown for which one description was paranoid schizophrenia. A majority of the bitterly divided state supreme court affirmed an award of workers' compensation benefits, citing testimony from his treating physician that, given a "personality predisposition towards the development of this illness," his job became "the straw that [broke] the camel's back" with the development of an "actual psychosis."[6]

The decision was important because of the way it combined several factual elements that prior cases had not combined: It did not require a single precipitating event, such as a physical injury or traumatic emotional shock, and it awarded damages when the claimant had predisposing tendencies. The majority and the dissent hurled citations to past cases back and forth—for example, cases involving physical injuries, mental injuries, and combinations of them. This is the way that lawyers operate; they take precedents seriously. But in close cases that involve the interpretation of language in statutes—for example, the phrase "arising out of and in the course of employment"—they will draw on considerations of public policy to rationalize their conclusions. The majority in this case quoted a Massachusetts decision in which the court referred to the purpose of workers' compensation statutes as "ameliorating the economic plight of an employee injured in the course of and on account of his employment" or his family if he died, with compensation ordinarily being "awarded for incapacity to earn and not for the injury as such."

The dissenting opinion, itself quoting other decisions, essentially viewed the cause of the plaintiff's illness as internal to him. It quoted a member of the workers' compensation board as saying that "[t]he disability arose out of the plaintiff's own feelings and misapprehension and from within himself completely," and expressed concern that upholding the claimant's award would lead to decisions giving recovery when a worker suffered a breakdown from brooding over the failure to get a raise. It quoted another court on the idea that compensation should not be given for diseases "to which workmen would have been equally exposed outside their employment independent of the relation of employer and employee." In terms that resonate in today's political controversies, it said that the workers' compensation act "was not intended to provide general health insurance to the workman."[7]

An interesting sidelight on this decision was social science research on the Michigan Supreme Court's decisions in workers' compensation cases. In a few of the cases surveyed, the court was unanimous, but in the others, the votes for and against workers' claims were perfectly aligned with Democratic judges voting for workers and Republican judges voting for employers. The researchers commented that this was "brute testimony to either the strength of party affiliation in Michigan or the unusual homogeneity of social attitudes among those judges who wear the party labels."[8]

A later decision of a Michigan workers' compensation referee may have borne out the worst fears of the dissenting judges. The referee ruled in favor of compensation for a worker, dismissed from his job, who had a psychotic break and began shooting in the Chrysler plant where he had worked, killing three foremen.

Another decision that would bear out those fears involved a woman who after being laid off was told she could transfer to another department where she could work as a foreperson.

In that job, with which she was "not pleased," she became depressed and hospitalized, and when she returned to work she again became depressed and eventually was found to be totally disabled. Although the workers' compensation board found that she was not entitled to compensation, a majority of the Massachusetts Supreme Judicial Court concluded she should have an award. It recognized that "layoffs and job transfers are frequent events, and that emotional injuries are more prone to fabrication and less susceptible to substantiation than are physical injuries." However, it concluded that it was "within the Legislature's prerogative to determine, as a matter of public policy, whether one of the costs of doing business in this Commonwealth shall be the compensation of those few employees who do suffer emotional disability as a result of being laid off or transferred."[9]

As in the Michigan case involving the assembly line worker, the court was sharply divided. The writer of the dissenting opinion declared that the majority had "expanded the scope of our workers' compensation law far beyond what the Legislature ever intended" with the results that "the critical distinction between workers' compensation and unemployment insurance is disappearing." He said there was no evidence that the claimant's "layoff was motivated by other than economic reasons or that the information was given to" to her "in a particularly stressful manner." Noting that in previous cases the court had "required a showing of one or more specific stressful, traumatic events as the cause of the emotional injury," he said that "[b]y departing from those limits, the court has opened workers' compensation to distressed claimants who have simply experienced economically inevitable terminations and transfers."[10]

Cases of this kind raise many questions of incentives that are familiar to readers in the healthcare professions and designers of products, questions concerning effects on behavior that may not have been considered when decisions are made. Just one example is that judicial decisions that are relatively liberal to workers with histories of emotional problems, advantaging particular claimants, may lead to more restrictive hiring practices designed to screen out predispositions to such problems.

Workers' compensation law presents another set of frontiers that may be likened to aspects of the duty problem discussed in Chapter 8, where injuring events are not the kind of occurrence that would ordinarily be predicted or where the claimant has a particular vulnerability. An interesting set of cases involved tornadoes. One worker was injured in some of those storms when he was working for his employer at a residence and another died when a tornado hit a motel in which he was staying while on a business trip for his employer. Both claimants won awards from a majority of the Michigan Supreme Court on the basis that their injuries arose "out of" and "in the course of" their employment. One opinion that supported the claimant said that "if the employment is the occasion of the injury, even though not the proximate cause, compensation should be paid."[11] Another said that "if a workman is engaged in the course of his employment when he is stricken violently from on High, whether by windstorm, hurricane, tornado, typhoon, cloudburst resulting from a flash flood, or say an earthquake, then whatever disabling or fatal injury is sustained by him has arisen out of the course of his employment as well as in the course thereof."[12] A very different view, one which matches an idea put forth in decisions in the torts cases discussed in Chapter 8, appeared in an opinion declaring that "[l]ightning, flood, tornados and estranged wives will always be with us, in this vale of tears." Digging into the historical reasons for workers' compensation, that judge said that those events "were the occasion of human injury when our forebears were tilling the soil with sharp sticks" and "not a byproduct of the industrial revolution." He concluded that such occurrences were not "in any sense the moral responsibility of those who profit by, or enjoy the fruits of, our modern industrialized society."[13]

There are numerous cases at the boundary of judicial choice, which some readers may think should be beyond the realm of liability but in which courts have awarded compensation. In one such case, an investigator for a county prosecutor would smoke on a courthouse roof where "he could think about the case he was working on," but where pigeons often came, leaving their droppings. His wife testified that she had visited him on the roof 100 or more times while he was there and observed droppings there. After surgery on a lung with a nodule suspected to be cancerous, a procedure followed by a stroke, he sought workers' compensation on the ground that a biopsy of the nodule disclosed a fungus and bacteria that his expert attributed to pigeon droppings. A state appellate court affirmed a ruling by an administrative law judge and a commission that the worker's "occupational activities" caused his infection, with accumulated disability benefits of $167,811 and monthly payments to his widow of $502, agreeing with the commission that the injury "arose in and out of the course of his employment."[14]

Workers' compensation law, as we have noted, is an exclusive remedy for workers who fall within the coverage of the statutes. However, that system sometimes bumps up against tort law, the civil action for personal injury, which often will be preferred by claimants because tort awards are likely to be larger than the detailed schedules enforced under the compensation statutes. In cases involving injuries caused by products used in the workplace, workers may get two bites at securing awards. For example, they may bring a tort suit against the maker of an industrial machine, claiming that it was defectively designed, at the same time they receive a workers' compensation award from their employer. But the legal bumping may occur when a product manufacturer, successfully sued by a worker in tort, tries to get a complete or partial recovery against the worker's employer on the ground that it was the employer's use of the machine that was entirely or partly responsible for the injury.

A lot of decisions will not permit the manufacturer to recover against the comp employer, emphasizing the exclusivity of the workers' compensation remedy. However, there are decisions that favor manufacturers, one of which came from a majority of the U.S. Supreme Court. In this case, which involved a rescue of refugees from the Vietnam War, a plane made by Lockheed crashed, killing 150 people. Among those who died was a civilian employee of the Navy. The United States paid death benefits to her survivors, to which they were entitled because she was covered by the federal workers' compensation statute, the Federal Employees' Compensation Act. The administrator of the deceased employee then sued Lockheed on the ground that the plane was defective. Lockheed settled that suit but then turned around and tried to sue the government for indemnity, that is, the entire amount involved.

As the Court summarized it, "[t]he Government did not dispute that it was primarily responsible for the fatal crash, nor did it challenge the terms of the settlement." The case involved the technical issue of the meaning of the statute, the language of which prohibited actions against the Government by an "employee, his legal representative, spouse, dependents, next of kin, [or] any other person otherwise entitled to recover damages from the United States ... because of the [employee's] injury or death." The government argued that this language barred Lockheed's claim against it, but the Supreme Court majority rejected that argument. It said that the language of the statute "was intended to govern only the rights of employees, their relatives, and people claiming through or on behalf of them"—that these were "the only categories of parties who benefit from the 'quid pro quo' compromise" adopted by the statute.[15] A dissenting opinion said that could be "no doubt that a principal purpose" of the statute was "to limit the amount that the government would have to pay on account of injuries to its employees" and that indeed "any workers' compensation statute exists in part to provide 'for employers a liability which is limited and determinate.'" Pointing out that the effect of the majority's decision was to require the government to pay indemnity—the entire amount, rather than to share liability—the dissent complained that it "greatly expands the liability to which the government may be subjected on account of injuries to its employees."[16]

Workers' compensation itself has been under attack from both sides. Employers have supported state laws that would enable them to opt out of the system, with provisions that cover fewer injuries and limit the amount of time during which benefits could be paid. At least one of these statutes has been struck down by the Oklahoma Supreme Court on the ground that it was "an unconstitutional special law" under the state constitution that created an "impermissible, unequal, and disparate treatment of a select group of injured workers."[17] By contrast, an attack from the employer's side produced a ruling by a Florida appellate court on technical grounds that blocked a suit by a workers' advocates group which argued that that the exclusive remedy provision of a workers' compensation law should be invalidated. The plaintiffs argued that the limited benefits paid under comp rendered the system unconstitutionally unreasonable as contrasted with the damages that could be recovered in tort suits, but the appellate court concluded that the plaintiffs did not have legal standing to bring their suit.[18]

11.2 Traffic Injuries

A separate category of activities for which no-fault systems have been proposed is traffic accidents, which at this writing have claimed well over 30,000 lives per year and caused millions of injuries. In practice, tort suits for vehicle injuries have been shown to overcompensate for minor injuries and to undercompensate for serious injuries. When people have to go to court to recover for traffic injuries, they may be subject to long delays in receiving compensation if they receive it at all. This situation is especially unfair to those who suffer severe injuries, and who may be grievously squeezed by delays and tough bargaining employed by defendants' insurers. The context of such litigation includes complaints by critics of the tort system about a "negligence lottery" in which litigants spin a legal roulette wheel with uncertain results. They also complain about the administrative cost—often wasteful cost—in a litigation-based system, and add a complaint about incentives to fraud by the fabrication of injuries. Critics have also targeted the fact that injured persons sometimes cannot recover at all if they were contributorily at fault, depending on state rules.

More or less half the states have passed laws that, to some extent, eliminate the fault-based tort action for injuries caused by motoring, with the clear intent to rid the courts of litigation. The effect of these statutes is to make first-party insurance mandatory for those injured in accidents, rather than remitting them to suits against injurers, where judgments are principally paid from liability insurance. None of these laws completely replace the tort action. All of them have "thresholds," a cut-off below which an injured person cannot bring a tort claim against her injurer, and the insurance policies for no-fault allow recovery only for economic loss and not for intangibles such as pain and suffering. Some thresholds are in dollars and some are verbal thresholds—for example, requiring that claimants show a fracture in order to bring a tort action. All no-fault insurance plans have dollar limits on coverage. Critics argue that dollar thresholds contribute to a tendency to inflate medical bills to get above those thresholds.

Serious arguments against no-fault systems are based on both philosophy and economics. Opponents contend that to eliminate fault from vehicle accidents is to diminish personal responsibility and that such schemes give morally undesirable advantages to those who could not recover at all under tort law. In particular, they argue that it would be wrong to allow no-fault recovery to drivers who are intoxicated or under the influence of drugs. They also argue that no-fault regimes will lead to more accidents, because motorists who do not fear being held liable for accidents will not drive as carefully. There are conflicting empirical data on this hypothesis. Other parts of the puzzle are that in some states persons with relatively minor injuries can get compensation only under no-fault whereas in other states they may receive greater sums from tort liability judgments, although they may not recover at all.

11.3 Medical Injuries

The statistics on injuries in the course of medical care are daunting. A much-cited study by the Institute of Medicine estimated that 44,000 to 98,000 deaths per year are caused by negligence, and more recent estimates put the numbers much higher. Other studies have reported a rate of adverse events due to negligence to be one percent of hospitalizations. The causes posited for these deaths, and many other injuries, are various: Insufficient checks on physician incompetence, the erosion of the doctor–patient relationship and resultant failures in communication, the lack of individual experience rating for insurance premiums, and unrealistically high expectations by patients. Along with these problems were concerns about costs—the costs of defensive medicine, the difficulty of measuring costs for victims, and the psychological impact of tort suits on doctors. Statistics indicate that negligent medical injuries are significantly underlitigated, with a very small percentage of potential claimants bringing suit. Additionally, those who sue face delay in the court system, a set of complex legal doctrines that present barriers to recovery, uncertainty about whether they can recover at all, and unpredictability of the amount of jury verdicts. The mirror image of those problems—uncertainty about ultimate results and amounts if claimants win—applies to doctors as well.

All of this has led to proposals to change medical malpractice law that would provide alternatives to the tort system. A plan drafted by the American Medical Association, briefly mentioned in Chapter 10,[19] would set up an administrative system under which a hearing examiner would review malpractice claims and make decisions subject to review by a seven-member board with full-time members, decisions of which would in turn be reviewable by a state appellate court. This alternative to tort suits has been justified on the basis that avoiding the delay and uncertainty of tort litigation would be a "quid pro quo" for injured patients analogous to that which justified the workers' compensation laws and would avoid jury trials. The proposal included a feature of "performance monitoring," which would require reports to a branch of the board of "all settlements and awards based on medical liability."

The proposal also included substantive "tort reform" changes in the law that would govern the decisions of hearing examiners. These included a set of factors for determination of reasonableness of physicians' conduct, and standards for qualifications of expert witnesses and for the use of manufacturers' instructions for medical products. Other proposals codified the doctrine of informed consent to employ a "reasonable patient" standard, would place caps on awards for noneconomic loss and punitive damages, and would require awards of more than $250,000 for future damages to use a schedule of periodic payments.

Some models have been advanced for no-fault compensation systems for medical accidents. Some features of these plans include elimination of payments for the first four weeks of disability, caps on pain and suffering, wage deductibles, and percentage limits on wage replacement. Another set of no-fault plans, adopted in two states, provided compensation only for "newborns with severe neurological impartments." Researchers found that these plans gave "substantial" protection to doctors against tort liability and "lowered premiums for almost all obstetricians," but at least at the outset, few claims were filed.

A problem for the fashioning of medical no-fault plans lies in the definition of compensable events. Various standards have been offered—for example, a definition of "adverse event" that would include injuries caused by "medical management" that result in either prolonged hospital stays or disability at the time of discharge. Questions of interpretation that arise under this kind of classification system parallel those in determining whether an employee was acting in the course of employment for purposes of workers' compensation.

Any relief from litigation provided for doctors by tort reform statutes is subject to constitutional challenge. Claimants whose recoveries may be barred or limited by such laws can claim that they are deprived of equal protection of the laws by the creation of categories that prejudice those with medical injuries as contrasted with all other injury litigants. They also will claim that these statutes deprive them of due process of law when those laws eliminate or restrict legal doctrines that would allow tort recoveries, and that they deprive them of the right to jury trial.

11.4 Terror

A compensation plan that was unique, limited to time and place, is the September 11th Victim Compensation Fund.[20] It was created in response to the crashes of three airplanes that took the lives of more than 2,700 people, most of them in and around the Twin Towers of the World Trade Center in New York, with another 40 who died when a plane crashed into the Pennsylvania countryside. It may surprise readers that this plan was almost an afterthought to legislation originally crafted to provide financial support to airlines grounded in the wake of the attacks, and was drafted under pressure in a space of 24 hours by a small committee. The fund provided financial relief for the economic losses of those who died or were injured and for their families. It also included awards for "noneconomic losses," which it defined broadly in at least eleven categories ranging from pain and suffering to mental anguish, loss of enjoyment of life, and the broad classification of "hedonic damages." This list was itself interesting because it named those categories in a way broader than the categories of noneconomic loss for which most states specifically give recoveries in regular tort suits. The rules under the statute established substantial minimum awards for eligible individuals—those who were at the attack sites and the personal representatives of those who died there. These minimums included $500,000 for representatives of a person who died with a spouse or dependent, established $250,000 as "presumed noneconomic losses" for those who died, and another $100,000 for the spouse and each dependent of those victims.

A remarkable feature of the fund was the options it provided for claimants. They could, without litigation, recover from the fund, or they could opt out of the fund and bring tort suits—for example, against the airlines and their security companies for negligence in permitting hijackers to board the planes, or against the World Trade Center for failing to design buildings that might have withstood the crashes. This option contrasts with workers' compensation, which is an exclusive remedy for covered employees who cannot opt out to sue in tort. The Trade Center itself, which recovered more than $4 billion from insurance, also sued the airlines.[21]

The fund law placed administration of its compensation system in a single person, the Special Master, who had a substantial amount of discretion under rules that were adopted within a few months. These rules provided a series of tabular charts that quantified "presumed economic loss" for categories of survivors in accord with incomes of those who died and also with their family status. Although those charts were precise down to the dollar, the statute allowed the Special Master to consider the "individual circumstances of the claimant," which the rules interpreted to mean that he could consider the "financial needs or financial resources" of claimants or their survivors. This was clearly a departure from the usual rules of tort damages, which do not include those factors.

A strength of the fund law was that claimants did not have to hire lawyers to get awards. However, one writer noted that a "cloud of lawyers" appeared "around the Fund," with 90 percent of those bringing death claims and 62 percent of those filing injury claims using lawyers.

The fund, which was uncapped as to dollar amounts, wound up paying out $8 billion, all from the general revenues. Its creation raised many questions. A fundamental one was whether the fund should have been created at all. For many, the shock to the nation as a whole was a sufficient basis for its creation, although questions were raised as to why the fund did not provide for compensation to "emergency responders" like police and firefighters who rushed to the scene.[22] Critics also cited the use of charts that employed the income of those who were killed as benchmarks for the amount of awards, with one argument being that the awards should be a flat figure, and a Republican politician saying that anything else would be "un-American." The amount of awards themselves roused an array of emotions, which provide evocative examples of the tensions surrounding the amounts of damages in traditional tort actions. One survivor said that an offer by the Special Master for the death of his spouse "spits on my wife, my mother-in-law, and my father-in law." On the other side came a remark made to victims' advocacy groups that "[w]e feel your grief, really," but "I'm just wondering whether we have to feel your greed, too."

As a practical matter, because of federal legislation governing suits against the United States, the government could not be sued for alleged negligence related to the September 11th attacks. However, a natural question was whether the fund, without saying so, represented a kind of expiation for the government's failure to respond to information that suggested not only that attacks were coming, but the chosen method of the attackers. One example of this kind of information was a briefing provided to the CIA director more than two weeks before the attacks that told him that "Moussaoui wanted to learn to fly a 747, paid for his training in cash, was interested to learn the doors do not open in flight, and wanted to fly a simulated flight from London to New York." I note in this connection that the most obvious defendants—those who plotted the attacks, including the nations in which they resided—did not then appear to be available for suit as a practical matter. I further note that until 2016, 28 pages of a report of a congressional investigation on September 11th had been held back because of the sensitivity of information on the involvement of Saudi Arabian nationals in the attacks. Underneath all of the argument about whether the fund was a good idea was what I earlier quoted as the "vale of tears" argument. Those who say it was not a good idea would argue that the vicissitudes of life affect us all in many ways we manage to cope with, without demanding compensation.

11.5 Oil on the Water

A very different kind of event, with catastrophic economic consequences but much less direct loss of life, was the BP oil spill in the Gulf of Mexico in 2010, which led to a specialized compensation plan and a varied menu of compensation litigations. Several corporations were identified as having negligently contributed to the spill, which affected people and resources along a wide swath of sea and land from Texas to the Florida panhandle. Even a year after the event, a report declared that its many impacts were still "uncertain[]" and "unknown." Lawsuits beginning within weeks turned into what I have called a multi-ring legal circus. Thousands of suits were consolidated into the tribunal I have described previously, the Judicial Panel on Multidistrict Litigation. BP agreed to establish a $20 billion fund for the spill to be administered by Kenneth Feinberg, who had been the Special Master for the September 11th fund. The complexity of the subject was evident in a remark by then Senator Sessions of Alabama, later U.S. Attorney General, that the offshore oil industry was "responsible for nearly 200,000 jobs around the Gulf of Mexico and over $13 billion a year in non-tax revenues for the gulf coast oil producing states."

It was apparent that the ordinary tort duty rules on time and distance discussed in Chapter 8 would be stretched if one tried to apply them to the spill. Feinberg plaintively asked, "What do I do with a restaurant in Las Vegas ... who says, 'We have lost 30 percent of our business because here in Vegas we are the only restaurant that has that Gulf shrimp,' and now it is gone and people are not coming to that restaurant?"

Beyond the $20 billion in the fund set up by BP, at the time of this writing there were many suits in process by litigants who had not filed under that fund. And there was another layer of payments, emblematic of the role of government itself in compensation for injuries. In 2016 a final settlement of about $20 billion was sealed on a civil damages suit filed by the United States and five Gulf Coast states. The judge overseeing that litigation said BP had been "grossly negligent" in causing the spill.[23] As reported, this settlement included a penalty of $5.5 billion plus interest for violations of the Clean Water Act, "$8.1 billion in natural resource damages, ... up to an additional $700 million ... to address any later discovered injuries to natural resource conditions that were unknown" and "$600 million for other claims." A related agreement required the company to pay approximately $5.9 billion to state and local government entities.[24]

The backwash of the BP spill exhibited a complexity of elements that went beyond the September 11th fund: a fund provided by a company, a multidistrict litigation, a multitude of private suits outside of that, and civil damages actions by the federal government and by state governments.

We have reviewed a number of compensation systems with both public and private inputs, which cover different kinds of activities and events. Threading through all of this discussion is the question of the effects on conduct of those who are potentially liable, or who have been held liable, for injuries caused by risky activities—effects produced by tort litigation, by statutory compensation systems, or by other funding schemes.

11.6 Broad Scale Compensation Systems

Utopians might prefer a system that compensated for all injuries, whether they occurred on the road, at work, slipping in the bathtub, or mountain climbing. Models of various kinds for such a system could be fashioned, and there has actually been one such system in operation—in New Zealand, although it has gone through a number of iterations. That country first adopted a scheme in 1972 for "injury by accident." One writer summarized the initial provisions of this law, which was described as "social insurance," as including "medical and rehabilitation expenses, compensation for eighty percent of lost earnings as long as disability continued, and lump-sum payments of up to $27,000 (N.Z.) for non-economic losses." The law broadly abolished the tort action, but it is interesting that after a decade of experience, the law continued to allow civil actions for punitive damages for "outrageous conduct."

A decade later, in 1992, the New Zealand Parliament made changes in the law that expanded a categorization of a type of activity that produced injuries. Specifically, it adopted a definition of "medical misadventure" which was almost two pages long, and which a commentator said made it likely that proceedings would "turn into actions to prove medical negligence or malpractice." It eliminated the lump-sum payments for noneconomic losses and changed the way that funds under the scheme were financed. For example, under the first law, payments for both work and nonwork accidents came from levies on employers, and payments for traffic accidents came from levies on vehicle owners. The later statute required employers to pay premiums only for work accidents and some industrial diseases. A new Medical Misadventure Account set premiums for healthcare professionals that might include "different fields of specialization, as well as different categories of health professionals." More generally, the later law provided for "experience rating" for "employers (including those who are self-employed), motor vehicle owners, earners" and those who paid medical misadventure premiums. A commentator described the later law as "embody[ing] five distinctive schemes of compensation" instead of the original general scheme for "injury by accident," with the new law amounting to an "accident insurance" law rather than a social insurance one.[25]

Even if one desired a social insurance system that covered all accidents, it would seem politically impossible that such a law would be passed in the United States. In this country, compensation for injury comes from a patchwork of laws. These include the kinds of compensation systems summarized previously. Beyond that, a substantial amount of money for the relief of injury victims comes from the Social Security disability program, which over the years has developed an arcane set of rules for defining disability, and which by 2016 was paying out $142 billion in benefits. Benefits under Social Security can be awarded only to people who have paid into the system for 40 covered quarters.

Those in need who do not qualify for Social Security may seek benefits under Medicaid, the joint federal and state program which is "the single largest source of health coverage in the United States" at a cost of $565 billion in 2016. Together with the Children's Health Insurance Program, Medicaid provides health coverage for more than 72 million people. The law requires participating states to cover low income families, certain groups of needy pregnant women and children, and persons receiving benefits under the separate Supplemental Security Income (SSI) programs. The SSI programs have three separate categories for persons with limited income or limited resources: Persons who are over 65, blind, or disabled.

We are now brought to the largest question of all, which covers all the kinds of injuries that may be caused by the activities in which readers of this book participate, and many other injuries and problems that afflict millions of people. This is the question of when, and how, we should compensate for misfortune in its broadest definition. That definitional problem includes how to construct the definition itself. Just one example is the problem of compensation for victims of terror. One may visualize a series of concentric circles, with the narrowest being victims of the September 11th attacks, the next one being victims of terrorism generally, and the more expansive ones beyond those being all kinds of crimes and personal injuries generally. In this diagram, the outermost circle is an even broader set of the vicissitudes of life. How potentially broad is that set? We may ask whether we should distinguish between physical injuries and emotional injuries or between physical disease and mental illness, always taking into account that there are blurry lines between and among those categories. Apart from those questions, we would ask if government should provide aid for victims of natural disasters. And then we move to the edge of the cliff: Does government have an obligation to provide compensation for those who were born poor or burdened by racial injustices?

Given the symbolism of the pervasive shock to the nation of the attacks of September 11th, we return once more to terrorism and pose another group of questions related to that topic. Why should the government pay out billions of dollars to those victimized by the September 11th attacks, but not provide payments to those injured and killed by the Oklahoma City bombing sixteen years before that? Should the government have paid compensation to those injured in the Boston Marathon bombings of 2013? How much, in dollars, do we as a people owe to soldiers who die in combat, for whose survivors the government now pays a lump sum of $100,000—gradually increased from an original figure of $6,000 to $12,000 and now to the present amount?

Finally, we can mention the private giving of more than $2 billion for relief and recovery efforts in the wake of September 11th and the fact that a charity fund provided more than $80 million to victims of the Boston Marathon bombing. Using these sums as an intellectual springboard, we can ask how much we should rely on the goodness of heart of people who reach out to their fellows through voluntary contributions.

Endnotes

1. *Peoria County Belwood Nursing Home v. Indus. Comm'n*, 505 N.E.2d 1028, 1029 (Ill. 1987).
2. *Johannesen v. N.Y. City Dept. of Housing Preservation & Development*, 683 N.E.2d 981, 984–85 (N.Y. 1994).
3. *Darco Transp. Co. v. Dulen*, 922 P.2d 594, 594–96 (Okla. 1996).
4. *Olsten of Richmond v. Leftwich*, 336 S.E.2d 893, 894–95 (Va. 1985).
5. *United Parcel Service of Am. v. Fetterman*, 336 S.E.2d 892, 893 (Va. 1985).
6. *Carter v. General Motors Corp.*, 106 N.W.2d 105, 108–09 (Mich. 1960).
7. Id. at 115–18 (Kelly, J., dissenting).
8. Ulmer, The Political Party Variable in the Michigan Supreme Court, 11 *J. Pub. L.* 352, 360–61 (1962).
9. Kelly's Case, 477 N.E.2d 582, 585 (Mass. 1985).
10. Id. at 586–87 (Hennessey, J., dissenting).
11. *Whetro v. Awkerman*, 174 N.W.2d 783, 786 (Mich. 1970) (T.J. Kavanagh, J.).
12. Id. at 789 (Black, J.).
13. Id. at 787 (Brennan, C.J.).
14. *Lankford v. Newton County*, 517 S.W.3d 577 (Mo. Ct. App. 2017).
15. *Lockheed Aircraft Corp. v. United States*, 460 U.S. 190, 196 (1983).
16. Id. at 201–02 (Rehnquist, J., dissenting).
17. *Vasquez v. Dillard's*, 381 P.3d 768, 775 (Okla. 2016).

18. State of Florida Workers' Advocate, 167 So.3d 500 (Fla. Dist. Ct. App. 2015), jurisdiction declined, 192 So.3d 36 (Fla. 2015) (Table).

19. AMA Project proposal, cited in Chapter 10, note 29.

20. I have explored this subject generally in Marshall S. Shapo, *Compensation for Victim of Terror* (Oceana 2005).

21. See In re September 11 Litig., 889 F. Supp.2d 616, 619 (S.D. N.Y. 2012).

22. In 2010, Congress passed a law providing compensation for "WTC Responders," the James Zadroga 9/11 Health & Compensation Act of 2010. H.R. 847, 111th Cong., 2d Sess. (2010).

23. Judge Approves $20 Billion Settlement in BP Oil Spill, NBC News, April 4, 2016, printed from the Internet, May 10, 2017.

24. Dept. of Justice, U.S. and Five Gulf States Reach Historic Settlement with BP to Resolve Civil Lawsuit over Deepwater Horizon Spill, Oct. 5, 2015, printed from the Internet, May 10, 2017.

25. Summarized from Richard Miller, An Analysis and Critique of the 1992 Change to New Zealand's Accident Compensation Scheme, 52 *Md. L. Rev.* 1070 (1993).

Conclusion

I have provided a review of the fundamentals of law and the legal system, particularly as they affect professionals in science, medicine, and the design and sales of products that may carry risk to patients and consumers—here described for convenience as "scientists." Readers also may consider the topics discussed here from their roles as ordinary citizens as well as professionals, and this review will pose questions for them to consider in both capacities.

One thing that binds together lawyers and scientists is analysis—both professions must be able to break down problems into their component parts in order to devise solutions. Ideally, both should emphasize evidence, wherever it leads, and should aim to be dispassionate in decision-making and steer away from ideologically based judgments. However, ideology often creeps in at the margins of law, and it even takes possession of the minds of scientists, despite their striving for neutrality in the choice of techniques and processes. An example of great topical interest today embraces the arguments over the validity of hypotheses about climate change.

A place where law and science have had a vigorous confrontation, one that continues in particular cases, is the process of rulemaking for investigational new drugs. The FDA revised its procedures in this area under pressure from activists in the HIV/AIDS community. Their arguments included the idea that as patients they had developed an expertise that qualified them to make certain judgments made by the agency's scientists. Another aspect of that story, which runs through many areas of the law, was the contention that patients should have freedom for choice about their therapies. In the face of that argument, regulators insisted that the only way to do good science—which meant science that was good for patients in the long run—was to use the established standards of scientific investigation, including randomized double-blind tests.

One place where law and science diverge often, although not always, is in the need to make decisions under time pressure on particular subjects. In courts, judges frequently must decide specific disputes, and in legislatures, elected representatives must cast votes in compressed timeframes. These decisions may be characterized as having experimental features. For example, when judges announce rules of law they can later change their minds. But they do not have the relative leisure afforded to scientists to go down paths of research that turn out to be dead ends and then to reformulate their hypotheses. The metaphor of large-scale experimentation over long periods of time applies to the marketing of medical products, where it may take years to decide that those products should not be sold because of data that gradually accumulates on dangerous effects.

An analogous set of contrasts exists with reference to matters of proof. Scientists may continue to generate propositions that they then attempt to falsify, but courts must make decisions right now about what they are willing to call truth. In all of these areas, decisions made by regulators place a political overlay on supposedly value-free questions of science and technology.

Politics is at the root of decisions that may generate incentives, in one direction or another, with respect to the taking of risks that involve the safety of others. Businesses and scientific experimenters will complain that constraints on their risk-taking will discourage innovation. Potential victims of injury will argue for one version or another of the "precautionary principle." This idea emphasizes risk aversion as opposed to risk-taking. The politics of this clash extends to the fashioning of laws made by legislatures and to their interpretation by courts and even to decisions by courts in individual disputes, for example, in cases involving product-caused injuries. Courts taking the precautionary principle route will concern themselves with the vulnerability of populations who cannot protect themselves against risks created by others. Throughout these arguments are disputes about how to weigh risks and benefits—and indeed how to define those categories.

For those in businesses and professions that generate risk to others, much depends on the governing law and who the decision-maker is. The most powerful law appears in constitutions—the Constitution of the United States and the constitutions of each state. The language of those documents may override laws passed by Congress and state legislatures and also court decisions.

Legislation is the next strongest kind of law in terms of authority. Its strength comes from the idea that on issues of public policy, a statute—the product of a process in which different interest groups compete in a public arena and often reach compromises—is the most powerful indicator of the policy choices of the people at large. This idea is the very essence of representative democracy.

It is the courts that decide disputes between individuals, between individuals and private corporations, and between individuals and governments. In theory, courts should be ideologically neutral. In practice, politics enters into their decisions—indirectly because the members of many courts owe their appointment to politically elected officials, and directly when judges are elected by popular vote, as is the case with many state courts.

The court system includes federal and state courts, and both may be governed by federal legislation, including laws that may be interpreted to keep state courts from deciding

cases in areas that are governed by federal laws. Although
courts frequently interpret legislation, a principal area of their
operation is in the common law, under which they apply precedent, create legal rules, and extend or limit those rules. An
important aspect of court proceedings is that parties usually
are represented by lawyers in an adversarial process. In trials
at least, judges do not step out of court to search for facts.
Rather, they are arbiters of legal arguments made by lawyers
or by parties representing themselves. This leads us back
to a point we made about proof: That judicial decisions in
specific cases represent a finding of truth in the context of
particular disputes. What truth is for those purposes frequently
depends on the opinions of paid experts.

Another major source of law is regulation. Regulation produces rules that govern the behavior of people in many activities and areas, including scientific experimentation, applied
medicine, the design of products, and the way employers run
workplaces. Typically regulations are issued by agencies created by statutes in such areas as health and safety. Those statutes are themselves the products of what may be prolonged
and bitter arguments in legislatures. They declare policy
preferences about such things as the exercise of personal
choice about exposure to risk, the use of cost–benefit analysis, tradeoffs between risks and benefits, and the protection of
vulnerable groups. They also embody assumptions concerning
the information about risk that is available to consumers and
patients, and their ability to process and act on that information. An interesting manifestation of how agencies resolve
controversy is the convening of scientific panels by the FDA to
assess particular medical products. Like judges on courts and
even legislators, members of these panels vote, and their votes
may determine whether a product is marketed, and what the
limitations may be on promotion of the product.

A branch of court-made law of particular interest to scientists and businesspersons is the law of personal injuries called
torts. Tort law is itself a legal industry, with specialists who

represent injured persons and defend parties who are sued. Potential defendants, quarreling with the application of tort rules that require them to pay damages, will demand to know what justifies such awards, which may affect their insurance rates as well as their public image.

There are several rationales for tort law. One lies in the simple idea that as a matter of individual justice a person who injures another should compensate the other. A related rationale is that tort judgments send a message that tells what society regards as right and wrong. The award of punitive damages communicates the most rigorous message of this kind. A quite different rationale is that imposing damages on persons who create risk acts as a control on how much risk they create—a deterrent to conduct that is economically undesirable. There are many arguments about the rationales of tort damages, principally about the category of intangibles called noneconomic loss, which includes pain and suffering. One set of arguments focuses on the amount of awards—is the "right" amount for a particular plaintiff's pain and suffering $250,000, or a million, or more? A vigorous debate about noneconomic loss stems from the argument that it is impossible to put a dollar figure on intangibles and that therefore such awards should not be given at all.

Tort liability applies to injuries caused by many kinds of activities and products. There are several kinds of conduct that may lead to liability in tort. As one might expect, these include intentional acts and negligence. But courts may also impose a strict form of liability for the sale of defective products and for activities that are especially dangerous. In the products area, liability may be imposed in tort for intentional or reckless misrepresentations about goods. It also may be imposed on commercial law theories—for example, breach of implied warranty—as well as on a tort basis, for statements that turn out to be wrong even if they were not made negligently or fraudulently. Some strict liability for products is standard, even though many people may feel that the only basis of liability for product injuries should be fault.

In the tort law of product liability, a particularly controversial subject is the design defect, with arguments about whether the better legal standard is a risk–utility test or a consumer expectation test. There has been a lot of argument about whether there should be liability for products well-established on the market that carry high risk. The product with the worst public health impact is cigarettes, and the courts, as well as some state legislatures, have varied in their response to cigarette-caused illness.

An area that has spawned much product litigation involves the question of when and how product sellers must give warnings about the hazards of their goods. In the hundreds of reported cases on the subject, one answer lies in the knowledge and sophistication of the product user. Courts may reject liability if the danger of a product is obvious. In the area of medical products, a defense that often proves successful for makers of medical products is the learned intermediary doctrine, but the physicians who are the intermediaries may themselves face malpractice suits. For claimants in product cases, expert testimony is typically a necessity, with the qualifications of experts being a subject of scrutiny. A contentious area has to do with whether circumstantial evidence can be used to prove a defect in a product, for example by showing that it failed in the first month of use or that it had a particular kind of flaw.

The law of medical malpractice has produced rules that differ from state to state. Among the different kinds of rules are those that govern the standard of care, with nuances involving geography and the availability of facilities, ranging from a national standard of care to "locality" or modified locality rules. As with product cases, there are disputes about the evidence—whether negligence has been proved and whether negligence caused an injury. Again arguments swirl around the use of circumstantial evidence, with questions about when it is appropriate to give to the jury the issue of whether a particular kind of maloccurence is itself evidence of a failure to use due care. And just as is the case with products, expert testimony is usually a requirement for plaintiffs in medical cases, although there are exceptions for injuries so obvious that laypersons can make judgments on their own.

Medical readers know that in many circumstances physicians must give "informed consent" to a patient, and may be frustrated by the many elements that some decisions have found are necessary for doing so. Those elements include not only the risks of a procedure but also its benefits, the existence of alternative courses of treatment, and even the risks of not having a specific procedure. Courts vary on whether consent should be elicited on the basis of a "professional" standard or one that considers what a reasonable person—not the particular patient—would want in the way of information.

A topic common to both products liability and medical malpractice is what weight courts should give to industry practice. One phrase used to describe this issue is "state of the art," to which courts have given different meanings, ranging from "customary industry practice" to "the aggregate of product-related knowledge existing at any given point in time." A cautionary statement from a much-respected judge, which will raise hackles for both product sellers and physicians, is that although common practice is often the proper standard for testing whether "reasonable prudence has been exercised," it is not always the proper measure, because an entire industry "may have unduly lagged in the adoption of new and available devices." A symbol of the power of judicial standard setting in many areas of the law is that judge's statements in the same case that an industry "may never set its own tests, however pervasive be its usages" and that "[c]ourts must in the end say what is required."

Another thing that joins together these areas of the law, and indeed is a major factor in all kinds of litigation, is the division of decision-making power between judges and juries. The usual legal mantra is that determining the law is for judges and assessing the facts is for juries. But there are many cases in which the judge may not be certain about the contours of the legal standard and may allow the jury effectively to make that kind of judgment. There are various procedural doctrines that courts use to decide whether a jury should get a case—for example, a rule that asks whether reasonable persons could decide for one party or another under the law as stated.

It may now be clear to readers, whatever their business or profession, that the possession of information about risk will often be crucial in litigation about injuries. Legal concepts frequently applied in favor of defendants when information is readily available to claimants often go under the label of "assumption of the risk." An associated set of doctrines uses terms like contributory negligence.

A philosophical basis for such doctrines lies in a premise of free will possessed by rational human beings. Various readers, including some who would benefit from the use of these defenses in litigation, may question the assumption of rationality, but it is an important theoretical foundation for those doctrines. The case discussed in Chapter 6 involving a head-first dive into an above-ground swimming pool is one example of how pervasive that assumption is. Other cases involve patients who refuse a proposed course of treatment that most physicians would say it would be irrational to reject.

An important aspect of consumer information about risk appears in products liability cases on sellers' duty to warn about the hazards of their goods. The lesson of many decisions is that the well-known devil is in the details of warnings. The cases vary about the level of detail that is required for a warning to be adequate. The rise of direct-to-patient TV commercials provides an example of the complex elements of the problem, including the factors of the level of statistical data involved, patient sophistication, the premise of free choice, and empirical questions about the ability to choose from the standpoint of both intellect and emotion. In the background are questions about the power possessed by defendants. Courts may cite extreme imbalances in either the possession of information or market power as grounds for holding that a bargain was unconscionable.

Especially difficult are cases dealing with injuries that could be termed unpredictable—as to the kinds of injuries, or the ways injuries happened, or occurrences involving intervening events, which may include crimes committed by third parties. The courts have used more than a dozen terms to describe the results they reach in cases of this kind. Principal entries in this derby of terminology are *duty* and *proximate cause*. As with the topics discussed previously, a crucial question is whether the court will give the jury the liability question, especially when the line between questions of "law" and of "fact" is blurry.

In all the cases in this category, the claimant's injury would not have occurred but for some act or omission on the part of the defendant, with or without an intervening cause. Courts will look to many factors in reaching decisions. Beyond the foreseeability or unpredictability of a particular kind of event, these factors include the incentives that a decision either way would create to avoid accidents, and the availability and affordability of insurance. Many decisions holding for defendants express concern that to allow liability in a particular case would lead to a parade of horribles—the imposition of liability that is limitless, and in the case of unforeseeable occurrences, unpredictable.

In the end, many courts rely, either explicitly or implicitly, on factors that are difficult to put on a chart or graph. The foundation of these factors include intuitions about the justice of cases and of fairness as derived from judges' understandings of culture. This is not to say that judges act as public opinion pollsters but rather that they have a sense of how ordinary people would react to a case from a standpoint of fairness.

Certainly one set of guides for judges in these cases is precedent. Insofar as they can, they reason by analogy from decisions in prior cases that present problems that can be said to be similar to the case before them. In the end, though, to restate what I suggested in Chapter 8, the law reflects the complexities and difficulties of living itself—and the nuances of our reactions, both intellectual and emotional, to the legal issues that grow out of those problems.

The problem of proof runs throughout injury litigation. Here I emphasize special problems that arise in cases involving scientific and technological evidence, cases in which there are almost always competing experts. The governing law in all federal cases, and in most state courts, is the Supreme Court's decision in the *Daubert* case. That decision rejected the view that a litigant must show that a theory had general acceptance in the field at issue, but rather named a group of factors to which courts might refer. Those factors included the testability of a hypothesis and whether it had been tested, whether it had been peer-reviewed, and the known or potential rate of error. The decision pushed courts to insist on special hearings to test out the qualifications of expert witnesses, and indeed drew from lower courts even longer lists of criteria—as many as 17 of them—for determining the admissibility of witnesses' testimony. We noted that courts have constructed various categories of admissible expertise.

Courts considering scientific testimony tend to reject what they view as anecdotal evidence and "inspired hunch[es]," and some require a showing that there has been acceptance by a "recognized minority" of experts. However, some decisions have been partial to "novel" hypotheses if a witness has been qualified as to her background and her methodology. There have been varying results with reference to the statistical strength of evidence on the occurrence of particular diseases claimed to be associated with exposure to specific products, with some courts requiring a showing of a doubling of risk but others leaving to the jury a determination on risk factors above 1.0. In Chapter 9, on the regulatory side, we provided an illustration of the ferocity of expert argument on medical evidence in the case of the diabetes drug Avandia, summarizing the differing positions taken by FDA panelists with respect to permission for marketing of the drug. On the tort side, we noted the settlement of Avandia suits brought by great numbers of plaintiffs.

Since tort litigation is a continuing topic of fiery dispute in both state and national politics, it was quite expected that legislatures would enter the field with statutes designed to lower the rate of injury suits and to limit the amounts that can be recovered in them. "Tort reform" statutes come in several flavors. Some modify the culpability rules for injurer conduct. Others effectively allow a state-of-the-art defense. Tilting to the side of plaintiffs, a few statutes, joined by court rulings, allow negligent claimants to recover something where previously they could recover nothing.

On the damages side, many statutes limit the amounts that may be awarded for noneconomic loss and punitive damages. Others effectively tighten the amount of time in which claimants can bring injury suits. Some statutes impose limits of varying kinds on lawyers' contingency fees. Still others require parties to submit disputes to arbitration. Counterpunches to these statutes occur in another chamber of decision-making, that of the courts. Continuing battles have been fought over the constitutionality of tort reform statutes, with plaintiffs arguing, sometimes successfully, that these laws deprive them of their rights as litigants without due process of law, or deny them equal protection of the laws by contrast with other claimants. Behind these battles is the question of whether courts or legislatures are the better lawmakers. Those supporting judge-made law against tort reform stress the importance of individualized justice. Those supporting reform statutes emphasize that legislatures are in a better position to collect economic data and to weigh competing elements of public policy.

I also have mentioned the broad spectrum of remedies, apart from tort law, that are designed to provide compensation of victims of injuries. A major activity-focused kind of program that eliminates the requirement that injured persons prove fault, which exists in every state, is workers' compensation, which annually pays out more money than tort judgments nationally. It provides compensation for the most obvious workplace injuries—for example, amputations from industrial machines and heart attacks from heavy lifting—and in many jurisdictions has included stress-based emotional illness. One decision even granted an award for illness caused by bacteria from pigeon droppings in a chosen work venue. Some states have enacted limited no-fault programs for traffic injuries. Far-reaching proposals exist, but generally have not been passed, that would compensate for injuries in the course of medical care; these proposals have been linked with suggested plans for tort reform.

Disastrous events with widespread consequences have led to payouts in the billions from a variety of sources. For the victims of the September 11th attacks, these included a special fund entirely based on government dollars and a large group of charitable contributions. For those harmed by the Gulf oil spill of 2010, many billions came from a fund established by an oil company and from civil damages fines paid to the government.

One country, New Zealand, passed a law establishing an overall social insurance scheme for "injuries by accident," abolishing the tort action, but somewhat retrenched on that legislation in the direction of a scheme with features more like accident insurance.

A patchwork quilt of legislative programs in the United States provides enormous sums for those who suffer injury and illness in many ways. A big program based on mandatory contributions by workers is the Social Security disability program. A set of categorical programs provides financial relief for needy persons. The largest of these is Medicaid, which in 2016 paid out $565 billion.

The existence of all the remedies and programs described in this conclusion leaves the reader with the question of when society, or component parts of it, should provide compensation for those who suffer misfortune—indeed, how to define misfortune itself.

There are others matters I leave for readers to consider. There is the question of who are the best decision-makers on issues of how society should respond to injuries—for example, judges or legislators. There also is the need to recognize the parallel existence of two cultures in our America. I have described one of them as a "justice culture," in which people angry at injuries caused by risky activities lean toward imposing responsibility on power holders and favor remedies for vulnerable persons. Another, a "market culture," tends to leave injury problems to the market itself, except in cases involving violations of crisply defined standards or conduct found egregious by consensus. The philosophical basis for this position includes a certain resignation about the human condition, epitomized by the idea that we all live in a "vale of tears."

There are some ideas that may unite members of both cultures. One is a belief in the dignity of the individual. Another is the idea that people should not take unfair advantage of others—although the definition of what is "unfair" often will excite further argument. What I said about punitive damages in another book may provide a good guide for professionals in the sciences and in business who wish to avoid liability as well as social condemnation: Behave sensibly. Act decently.

Now a few concluding thoughts about the contributions of lawyers to solving problems of the sort on which this book focuses. One of these is the observation that lawyers are trained to conceptualize problems, and solutions, in words, and that words, as it has been said, can be better than logarithms. Another is that lawyers, at their best, are good at judgment. A very fine judge defined "judgment" to include "an ability to gauge in advance the reactions of others to events and arguments; a sense of calm or self-discipline, enabling one to separate and prefer the reasoned response to one based on emotion; a willingness to make decisions and to do so based on incomplete data; a certain seriousness of mind, and perhaps an instinct for order or pattern."

Perhaps all readers will agree that the end of law is justice, although with the understanding that the idea of justice will mean many things to different people. Scientists and lawyers will agree that judgment requires a way to impose structure on unstructured data, a task that daily confronts people in both professions. It is in the spirit of that recognition that I conclude that scientists and lawyers should make love, when they must do so, like porcupines—very carefully.

Index

Printed in the United States
by Baker & Taylor Publisher Services